THE END

IS

NOT

NEAR

THE END

IS

NOT

NEAR

HOW THE CULTURE OF FEAR
HAS
CORRUPTED DEMOCRACY,
BUILT AN EMPIRE,
AND
ERODED OUR INTELLECTUAL LIFE

JEFFERY L. IRVIN JR., PH.D.

CREATESPACE

CHARLESTON, SC

Contents

WHAT GOD AND SCIENCE HATH WROUGHT

Preface

That's great, it starts with an earthquake, birds and snakes, an aeroplane–
Lenny Bruce is not afraid.

REM, *It's the End of the World As We Know It (And I Feel Fine)*

Scroll through the guide on your cable box or dish and you will find programs profiling all manner of end-of-the-world scenarios. Whether it is the History Channel's latest documentary on Christian apocalypticism or the Mayan Calendar, or Prepper reality shows on National Geographic and the Discovery Channel, you will find a plethora of programs that showcase the apocalyptic mindset. Add to this the increasing concerns about climate change and you have a confluence of forces that are resulting in a widespread anxiety about the world around us, a phenomenon that sociologists have designated *the culture of fear*.

This book began as a tongue-in-cheek treatment of fear and how it is used to manipulate the public. It was originally going to be titled *We're All Going to Die! Your Guide to Enjoying the Coming Apocalypse*. I was going to dispense nuggets of wisdom like "Never pass up the opportunity for a good bowel movement; you may not get another" or "Always get a second opinion, and ignore that one too." I was hoping to do for our general social anxiety what Stanley Kubrick had done for Mutually Assured Destruction (MAD) back in 1964. After all, why cry when you can laugh?

My initial inspiration for this book was sparked by two things: Jon Stewart and Stephen Colbert's "Rally to Restore Sanity and/or Fear," held on the National Mall in October 2010, and the predictions of engineer-turned-prophet Harold Camping. I was in Northern California at the time and used to drive by a sign that predicted the world would be coming to an end on May 21, 2011. I had done extensive research on apocalyptic thought while writing my master's thesis in American history, so I decided this was yet another *amusing angle* I could add to the book.

Being by nature a bit anal, and steeped in research methodology, I could not help but pick up a couple of books on *the culture of fear*. This inevitably led to a wide variety of reading that took me over a year to complete. Writing satire would have been so much easier. However, as I dug into the existing research on the culture of fear it was clear this story required a more sober approach. I could no longer be so cavalier about something that adversely affects millions of people in the United States.[1]

The culture of fear is a psychologically legitimate phenomenon. It is no laughing matter. It is exacerbated by the modern media, politicians, pundits, and those purporting to be experts on various topics. It is also clearly a close cousin to Christian apocalyptic thought, which has been part of the fabric of American history for centuries. Both the culture of fear and apocalyptic thinking lead to common social and psychological maladies, but the worst maladies are individual paralysis and infantilization. These are particularly bad social and psychic problems because they encourage us to turn away from traditional political solutions, which prompts us to greater social and political insularity. That increasing insularity makes social and political action even more unlikely when it comes to solving common problems, and it ultimately leads to the only logical action for the individual: *escape from what is thought to be an oppressive society dominated by large unaccountable corporations and godless men*. While some still look for a messianic figure in the form of a political, business, or cultural, leader, others prepare for the inevitable destruction of *the world as we know it*.

A case in point is the popular book *How to Survive the End of the World as We Know It: Tactics, Techniques, and Technologies for Uncertain Times* (2009). In this book the author, John Wesley Rawles, encourages everyone to develop a "bug-out plan" in preparation for the inevitable collapse of society. Rawles claims to be a former intelligence analyst for the military. He is said to live in an undisclosed location somewhere near the Rockies. He is also an apocalyptic-minded Christian, who believes that a time of religious persecution is at hand. That is why he is encouraging Christians to migrate to the eastern portions of Washington and Oregon, or to Idaho, Montana, and Wyoming. There he hopes to create what he calls an "American Redoubt," a stronghold that will be able to defend itself against the inevitable unbelieving horde that will be displaced by the crumbling of "the world as we know it."

If this message sounds familiar maybe you used to watch the now defunct Fox News program hosted by Glenn Beck. For an hour each night the audience was treated to the tergiversations of an individual who while wailing about our inability to do anything to save ourselves hawked gold and survivalist gear.[2] Did Mr. Beck listen one too many times to that old Mike and the Mechanics song, *Silent Running*? Don't forget the ammunition!

Recently I picked up another book, *After America: Get Ready for Armageddon* (2011), written by the Canadian conservative pundit Mark Steyn. He does not suggest heading for the hills just yet. He thinks there is still time to rescue America from the coming Islamic horde and their greatest enabler, Barack Obama. However, he does say it is too late for Europe. This book is a perfect representation of how those on the right of the political spectrum tend to couch their arguments in extreme language, even when they are arguing for banal policies like privatizing Social Security and Medicare. Another example of this use of apocalyptic language are the books of Ann Coulter. Her most recent book, *Demonic: How the Liberal Mob Is Endangering America* (2011), takes to task what she and the far right calls "liberal secularism," which is in their minds a loose conspiracy among "liberal elites" to destroy all religion, eliminate religious freedom, end private enterprise, and make the state the supreme arbiter of all human relationships. The absurdity of these arguments is exceeded only by the passion with which they are disseminated.

This is not to say that the left has not produced similarly charged works. For example, Chris Hedges's *American Fascists: The Christian Right and the War on America* (2007) explores what can only be called an "evangelical subculture," which has fused American Exceptionalism with Christian eschatology, and which includes a modernized version of the "wealth gospel." However, the major difference between left and right pundits is that those on the right are forced to infer the motives of the left while those who make up the Christian Right are unapologetically open about their unquestioning support for Israel, and their hope that this support will lead to Armageddon and the speedy return of Jesus Christ.

We will talk a little more about these types of books when we discuss the role media plays in keeping the culture of fear alive in the American consciousness, and their role in feeding America's long tradition of "civic millennialism." For now, let me explain what this book hopes to achieve.

The book is split into four sections. The first part of the book introduces the reader to culture of fear and why human biology and psychology make this phenomenon possible. The second part explores how politicians, the media, and self-appointed experts exploit our natural proclivity to fear the unknown and intractable. The third part of the book explores what I call *the close cousin of the culture of fear*, that is Christian apocalyptic belief. That brings us to the fourth section of this book which attempts to pull all of these things together, providing an explanation for why the culture of fear has so effectively hobbled the American democratic process.

The conclusion is clear: *the culture of fear in America has led to a political system that is democratically unresponsive to the needs of the majority, it has saddled us with a foreign policy that is unsustainable and self-destructive, and it has given birth to a society geared solely toward satisfying our most materialistic, Machiavellian, and narcissistic desires.*

As an historian I am not naive enough to believe that things were much better in the past. We have always been driven by fear to one extent or another. Today's fears, though, are largely unjustified, and they are made more problematic by the complex society in which we live. As we will learn in the following pages, fear can be a very effective tool for survival when out in the wilderness. It is not a mistake to overestimate danger when you are alone in a jungle, since there are plenty of predators who would like to make you their next meal. However, in a modern society we are driven by fears that are mostly illusions. Upon examination we learn that what we fear the most is statistically what we should fear the least, and that if we returned to traditional political action we might be able to solve the problems that lead to our pervasive anxieties and fears.

I argue in this book that in order to diminish the worst effects of the culture of fear and apocalyptic thinking in America we must engage in a conscious process of moral renewal, but not in the traditional sense. In early American history preachers like Jonathan Edwards, George Whitefield, and Charles Finney, would have called America back to faith and morality. Of course, they would have done so using fear, as evidenced by Jonathan Edwards's famous sermon "Sinners in the Hands of an Angry God."

> O sinner! Consider the fearful danger you are in: it is a great fur-
> nace of wrath, a wide and bottomless pit, full of the fire of wrath,
> that you are held over in the hand of that God, whose wrath is
> provoked and incensed as much against you, as against many of
> the damned in hell. You hang by a slender thread, with the flames
> of divine wrath flashing about it, and ready every moment to singe
> it, and burn it asunder....[3]

That was the eighteenth-century preacher's way, but today we cannot afford to use this dangerous tool; fear cannot achieve the greater good in a modern society. Instead, we must start with a central reality rooted in the human condition: our frailty and limitations as human beings. This is something traditional religion sometime reminded us about, that is before the Enlightenment renewed Western society's pre-Babel faith in mankind's ability to achieve just about anything. To make matters worse the modern Christian church has commoditized, sanitized, and packaged its message to appeal to a congregation treated more like consumers than parishioners. This has robbed Christianity of its moral force in the modern world. The modern marketing of Christianity has made faith merely a lifestyle choice.

This is not the first time this has happened. The Roman Catholic Church abandoned its moral imperative in the middle ages, preferring the trappings of political power. This institution eventually paid the price when Martin Luther led a revolt against the political corruption of the Church in the early sixteenth century. Yet, even today we are still saddled with this sclerotic religious organization, which prizes its institution and tradition over its original moral mission. How else can one explain the widespread cover-up of priestly abuse against children, or policies that actually increase suffering rather than alleviate it?[4]

Our frailty as human beings must be the starting point of any discussion about how to build a better society because no economic, political, or technological advance will ever diminish that frailty. Sure, we might be able to nibble at the edges, give ourselves a few extra years on the planet, but in the end we all remain subject to the laws of the universe. We will all grow old and die, or be struck down "before our time" by illness or accident. Even without physical maladies or old age we all will continue to be subject to the vicissitudes of ego and desire, which themselves cause much of our suffering. So, it is only with the acknowledgment of our human weaknesses that a real moral dialogue can begin, and if you continue to read I believe you will understand why such a moral dialogue has now become imperative for our social survival.

Jeffery L. Irvin Jr.
May 2013

PART ONE

A BRIEF INTRODUCTION
TO THE CULTURE OF FEAR

Chapter One

Be Afraid, Be Very Afraid

In time we hate that which we often fear.

William Shakespeare, *Antony and Cleopatra*

Are you anxious or afraid? If so, you are not alone. You have something in common with millions of your fellow Americans because anxiety and fear appear to be running rampant in the United States. This is true even though there is plenty of evidence that we live in what can modestly be called "the best of times." The truth is that in a modern liberal, democratic, and capitalist society there is very little for us to fear on a daily basis. We have greater longevity, greater wealth, greater leisure, greater freedom—the list goes on.[1] Yet, a recent newspaper article claims that one in ten Americans are using anti-depressants, now prescribed more often for anxiety disorders than for depression.[2]

What is going on here? Why are so many so anxious, why so afraid? To begin answering these questions we start by exploring a phenomenon known as "the culture of fear." What this is will become clear over the next several chapters, but as you read keep in mind that what we call "the culture of fear" is primarily a manufactured phenomenon, a response to perceived social, political, and economic uncertainty. It is this uncertainty that explains why the culture of fear is such a powerful phenomenon. It also explains why apocalyptic thought, the subject of the part three of this book, is the close cousin of the culture of fear. We fear that which we cannot understand, that which we cannot control, and that which reveals the inherent weakness of being human.

The culture of fear is possible because we are fundamentally afraid of what we are: *a decaying piece of flesh with hopes and dreams that can be annihilated in an instant*. The culture of fear is made reality by those who sow the seeds of despair to accomplish some purpose, whether nefarious or benign. That is why most of us are not able to accept that we are motivated by fear on a daily basis, even as we contend each day with varying levels of personal anxiety. The anxiety and fear with which most of us live on a daily basis is low-grade. We do not pay any attention to it until a crisis forces us to examine the basic foundation on which our life is built. Personal tragedy and general chaos become the crucibles through which we learn about ourselves and our society. So, the *culture of fear* is always present in one form or another, and when times of crisis occur we all look for a ready-made narrative that is effective at explaining things and at preparing us for the other shoe to drop. Whether that shoe drops or not we hold on to these narrative explanations, for who knows when they might not be needed?

We are frail creatures who forget that living in a complex society is a very effective way of supplying our basic wants and needs. Most–unfortunately not all–who live in an advanced industrial society do not have to think about where their next meal is coming from or whether they will have a place to sleep. However, when personal tragedy or social crisis rips off the thin veil of society our weaknesses are exposed, along with the limitations of society. During these times of crisis those who manufacture the culture of fear pounce. They want to make sure you know that during any crisis they have just what you need to even the odds, or give you an advantage. The danger inherent in this manufactured system of fear is that it causes us to forget that in the long run social organization itself is the best way for us to even the odds. The best thing an individual, a family, or a community, can do is to keep their society strong, healthy, and responsive to the needs of the many. However, do not think this will provide you with total security and certainty. That is not what the social contract promises.

Living in a society is ultimately a trade-off. In return for a degree of security and predictability we exchange a certain amount of our freedom. Society always costs something; however, when the costs exceed the benefits—as it does for some—then society becomes an albatross around the neck. Those estranged from society begin to look for ways to limit the reach of their society. Ironically, this makes society even less effective in addressing their needs since an effective society requires the participation of all. The growing ineffectiveness of society further alienates the already disaffected, and this vicious cycle creates the perfect environment for the culture of fear to do its work.

Disaffection becomes particularly problematic when it begins to influence the middling classes, as it has the last several years, especially since 2008, when the financial crash decimated the global economy. In the United States this has always been less of a problem because of the American myths of economic progress and personal achievement; however, these myths are being challenged every day by a reduction in the United States' share of the world market. Greater disparity of wealth, a growing poverty rate, and the lack of career opportunity for the college graduate and skilled worker are all results of economic globalization and of government economic policies that favor the multinational corporation over the general economic health of the country. These are conditions that create the perfect environment for a culture of fear to thrive, and what do we get as a result? We get a large minority of the population afraid of change and the future. We get a culture of fear, which paralyzes and infantilizes far too many. The culture of fear makes people fully aware of their inability to address through their own effort the intractable, and often illusory, problems that beset them. At that point, they give up, or hope that someone, somewhere, will come to the rescue. Consequently, the paralysis and infantilism that results from the culture of fear leads to either passive dystopian nightmares or active utopian fantasies, neither of which is a good foundation on which to build a modern and secular society.

At this point you may be thinking that the culture of fear has no effect on your life. You might be right, if you mean that you are not directly affected by it because you are not consciously anxious or afraid of the world around you. The culture of fear is something that occurs most of the time at the margins of society. It is most prevalent among the vulnerable, or those who believe themselves to be more vulnerable than they are. The culture of fear has an inverse relationship with how effective society is at addressing the concerns of the many, so as society becomes less effective at addressing those concerns the culture of fear grows more appealing. The culture of fear is also made palpable by modern media. Literature, movies, and even the nightly news, are the chief ways in which fear is inculcated to the members of a society. These mediums feed us a subtle message: the idea that something in our society is just not right, that dangers, which no one wants to talk about, are much more likely to exist than they really are.

A good example of this is the recent movie *Live Free or Die Hard* (2007) in which our hero, John McClane, is pulled into rescuing the whole country from a group of terrorists who are trying to shut down the whole country via the Internet. This brings us to the whole debate about whether movies, television, music, and video games, represent society or whether they shape it. The answer is, "Yes. It does both." This latest offering in the John McClane franchise reflects our own concerns about Internet security, the fragility of our complex society, and the willingness of unscrupulous individuals to prey on the weak. It reflects existing concerns but it also makes them seem more real as our imaginations get carried away by the story on the screen. That is why when we heard in 2011 about hackers interrupting operations at a water plant in Illinois we were already *primed* to believe that it was true, and that we are a lot less safe than we might be. It turns out that one of the plant's pumps had just burned out.[3]

My view of the culture of fear has been largely influenced by the work of two social scientists: Frank Furedi and Barry Glassner. I will make extensive reference to their work, and the work of journalist Dan Gardner, in the following pages. Where I most disagree with these individuals is that I believe media (literature, film, television, and news) has a greater degree of responsibility for keeping the culture of fear alive. However, I realize this is a chicken and egg paradox since this type of media would not be consumed unless there was a demand for it. This reveals an interesting aspect of fear: *we sometimes like to be afraid.* There is something about being afraid that—at least after the fact—gives us a greater appreciation for life. This is why we engage in extreme sports and jump out of airplanes with nothing but a silk sheet and ropes strapped to our back. Surviving is a rush, even when we are not likely to die. We will examine this psychological aspect of fear in a later chapter.

***

Now, let us get more specific. What is the culture of fear, and how pervasive is it? Does it affect everyone? Is it all in the perception of the individual? All of these questions are a little problematic since it is difficult to quantify how much fear and anxiety individuals experience on a daily basis, and over time. However, we can try to measure the level of fear indirectly through the response people have to certain news stories and rumors, through the popularity of conspiracy theories, or through the success of utopian and dystopian literature and film. I mentioned above the increased use of drugs to address our growing anxiety about daily life, but we could also talk about the increased consumption of novels and movies that explore the dystopian theme, for example, the popular trilogy by Suzanne Collins, which began with *The Hunger Games* (2008)—now a film. This type of literature and film is part of long list, among which even the Harry Potter series could be numbered.

One novel in particular directly addresses *the culture of fear*, Michael Crichton's 2004 techno-thriller *State of Fear*. In this book Crichton takes on the issue of global warming, suggesting that it is part of a larger effort on the part of disparate interest groups to make money and gain power. This book is not pure fiction as evidenced by Crichton's extensive bibliography. However, the novel is clearly a polemic, a Socratic dialogue meant to convince the reader of two things: 1) climate change may not be as great a problem as scientists have made it out to be, and 2) it is possible that some within the environmentalist movement have political, social, and economic agendas which they disguise through activism. I will not comment on whether Crichton was right about climate change, but I do think he was right about the alarming growth in the use of fear-mongering in modern society.

About two-thirds of the way through the novel Crichton introduces Professor Norman Hoffman, who claims to be a specialist in the "ecology of thought." Professor Hoffman's thesis is that since the end of the Cold War there has been an increase in the use of specific code words that are meant to heighten the fears of individuals within society. This fear-mongering tactic, says Hoffman, is used by what he calls the PLM (the politico-legal-media complex), whose primary goal is to keep people afraid, compliant, and looking to their governments and other leaders for answers.[4] One is reminded of H. L. Mencken's quip that "The whole aim of practical politics is to keep the populace alarmed (and hence clamorous to be led to safety) by an endless series of hobgoblins, most of them imaginary."[5]

Crichton clearly modeled Professor Hoffman on the two professional sociologists I mentioned above: Barry Glassner and Frank Furedi. In fact, in the novel Hoffman is a professor at The University of Southern California, the same place Glassner worked before moving on to Lewis and Clark College in Oregon. Hoffman goes on to claim in the novel that he has discovered through statistical analysis a virtual conspiracy by politicians, the media, and the legal system to keep people in a perpetual "state of fear." Furedi says as much in his own work when he talks about the use of the term "at risk" in UK newspapers. Based on

Furedi's count the use of the term "at risk" in newspaper articles went up nearly nine-fold from 1994 through 2000. In 1994 the term "at risk" was used a total of 2,037 times while in 2000 that number had shot up to 18,003 times![6] One has to ask, did the world really get that much more dangerous between 1994 and 2000?

It should be pointed here out that Crichton made a literary career out of questioning the role of science in society—a tradition that extends back to the Greeks. In books and films like *The Andromeda Strain* (1969), *Westworld* (1973), and, probably more well-known, *Jurassic Park* (1990), Crichton rightly encourages us to deal with the limits of human knowledge and technology. He often asks the question, what would happen if this did not work the way we predict? So, it was well within Crichton's traditional critique of science that he questioned the validity of climate research, but more important for our discussion he addresses why and how the culture of fear is manufactured. My reading on the culture of fear has led me to two conclusions: 1) *people are unable to properly measure risk in a complex society*, and 2) *there are many in society willing to exploit our inability to properly measure that risk*. The next several chapters will be devoted to digging a little deeper into these two facets of the culture of fear.

***

How do we know what to do in any given situation? Well, some situations are easier to evaluate than others. If a large object is hurtling toward you it is best to just get out of the way, but what if the danger is not so obvious or immediate? For example, what do you do if you live in a society that appears to be in decay? What can you do? If you listen to your gut only two answers will come to mind: *fight or flight*. Flight is always the logical choice unless you are backed into a corner. However, is it that easy to run away from a modern society? How many of us are actually backed into a corner? Some statistics suggest that nearly half a million Americans have already abandoned society,[7] but where does that leave the other 314 million? How many more would like to escape but cannot?

Evolutionary biologists will tell us that the reason the fight-or-flight response is so strong is because we evolved to react to very simple situations where life and death were clearly on the line, and it is difficult to break a habit acquired over millions of years. Journalist Dan Gardner presents an interesting hypothetical when he ponders how a Neanderthal would react to being transported to the modern world and waking up in Times Square.[8] What would be his first reaction? It would most likely be terror, and his first response would probably be running to find an environment similar to the one in which he had fallen asleep. If he made it to Central Park he might be less afraid, but he would still be anxious as he observed all the human activity there and the strange animals pulling wheeled carts around the park. What kind of magic would a wheel seem to a Neanderthal? The Neanderthal would be simply out of place in the modern world, and so are we in some respects, because we still possess all the adaptations associated with the primal brain. We will return often to the question of human biology and brain development throughout the rest of this book, but right now we have to move on to explain the immediate reasons for why the culture of fear exists.

As mentioned above, one of the reasons why the culture of fear can exist is because we do not have the intuitive ability to measure statistical risk. Experiments done by Paul Slovic and Daniel Kahneman show a large disparity between what we perceive as risk and the actual mathematical probability of risk.[9] We tend to be too optimistic when there is no call for it, like when we play the lottery. Conversely, we tend to be too pessimistic when it comes to losing something like a court case, even when the evidence is strongly in our favor. The main reason for this is our predilection for storytelling. We tend to believe whatever fits into a commonly accepted narrative, we are always looking for what "sounds right." In other words, we trust our gut rather than our head. This is the common thread running through all the literature on the culture of fear: *we simply lack the intuitive ability to evaluate statistical risk.*

Most people in modern industrial societies are not concerned with survival; their concerns are more social, more symbolic, and more intangible. This makes risk assessment more difficult for those who rely solely on their primitive fight-or-flight response. That is not to say this system of risk assessment is useless. It may be very handy in many situations, but a proper basis for risk assessment in a modern society is statistical and probabilistic. This more objective method of risk assessment tends to encourage the long-view because it evens out the bumps in the road and keeps us from being too optimistic or too pessimistic. It also helps to rescue us from those who would use our innate fears to manipulate us for their own benefit.

If we looked at the world more rationally, how many of us would have invested in companies in the 1990s that had no revenue but whose shares were selling for hundreds of dollars? How many of us would have continued to invest in a housing market that was clearly becoming a bubble by the end of the 1990s? How many of us would continue to believe that going further into debt makes us more prosperous? All of these absurdities are a product of ignorance about how the economy works. They exemplify our inability to understand the basic statistical rules underpinning most situations of risk and reward in a modern and complex society.

There is a lot more evidence that we are unable to properly measure risk. Take, for instance, the fact that it is no longer satisfactory for us to be able to judge risk; we must eliminate it altogether, even if that means giving up on the common biological act of pair-bonding. These days we are warned about "toxic relationships," and the young are warned not to bother since any relationship they start is fated to fail.[10] Doesn't the 50% divorce rate prove it? Of course, the irony here is that the increased aversion to risk makes failure more and more likely because we have no stomach for the slightest risk, and we demand too much when it comes to our emotional, social, and financial satisfaction. The aversion to risk ignores the fact that pair-bonding is a naturally integrative experience that requires compromise, a roughly equitable process of give and take. This excess of caution is not good for society; however, we are fortunate that most people ignore these warnings and continue to pair-bond—otherwise the species might in short order cease to exist.

There are many recent explanations for why we cannot judge risk properly. One is called the *Pygmalion Effect*. This is when something dominates the way we think because of how we have framed the issue. In other words, we filter all events through a narrative to which we have become wedded. *Road rage* is a good example of this because although death on our streets is a major problem, sudden outbursts of road violence are not a major problem. There are far more systemic problems like easy access to handguns, a transportation infrastructure that is not keeping up with increased demand, or drunk driving, but these problems are not sexy enough; they lack drama, and they require extensive social and political coordination to solve.

In the mid-1990s road rage became the subject of hundreds of segments in the news cycle, and rather than seeing this for what it was, a small and temporary spike in violence on our roadways, it was seen as the beginning of a trend. It was viewed by some as part of a larger trend in the downward spiral of society into barbarism, an idea that fits into a general narrative of cultural decline, which has existed for centuries.[11]

Arnold Nerenberg, a self-appointed road-rage expert contributed to the hysteria about road rage in America, and also saw it as part of a systemic social and psychological problem. He was sought by all the media outlets when he let it be known that he was a "road-rage therapist." He even had a website, www.roadrage.com—now defunct. During his appearances on radio and television Nerenberg made categorical statements about a widespread and "contagious" psychic disease that was debilitating Americans and leading them to engage in sudden acts of violence on our roads. He made these claims even though he was not a professional researcher in this area and even though he had no statistical backing for his claims. In fact, from 1990 to 1996 traffic incidents involving violence went up by a total of 671 in all fifty states. Yes, this was an increase of 59% over the 1,129 incidents of 1990, but when compared to the overall population these statistics hardly indicated an epidemic or a trend. However, the press and the self-appointed experts made sure the raw numbers did not reach the public. They made sure the public only heard that incidents of road violence had gone up by "over fifty percent."[12]

Each incidence of violence is a tragedy, but to conflate those tragedies with general trends and to scare people into thinking things are worse than they are only contributes to an unnecessary climate of fear. For instance, at the same time this small spike in road violence grabbed society's attention there were 17,000 people killed each year because of drunk driving.[13] You judge. Which is worse, 17,000 deaths resulting from drunk driving each year or the 200 deaths annually attributed to road rage? While you decide remember this, the media often got the story wrong. For example, in one incident attributed to road rage it was found that a woman who was shot and killed alongside a California highway had been stalked, not randomly chosen, before she was robbed. She was also only killed when it was discovered she was a state corrections officer.[14] This was clearly not road rage, but the situation does raise thorny questions without simple answers, like the easy access to guns in our society. This may be why we have to have a simple answer like road rage to explain it, because there are just too many people who do not want to have a real conversation about Second Amendment rights or the American proclivity for violence.[15]

What this recent episode of road rage hysteria illustrates is that the media, politicians, and self-appointed experts are always eager to whip the public into a frenzy over things that most people will never encounter. Larger, more systemic, problems like the pervasiveness of guns, racism, homophobia, and gender discrimination are given short shrift because they are not seen as pertinent to the "core" problems of society. The general populace has been convinced that the problems they should be most concerned about are illicit drug use, teen pregnancy, rampant crime, the assault on "family values," etc. However, these "pseudodangers" take center stage in a classic attempt by politicians, the media, and so-called experts to engage in political, social, and economic, misdirection. Their goal is simple: *to make money and to gain influence and power while avoiding solutions to any of the systemic problems facing our society.*

Rather than accepting the fact that social structures often play a central role in creating and perpetuating the problems that individuals, families, and communities face, we blame everything on the individual—even when those individuals are the victims of what we might call "acts of God." This fits the common narrative of American success, a success always attributed to hard work–never chance. It becomes nearly axiomatic that all the problems we face as a society are because of bad apples, never a result of congested highways, easy access to handguns, and high-stress lifestyles.[16]

This is not an excuse for bad individual behavior. We must hold individuals to account for their actions. However, if building more roads, increasing public transit, reducing access to handguns, etc., could help reduce the level of stress and violence in society should we not at least be talking about it? Our inclination to create scapegoats for the persistent problems of society only makes the problem worse since we use this as a moral justification to ignore structural problems that could be addressed through social and political action. How might a more effective system of democratic action solve our problems, and allay our fears?

In addition to the *Pygmalion Effect* researchers have discovered what has been termed the *availability heuristic*. This is a more personalized version of the Pygmalion Effect. This is when we see ourselves in the news, as personally part of the drama. In other words, we filter the news through an already dominant narrative in which we play an active part, no matter what is happening. That is why when we see a random act of violence on our highways we immediately think it could happen to us, even though it is a very remote possibility. After all, we all use the highways to get to work, we all know how aggressive people can get when they drive, and there is clearly an increase in this violence. You could be next! This is why parents want to know where their kids are when a child goes missing, even if the story they have heard about is happening several states away.

The *availability heuristic* explains why it is so easy for others to convince us that "small risks" are actually frequent and pervasive. In cooperation with the media and politicians, "would-be experts" prey on our "deeper cultural anxieties" so they can make a quick buck and garner more power and prestige for themselves. This is not a cabal, though; it is merely a naturally occurring symbiotic relationship between the media, politicians, and so-called experts, and it is built on whatever happens to be the *fear de jour*.[17] For example, the media dubbed the summer of 2001 as "the summer of the shark," even though there were less shark-related deaths that year than the previous year. In 2000 there were twelve shark attacks that ended in death while in 2001 there were five.[18]

If you are still unconvinced that the culture of fear is a manufactured phenomenon, or you have a difficult time conceptualizing it, then maybe a few more examples will help you to see how the dangerous world imagined by some is completely disconnected from reality. The following examples of the culture of fear illustrate two things. The first is that the persistent and general belief that crime is on the rise is not borne out by the statistics. The second thing is that what we think are the most crucial social problems in our society are frequently small problems when compared to the more pressing problems we ignore. Both of these distortions of reality can be laid primarily at the feet of a media that chases stories that bleed.

In the 1990s it was widely believed that crime was on the rise. Murder, child abduction and abuse, and what was called "granny dumping," appeared to be rife and growing problems. The statistics, though, told a different story. These things did happen, but they were far rarer than the media and so-called experts were leading us to believe. All the stories that dominated the headlines during the 1990s also ignored one simple fact: *most of these crimes were committed by relatives or other trusted members of the community in which these victims lived.* Again, though, these stories did not represent any statistical uptick in these heinous crimes.

Some have suggested that these stories dominated our national conversation because they masked our general concern over the breakdown of family and community. In the case of 'granny dumping" it may have been our shared guilt at abandoning the elderly to nursing homes, often to some of the lowest paid and most economically vulnerable people in our society, people who might be more prone to view the elderly as easy prey.[19] In other words, society's apotheosis of economic gain over the last forty years may have thrown into question all that we believe when it comes to "family values." The "epidemic" of "granny dumping" and "granny abuse" may have just been an attempt to shift the burden of our own moral and familial guilt to others.

It is curious that Americans in the 1990s saw crime as society's greatest concern, especially since statistics showed that crime was on the decline. This disconnect from reality is addressed in Steven Levitt and Stephen Dubner's best-selling book *Freakonomics.* In a chapter entitled "Where Have All the Criminals Gone?" the authors attempt to figure out why there was a dramatic reduction in crime during the 1990s, especially when people were predicting that gangs of *super-predators* would soon dominate some sections of the urban landscape. Remember all those calls for "gang task forces"? What Levitt and Dubner find is interesting. For example, all the things that were done in the 1990s from "innovative policing strategies" to the "increased number of police" on the street were not enough to explain the sudden drop in crime during the 1990s. There was little or no statistical correlation between these factors and lower crime in the United States. So, if it was not the actions taken by government and law enforcement, what could it be?

Levitt and Dubner concluded that along with two or three supplementary factors the main reason crime went down is that the forecasted rise in *super-predators* never occurred. Why? Because, they were never born. Yes, that's right! *Roe v. Wade* had effectively curtailed the birth of the next criminal class. As controversial as this idea might be the authors make clear that they are not arguing for or against a liberal abortion policy, they are simply trying to answer the question "Where Have All the Criminals Gone?" The short answer is that they were never born.[20] There could be other explanations like the nominal increase in prosperity during the 1990s, but then how do we explain the last decade which has seen an increase in poverty with no statistical uptick in crime? According to FBI statistics, the crime rate for both violent and property crime has either continued to decrease or leveled off.[21]

The belief that crime is increasing when it is actually decreasing, or stabilizing, is not the only way in which we get the story wrong. We also get it wrong when we think that certain types of crime are more rampant than they are in reality. For example, all the hand-wringing associated with the use of illicit drugs seems quite unnecessary since prescription drug abuse is a far more serious problem, causing more deaths and heartache each year than any illicit substance. Is it possible that the focus on illicit drugs is an attempt to draw attention away from the problem of prescription drug abuse, which is often mixed with alcohol abuse? What about economics? Could the "war on drugs" actually be an attempt to protect the reputation and profits of the pharmaceutical industry?

Let's take the "roofie" scare of the 1990s as an example. Stories about this drug were clearly more exotic than someone stealing their mother's Xanax and washing it down with a bottle of vodka. Stories about roofies, and the "inevitable" rapes that followed, played better in the press and on nightly police shows—of which there seem no end. Stories about roofie abuse fit the prevailing narrative of amoral teens running amok in a society that is going to hell in a hand basket. The reality about roofie use may have been quite different.

To start with, the roofie—*Rohypnol*—was originally developed by a Swiss pharmaceutical company to help people with sleeping disorders. Of course, just because a drug is legal and has only one legitimate purpose does not mean it cannot be abused. So, during the 1990s it was claimed that this "date-rape drug" was being used extensively by would-be predators. However, one study that looked at 1,033 cases of rape in which the victims also claimed they had been drugged found that only six had Rohypnol in their systems. The less surprising find was that nearly all of them had alcohol in their systems. Again, this indicates an unwillingness to deal with a larger but legal problem, namely alcohol abuse among the young. So, this false drug scare managed to draw attention away from an even bigger problem on college campuses: non-consensual sex between men and women known to each other, and often involving alcohol.[22]

What are we to take away from all of this? Should we have no fear? Can all of these things be explained away through statistics or blamed on a few rotten apples in society? Or, are there more structural reasons why we are so animated by fear in the modern world? The truth is that the world is not a carefree place, although many would like to create such a Disney-fied world. It is also true that the world is not a complete cesspool, but that does not mean we will never be a victim of time and place. What the work of Glassner and Furedi shows is that, for one reason or another, societies are constantly manufacturing new bogeymen, and the only logical reason for them to exist is to be keep people in a perpetual state of fear.

The problem from a social perspective, writes Glassner, is that these "fear mongers have knocked the optimism out of us by stuffing us full of negative presumptions about our fellow citizens and social institutions."[23] This lack of optimism and trust paralyzes us socially and individually, creating an environment more conducive to phobia and passivity rather than courage and action. This is an assessment shared by Frank Furedi who argues that safety has become a fetish in Western society. Safety for safety's sake is the rule, and those who violate it are seen as morally deficient, or even dangerous.

Furedi provides us with a list of things that scared people during the first half of 2001, prior to the attack on the World Trade Center. From the brief scare about *deep-vein thrombosis* that was supposedly linked to long-haul air flights to the fear that childhood immunizations were subjecting children to the risk of autism, the west has been assailed by all manner of "risks" lurking around every corner. In fact, the West has been bombarded every year by thousands of news articles that designate nearly everything we do as "risky" behavior. The increasing use of the term "at risk" was mentioned previously. Much of this attitude could be attributed to a loss of faith in mankind's ability to solve its own problems, which leads to the assumption that risk should not only be minimized but eliminated altogether—a goal that is clearly impossible. The problem from a social perspective is that a culture of fear ultimately leads to lower expectations, limited growth, and a lack of innovation.[24] These things are of paramount concern to a society geared almost solely toward material well-being. So, the culture of fear becomes an impediment to achieving what our society most prizes: *safety and wealth.*

As mentioned previously, by any statistical measure those in the West are wealthier and healthier than any group in history has ever been. Yet, we still insist on turning every banal experience into a major crisis. For example, when it comes to the religious moralist or the environmental activist the problem of risk in a complex society fits into their general narratives of a world that is falling apart because of sin or material excess. The former see the risks of modern society as the beginning of God's judgment; the latter see it as the revenge of a planet that has been raped and pillaged by mankind.[25] These folks propose two revanchist solutions: a return to traditional religion and morality, or a return to subsistence living. These solutions, though, only alienate the majority who happen to like the benefits of a complex, modern society, even though they might not like all the costs associated with it.

For example, Furedi suggests that excessive risk aversion might be a response to the wholesale violence of the first half of the twentieth century, a period that showed how politics and science could get out of hand, first in the form of fascism and totalitarianism, and then in the form of the atomic bomb.[26] It could also be a response to the complete individuation of society, a phenomenon that makes risk-taking even more dangerous since the risk is not shared by an extended family or the community. This growing atomization of Western society leaves the individual completely on his own, making mere survival, not growth, the only reason to exist.

The social upheavals of the 1950s and 1960s began to leave the individual with only himself as a reference point. In this situation the state becomes a foil, not a help. Family, friends, and community have become hindrances to personal fulfillment. The individual is left with no rules about how to behave in society; he begins to fear and loath everyone around him since they can only be viewed as competitors for scarce resources.[27] At the end of the 1970s Christopher Lasch called this the "war of all against all," a phrase taken from the work of the seventeenth century political theorist Thomas Hobbes. There is no evidence that things have changed much since Lasch wrote his seminal work *The Culture of Narcissism* (1979).

Is it also possible that our aversion to risk has a lot to do with the lack of concrete political and social achievements of an earlier age? For example, many of our political and social problems have now become "medicalized." Political and social oppression is now *victimhood*, made up of a series of psychological maladies that well-trained professionals have quantized and diagnosed, and there is no cure. So, these professionals teach us how to live with these maladies, or ignore them through the miracle of modern pharmacology. In this day and age everyone becomes a *victim* within the *cult of the riskless society*. After all, it is now immoral to take risks, because those who do take risks put not only themselves but the rest of society in danger.[28] The risk-taker can only brutalize, making everyone else a victim. Every year more and more neuroses, psychoses, and behavioral disorders are being "discovered." We have become in large part a society of the walking-ill, or as Susan Sontag might call them "the metaphorically sick." The abused and the abuser become celebrities, and every manner of personal weakness that gets the medical nod lowers the expectations we have of ourselves and society.[29] It denigrates the experience of the truly sick, making the suffering of the leukemia patient equivalent to that of the sex addict.

The insidiousness of the riskless society is exemplified in the way fear is sometimes used to achieve a very well-meaning objective. For example, the peril of sun exposure and its association with skin cancer has been in the news for the last thirty years. However, some have overstated the risks of skin cancer in order to keep people out of the sun altogether, and to hopefully save more lives. The truth is that human beings need sun—about twenty minutes a day—in order to activate the vitamin D in their systems. It has also been suggested that moderate exposure to the sun helps to build a tolerance against sun-related cancers, at least for those without a genetic predisposition for cancer. In other words, we have sacrificed the well-being of all because experts believe the public cannot handle nuanced instructions about how to properly care for their skin while in the sun.[30]

Yet another result of the culture of fear is that it has created a coterie of unelected advocates who stand between us and our elected representatives, allegedly to push for government policies that will benefit us. These "oligarchic" organizations claim to represent people in what is the only safe and unobstructed activity left to those in the West: *shopping*. This is one reason why we should lament the rise of these unelected, and often shadowy, *consumer advocacy groups*, because they end up creating one more layer of separation between us and our elected representatives. Rather than being good for us these self-appointed protectors are further proof that the electorate has lost touch with the social and political institutions that at one time were used to address the problems associated with living in a complex modern society.[31] This lack of direct involvement in the political process makes it easier for the culture of fear to thrive. It makes our political institutions appear ineffectual, which keeps people looking to anyone who will step up to protect them from a risky society that threatens to overwhelm them.

Unelected consumer advocates are not the only ones who claim to "have our back." Security companies are often viewed as the next best way of protecting us from the increasing dangers of a society run amok. The Security Essen trade show in Germany is a place where one can flit from exhibit to exhibit learning about the latest products in personal security. There is software to curtail "stranger danger," there are tasers, and, of course, there is pepper spray. One can also find a fence that makes every schoolyard a safe "compound" for children at play.[32] Again, one must ask, is all this really necessary? Is the world really that dangerous a place? Any objective analysis shows that, with the exception of war zones, the world is a far less dangerous place than we have been led to believe. Some have even suggested recently that this is the most peaceful time we have ever seen in human history.[33] Yet, many just will not believe it.

The culture of fear is largely a manufactured phenomenon. It benefits those who provide solutions for a fear they themselves create and spread. We will never rid ourselves completely of the culture of fear, because it is rooted in the weakness of the human condition and the limitations of society, but maybe understanding it a little better will help us to diminish its role in our society. That alone is a good reason to keep reading, and to hopefully learn why we need to stand courageously with others, even when the odds seem to be against us.

***

When I was a kid I used to sneak up late on Friday nights and watch old horror films. These films were what we would call "B-movies." The ones I liked the best were produced by the Hammer and Hammer studio. They usually featured Christopher Lee as Dracula and Peter Cushing as the intrepid Van Helsing. These were decidedly cheesy productions, which even I knew as a kid. However, one night the station chose to run a film called *Let's Scare Jessica to Death* (1971). This was a well-acted and graphic film, one in which throats get ripped open and the blood flows. The graphic violence was frightening enough, but what really scared *me* was the idea that there is sometimes a difference between what the mind sees and what is actually there. This was due to the fact that the main character of the film had just been released from a mental institution, so the viewer is left to wonder whether all this is really happening or if it's just in Jessica's mind. For some reason the thought that someone could lose their hold on reality made me more afraid than any monster.

When we talk about the culture of fear, or fear in general, we are entering into a world similar to the one I encountered with that old horror film. We grow uncertain about the dividing line between reality and fantasy. Real and imaginary fears become indistinguishable. Often we cannot put our finger on why we are anxious or afraid. We just know something is wrong, that "something wicked this way comes."

This feeling of uncertainty is the starting point for our examination of the culture of fear. We have made much of it the last few pages. To understand it fully, though, we must now dig deeper. We must explore that gnawing unease we all have about the world around us, an unease we all experience at some point in our lives. Most of us experience it only intermittently. Others live with it all the time. As we dig deeper into this subject it will become clear that we are all subtly influenced by the culture of fear, but that most of us only really feel it during times of personal or collective crisis. There are good reasons for this and they are rooted in our biology and psychology, but before we explore these aspects of fear, let us examine the last century of fear in the West.

Chapter Two

A Century of Fear

I know not with what weapons World War III will be fought, but World War IV will be fought with sticks and stones.

Attributed to Albert Einstein

In 1964 Stanley Kubrick gave us with his own dark take on Mutually Assured Destruction (MAD) in the film *Dr. Strangelove or: How I Learned to Stop Worrying and Love the Bomb*. The opening scene shows a paranoiac U.S. general, appropriately named Jack Ripper, starting a countdown toward nuclear annihilation. He does this by initiating an unprovoked first strike against the Soviet Union. After an unsuccessful attempt to stop the madness the Pentagon begins to make plans for the inevitable counterstrike. As the movie nears its conclusion Dr. Strangelove, an ex-Nazi scientist and now Pentagon advisor, suggests that the government bring lots of attractive women into the bunkers so they can more effectively repopulate the earth after the nuclear war destroys civilization. Anyone who enjoys absurdity will love the scene in which Slim Pickens hops on one of the nuclear weapons heading to Moscow, riding it like a bull in a rodeo.

Not everyone saw a reason to laugh at our impending destruction as a species. Sidney Lumet's film *Failsafe*, which came out the same year as *Dr. Strangelove*, took a more dour view of the nuclear-annihilation scenario. In this film a series of electrical malfunctions and human error lead to an atomic bomb run on Moscow. When it is clear the bomb run will succeed the President of the United States, played by Henry Fonda, tries to make a deal with the Soviets. In exchange for not retaliating with a full-scale nuclear strike against the United States the president proposes letting the Soviets bomb any U.S. city they choose. I will not give away the end.

Both of the films mentioned above came out after the Cuban Missile Crisis of October 1962, a moment when many thought we were on the brink of nuclear annihilation. However, these were not Hollywood's first forays into the subject of the *secular apocalypse*, and they would not be the last. The 1959 film *On the Beach* is set in post-war Australia where the last remaining survivors of a nuclear holocaust await their impending doom from radiation poisoning. It is only a matter of time before everyone is dead, so the movie explores what these people choose to do with their last remaining days.

All of the movies mentioned above were based on novels written in the late 1950s. These novels were written against the backdrop of post-World War II prosperity in the U.S., an escalating "Cold War" between the U.S. and the Soviets, and growing racial tension between whites and blacks in the United States. Oddly enough many today view the 1950s as an idyllic time, maybe because the United States was at a moment of political and economic ascendancy, and the social revolutions of the 1960s had not yet begun to *destroy society from within*. With shows like *Ozzie and Harriet* and *Leave it to Beaver* to come home to, and with a well-distributed economic prosperity made possible by unions and high-wage manufacturing jobs, it was easy for most to ignore the underlying social, economic, and political problems that faced the country.

However, not everyone could ignore these problems, which is why the turbulent 1960s brought about so much change, and confirmed within the American mind the general conviction that nuclear annihilation was almost inevitable. The destruction of the human race was so palpable that it even played a role in the 1964 presidential race between Barry Goldwater and Lyndon Johnson. In a now iconic piece of film a little girl is pulling the petals off a daisy and counting them. As she gets to the last petal and looks up a tinny, southern voice begins another countdown, a countdown that ends with film footage of a nuclear explosion. The voter is then warned about voting for anyone other than Lyndon Johnson. The ad only ran once, but it was a powerful use of fear. Johnson won.

Of course, by the end of the 1960s the fear that some right-wing extremist would *push the button* had given way to fears of crime, racial violence, drugs, vigilantism, government conspiracies, etc. These fears would be captured in the 1970s by films like the Dirty Harry series and the spy-thriller *Three Days of the Condor* (1975). So, the threat of nuclear annihilation was often crowded out by more provincial concerns, and by the U.S.'s impending loss of the war in Vietnam, all of which sapped American confidence. Nuclear annihilation also seemed to become less of a possibility as Nixon recognized Communist China and started a policy of détente with the Soviet Union. The latter policy led directly to the Strategic Arms Limitations Talks (SALT) of the 1960s and 1970s, an attempt to reduce tensions between the U.S. and the Soviet Union through a reduction in "defensive" nuclear weapons.

However, fear of nuclear annihilation made an encore appearance after the election of Ronald Reagan in 1980, primarily because Reagan was perceived as a bit of a cowboy when it came to foreign policy. The thought that Reagan might shoot first and ask questions later petrified many. This is ironic since the reality was that Ronald Reagan was deathly afraid of nuclear weapons and would later seek to reduce the nuclear arsenals of the U.S. and the Soviet Union through START (Strategic Arms Reduction Treaty) negotiations. These negotiations eventually led to a treaty signed by George H.W. Bush in 1991. However, the treaty was only a nominal step toward arms reductions. It failed to significantly reduce the threat of nuclear weapons. So, even with attempts in the 1970s and 1980s to address the massive stockpile of nuclear weapons held by the U.S. and the Soviets, there was still a growing concern that nuclear annihilation was almost inevitable, that it could result from mistakes made by the military or teenage hackers. The early 1980s saw several movies resurrect the theme of nuclear annihilation.

Keeping the message of apocalyptic destruction going in the 1980s, John Badham's *Wargames* was released in June of 1983. In this film a hapless, underachieving teenager mistakenly dials into a Pentagon computer and begins what he thinks is a game called "Global Thermonuclear War." It turns out to be a sophisticated gaming scenario run on a computer called WOPR (War Operation Plan Response). This leads to the possibility that WOPR will initiate a first strike against the Soviet Union because it thinks the scenario is real. The irony in the movie is that WOPR had just replaced humans in the missile silos because several teams had failed a test to launch their missiles when told to do so. Because of this failure WOPR is given control of all the missile silos. A similar plot line propels the movie *Colossus: The Forbin Project* (1970), but with far less sanguine consequences.

In November 1983 the TV movie *The Day After* was released. It was seen by an estimated 100 million Americans. It showed what might happen were the U.S. and the Soviets to engage in a skirmish that led to an all out nuclear confrontation. The movie was particularly frightening because of the special effects and the lack of a music sound track. It made nuclear annihilation for many seem all too real. The film was later released to theatres around the world and a friend of mine from New Zealand told me that she spent all her allowance on candy the same day she saw the movie. She was convinced there was little time left to enjoy life.

It is understandable how a child might have reacted to such things. The year before these movies came out my high school class read *Alas, Babylon* (1959), another post-nuclear war novel. I had been fed on a diet of disaster movies and post-apocalyptic movies in the 1970s, so I understood what it was like to live under the cloud of mass death every day. In fact, in a sixth grade class I once announced that we had enough nuclear weapons to destroy the world ten times over. I can still see all those blank stares coming from the other students, and the worried expression of our teacher as she quickly tried to change the subject.

In most of the movies within the nuclear-annihilation genre there is almost always some fluke that leads to nuclear war. The writers and directors of these movies want us to consider the possibility that these weapons are too dangerous to possess, even with the best safeguards and procedures. Rarely is a nuclear war the result of simple escalation like in *The Day After*. There is an interesting passage related to this idea in David Halberstam's *The Best and the Brightest*. According to Halberstam, Washington policy-makers had already concluded in the early 1960s that the use of nuclear weapons, even so-called "tactical nuclear weapons," was simply out of the question. The Pentagon agreed. If nuclear war was to come, they said, it would not be the conscious and considered decision of any leader within the U.S. government to engage in a first strike.[1] What was left but an accident or a malfunction of some sort?

This brings us to an interesting point in our consideration of fear and its cultural impact. Much of the fear that we will talk about throughout this book relates to our own inability to imagine that we have a handle on the world around us. We just cannot shake the thought that the world has grown too complex and that the slightest jarring of the system will lead to total collapse. We do not know whether this is true or not, but *we feel it*. Chaos surrounds us, waiting for its moment.

One of the goals of this book is to trace the source of that feeling of impending doom. So, I have spent a lot of time profiling movies in the last few pages. I will continue to do so throughout this book. The reason for this is that cultural fear is largely disseminated through literature and film, especially *secular-based, apocalyptic-themed* books and movies where human destruction results from nuclear war, super viruses, biological weapons, etc. These themes are to be distinguished from those associated with American evangelical and millennial religion, although, the secular apocalypse is informed by the apocalyptic themes of Christianity. This is evidenced in the common use of Christian *eschatological* terms like *rapture, millennium, judgment day*, and *Armageddon*. All of these terms have made it into the general lexicon of American speech and thought. We even use these terms to describe the weather, as we did a couple of years ago when a big snow storm hit the East Coast. We called it "Snowmageddon." That is why we cannot ignore the influence of these Christian themes when it comes to our discussion of fear and its cultural impact. So, we will deal with them below, in part three of this book.

The goal of this book is to help us understand how human fears are connected to our various conceptions of mankind's ultimate end. I do this by addressing the issue of why we are so susceptible to fear, and identifying what we fear most. Fear is an integral part of our DNA and psychology, which is known to anyone who has ever taken a basic psychology course. The *fight-or-flight* response is universal in the animal kingdom, and ten thousand years of civilization has not been long enough to counter millions of years of evolutionary development.

One of the tasks of this book is to distinguish between legitimate and illegitimate fears. The latter are used by politicians, pundits, and other unscrupulous individuals to gain power, profit, and prestige. One of the common characteristics of a legitimate fear is that the danger is unequivocal. There is also a clear response that can be taken to address legitimate fears, even if that response is simply to *flee*. One characteristic of an illegitimate fear is that the problem appears intractable, leaving us feeling helpless to respond. This *loss of agency* is another important theme throughout this book, since I will argue that modern fears and anxieties rarely lend themselves to clear-cut solutions.

First, though, we must lay some groundwork for our journey into the world of fear. I am much indebted for the rest of this chapter to the work of Joanna Bourke, whose book *Fear, A Cultural History* (2005) gives us great insight into the last hundred years of thinking about fear and the human condition. What we learn is that fear is a perennial part of the human experience, which some consider a necessary part of the maturation process but which others see as the chief enemy of human progress. Is it possible they are, to some extent, both right?

We start at the turn of the nineteenth century when many in both the United States and the UK began to experience an inordinate fear of being buried alive. This fear was so widespread that people began to demand more certainty when it came to the pronouncement of death, and more certainty that one was actually dead prior to being buried. Being buried alive did happen, but it was very rare. To meet the demand for certainty in death dozens of patents were filed for customized coffins equipped with things like air holes to the surface or an electric button that could be pushed to let someone know that "Hey! You guys buried me and I'm not dead!" One particularly gruesome request was made by a woman who wanted her heart removed prior to being buried.

This was not a new fear. Edgar Allen Poe had explored this long-held human fear in his story *The Cask of Amantillado* (1846), and Bram Stoker's *Dracula* (1897) may have fed these fears at the end of the nineteenth century, especially with all its talk of the living dead. Maybe that is why another woman at the end of the nineteenth century had a coffin designed with a stake mounted to the inside of the lid? This ensured her heart would be pierced when the lid was closed.[2] She would not have to worry about being buried alive.

One of the important issues addressed by the relatively new subject of psychology was how crowds react to disasters. The goal was to explain panics. Of course, in the early twentieth century there were the usual suspects, common to a chauvinistic and male dominated society. Hysteria was most often attributed to gender—women being more susceptible than men, although the vagaries of certain races and classes were also seen as likely culprits. It was thought by many that the responsibility of the *noblesse obliges* was to maintain their heads when all around were losing theirs. However, research showed how wrong this idea was in practice. The cultural elites appeared just as susceptible to panic as the *unwashed masses*. For example, the panic at the Iroquois Theater in Chicago, which occurred on December 30, 1903, cost 600 lives and provided psychologists with their first major case study about how people of all classes and gender react to unexpected events. Psychologists and sociologists at the time blamed the panic on the usual suspects: *gender* and *class*. However, in the case of the Iroquois Theater there was a much simpler explanation: the fire department had allowed numerous fire regulations to be ignored and the sole fireman on the scene was inadequately equipped to handle the curtain fire. Several decades after the Iroquois Theater fire psychologists and sociologists were beginning to understand that anyone can be subject to panic. Whether we panic or not depends on the situation, and one's mental state at the time. It has little to do with gender or class.[3]

In the early twentieth century some thought emotional states could be transferred to the fetus during gestation, which is why women were encouraged to remain calm during pregnancy. After giving birth it was also believed that the mother was the most influential force in passing on the right kind of temperament, a temperament that made it possible to deal with fear. Mothers were encouraged for a time to keep their children as free as possible from fear; however, the pendulum swung the other way when some suggested that a lack of exposure to fear was feminizing boys. This pendulum swung back and forth throughout the decades of the twentieth century, usually in response to something happening in society. For example, during the Cold War there was a concern that young men lacked the "manliness" needed to protect the country.[4]

This is still a concern as evidenced by the recent publication of Conn and Hal Iggulden's *The Dangerous Book for Boys* (2006). In this book boys are encouraged to build tree houses, explore nature, and generally learn how to be self-reliant. These are not such bad goals in and of themselves, but taken to an extreme we begin to hear calls for a new breed of men, "real" men. One man who is thought to have answered that call is Eustace Conway, who is thought by some to be "the last American man." Conway lives on his own thousand-acre preserve near Boone, North Carolina. He lives almost completely off the land, an attempt to escape what he considers to be the worst aspects of American culture, especially consumerism and corporatism. Conway was recently profiled in Nick Rosen's *Off the Grid* (2010), which is a catalogue of disaffected Americans who, as the subtitle of the book puts it, are seeking "more space," "less government," and "true independence." So, the debate about "manliness" continues, along with our struggle against fear.

In the mid-twentieth century there was an attempt to understand fear as merely a biological phenomenon. For example, nightmares were seen as the body's way of ordering conscious experience. This challenged the ideas of Freud and others. Freudians believed that nightmares were rooted in repressed desires or personal conflicts. Similar to nightmares, phobias were seen as emanating solely from the brain, which is why in the 1950s and 1960s lobotomies were used in extreme cases of "chronic fear." ECT, or electroconvulsive therapy, was also a popular tool for alleviating the psychic pain of constant fear. Even today there is no generally agreed upon response to phobic behavior, although a combination of conversational therapy, desensitization, and drugs have been found effective in moderate cases of chronic fear.[5]

One of the most interesting observations in Joanna Bourke's book is the relationship between self-identity and fear. As she writes, "Psychosurgery reduced fear by blunting any sense of self-identity."[6] This is an interesting point to which Bourke returns in a roundabout way throughout the rest of her book. This is clearly one of the most important points to be made about fear, because fear is ultimately a very personal experience. One might even argue that it is absurd to say that a society can experience fear. What we are really saying, with phrases like "the culture of fear," is that enough individuals within a society are experiencing enough fear that it appears to be a social phenomenon.

Individuals experience fear on many different levels, but it is especially keen at a primal level, when it involves physical survival—or a perceived question of survival. During these times when life is threatened the *fight-or-flight* response is engaged, and Bourke suggests that as we have moved closer to the end of the twentieth century the natural fight-or-flight response has been short-circuited by our inability to do either. We are unable to run away and we are unable to define in concrete terms what threatens us. This has ultimately become the source of our modern, collective anxiety, which becomes naked fear during times of social crisis.

An example of how this system of fight-or-flight is short-circuited can be seen in how men react to modern warfare. In a modern war a whole host of physiological reactions are observed during combat, including diarrhea, evacuation of bowels and bladders, abnormal heartbeats, etc. These physical reactions appear to be a natural response to the anxieties that buildup in a modern war zone, a place where the fight-or-flight response is often not a feasible reaction to those anxieties. This was particularly true in World War I where trench warfare was the norm. What has been found is that modern warfare creates an increase in anxiety rather than fear, and that anxiety is more difficult to deal with than raw fear. This helps to explain why modern soldiers are subject to the longer term effects of PTSD (Post-Traumatic Stress Disorder). Men cope differently in battle. Some harden quickly to the conditions while others need coaxing or castigation. However, extensive durations of inactivity, and not knowing when the danger will come but believing it to be imminent, causes increased anxiety for even the most hardened soldier.[7]

Increased anxiety can also be found among civilian populations during wartime. In examining the bombing of Britain during World War II it was found that civilians during the German bombing campaign were quickly acclimated to the dangers and soon went about their normal business. Even neurotics adapted well to the situation. However, on March 3, 1943, one hundred and seventy-eight men, women, and children were trampled to death due to a panic at Bethnal Green, the entrance to a bomb shelter. This proved that panic could still take hold of people who had effectively dealt with the stress of previous bombings.

In this particular case people may have believed the Germans were re-taliating for a large Allied bombing campaign that had just been carried out against Berlin. It was also shown that this particular area of London was prone to believing that it had been infiltrated by a host of immigrant subversives, an example of the natural xenophobia associated with any war.[8]

Two more examples illustrate the role anxiety plays in creating a full-blown panic. In 1926 Father Ronald Knox performed a satirical production on BBC radio called "Broadcast from the Barricades." It was a fictional account of the unemployed rising up in London and begin-ning what many thought was a real civil war. Bourke says that the socio-economic conditions of England at the time are the best explanation for why people took this broadcast seriously and began to panic. The Brit-ish people were already expecting something like this to happen and so ignored the repeated announcements that the production was fictional. This panic, however, was nothing compared to the one caused by Orson Welles's production of *The War of the Worlds* on October 30, 1938. Over a million people claim to have taken the broadcast seriously. However, many later claimed that they really thought it was an invasion of the Japanese or the Germans. Again, this shows how the socio-economic and political situation of the time influenced people's perceptions. The Great Depression and war fears contributed to the general sense that bad things were about to happen to American society.[9]

At the end of the twentieth century we find that we are no less fear-ful than we were at the beginning of the twentieth century. In fact, since 1945, after the detonation of two atomic bombs over Hiroshima and Nagasaki, we have had reason to fear more than any previous genera-tion. Modern fears of death, disease, and pain—in the form of cancer, HIV, and prolonged decrepitude—have taken hold of us at the end of the twentieth century. In large part we have substituted the fear of nu-clear annihilation with the fear of child molesters, violent crime, and a world full of man-made chemicals that will eventually kill us all. Climate change, super-viruses, and all manner of theoretical risk scenarios have convinced us that the dangers we face are pervasive and persistent. More importantly, we are convinced that these are dangers from which we cannot flee and against which we cannot fight. Again, the inability to engage in our natural fight-or-flight response in the presence of perceived dangers has created increasing amounts of anxiety. After all in a world beset with murky and ghostly risks, where is there to go and who are we to fight?[10]

It is not difficult to understand how the culture of fear thrives in the twenty-first century. We are subject daily to the fear-based milieu generated by politicians, pundits, and so-called experts. These individuals are willing to prey on our natural propensity to fear the unknown. They do so in order to enrich and empower themselves.

We may never be able to rid ourselves completely of fear, but we may be able to mitigate its effects through a better understanding of ourselves and the world around us. That is what I aim to do throughout the rest of this book: *convince you that most of the fear and anxiety with which you live in our modern world is manufactured, an illusion meant to deceive and control.* Only then can we hope to fight against the culture of fear through social and political action. By working together we can hope to reduce the amount of fear in our society, even the fear some believe to be politically healthy.

So, how can we better understand the fears that motivate us? In the next two chapters we will explore the biological and psychological roots of our greatest fears, and this will make it easier for us to understand why we are such easy prey for *the makers of fear*.

Chapter Three

The Biology of Fear

Most species do their own evolving, making it up as they go along, which is the way Nature intended. And this is all very natural and organic and in tune with mysterious cycles of the cosmos, which believes that there's nothing like millions of years of really frustrating trial and error to give a species moral fiber and, in some cases, backbone.

Terry Pratchett, author of the Discworld Series

None of us like to admit we are afraid. Fear is an admission of weakness, and in a society that prizes strength it is simply not acceptable to admit that we are scared or uncertain about ourselves, or the future. Instead we prefer to live with the illusion of power, usually sought through economic, political, or martial prowess—or the promise of these things. This illusion and its accompanying myths of self-sufficiency—as opposed to self-reliance—keep us operating without complaint in an environment that is ultimately corrosive to individual initiative. We are told we can do anything, that "the world is our oyster," but deep down we know it is not true, and the anxiety manufactured by this realization leaves us feeling scared and impotent. This is the true source of the culture of fear: *our underlying biological susceptibility to a fear rooted in our inability to know or control the environment around us.*

It is not difficult to understand where this proclivity comes from if you read modern-day works on psychology, philosophy, and human evolution. We are a species that has spent the bulk of its existence running away, only fighting when backed into a corner. This is nothing to be ashamed of; after all, running away is a smart thing to do when six hundred pounds of man-eating muscle and bone is chasing you. Within the last fifty thousand years or so human organization has ameliorated many of the conditions that made fear such a handy response to the unknown. Today large areas of urban development protect us from the worst uncertainties of nature. So much so that many bewail our loss of courage, our inability to understand how "red in tooth and claw" life really is.

In trying to understand why we react the way we do when swamped by the unknown, or an event which gives us the sense we have lost control over our lives, many have begun to study how the brain processes data during episodes of stress. This research is, even after a hundred years, still in its toddler stage, but we are making great strides by using the model of behavioral psychology and the technology of functional magnetic resonance imaging (fMRI). We have learned a lot of interesting things the last few years.

Back in the 1980s there was an anti-drug commercial where an egg was held up in front of the camera while a voice-over said, "This is your brain." The camera then pans to a skillet. You hear the egg being cracked and see it dropped into the pan. As you watch it sizzle the voice-over continues, "This is your brain on drugs. …Any questions?" A similar commercial could be made today using an fMRI video. We could show a brain functioning normally and then we could show what happens when the subject is suddenly frightened or made anxious. What researchers have learned so far is enough to "blow your mind." What will bowl you over is that all this research into fear and biology has begun to reveal how little we consciously control ourselves. In fact, it could be argued from what researchers have learned that our unconscious mind exerts far more influence over how we consciously behave than we ever imagined. In other words, we are more likely to be influenced by our stomach and colon than our conscious mind, but we never realize it.

***

Fear is part and parcel of being a member of the animal kingdom. Without it few of us would survive a day in the wild, or maybe even on the streets of New York City. The most fundamental fear, which every member of the animal kingdom experiences, is the fear of death. Some might argue that only humans can fear death because only we can *conceptualize* it, that only we can ruminate about it. However, watch a leopard chase a gazelle and still try to argue that the fear of death does not motivate the gazelle to move as fast as it can. Granted, gazelles probably do not sit around worrying about death as humans do these days—to the terrible disappointment of pharmaceutical companies pushing happy pills—but that does not make their death any less traumatic when it comes. It also points to something we share with the rest of the animal kingdom: an autonomical, biological, and chemical system that responds to all perceived external threats.

It can be safely said that without this defense mechanism evolution would not have been possible. Imagine a species completely devoid of fear. How long do you think that gene pool would have survived before the last remaining member crawled out on a loose branch that had sprung from the side of a high canyon wall? Maybe such a species once existed?

If we want to understand fear and the role it plays in modern society, we must first look to the biology and chemistry of the human body. Now, I am not a medical doctor, so anything I say throughout the rest of this chapter represents my knowledge of the prevailing literature. As with all scientific fields, theories change, and some are even discarded. New research continues to provide us with deeper and better insights into how our bodies and minds work. Having said all this, I am confident that the general conclusions drawn in this chapter regarding fear will prove accurate. In short, we have a good general idea of what happens to the human body during those moments when our autonomic systems react to the unexpected or to life threatening situations.

The fear of death is a visceral experience, prompting what psychologist call the *fight-or-flight* response. There are a whole host of physical symptoms associated with this type of visceral fear: increased heart rate, a surge in adrenalin, and the release of chemicals in the brain that shut down some sections while activating others. These chemicals operate as part of what doctors call the *endocrine system*. For example, one of the chemicals involved in regulating neurotransmitters in the brain is Gamma-Aminobutyric Acid (GABA). Researchers think this chemical regulates the neurotransmitters in the brain, acting as a sort of governor that allows the brain to operate at a manageable speed. It has been shown that when GABA is not present in sufficient quantities the result is fear or anxiety, which is why popular anxiety drugs like Valium are thought to trigger an increase in GABA production, thus calming the brain. Think of it this way: the brain is an electrical system, and when GABA is present the electrical impulses are regulated; when GABA is not present the electrical impulses are unregulated, leading to what we might call an *encephalic storm*.

The complexity of the chemical cocktail in our brains was made clear to me a decade ago when I read through James Austin's *Zen and the Brain: Toward an Understanding of Meditation and Consciousness* (1998). The book is not as New Age as it sounds. Austin is a medical doctor and practicing clinician at the University of Missouri's Health Science Center. He is also a practicing Zen Buddhist. His interest is in how the brain responds physically and chemically to meditation, which has now been studied for decades. Early studies focused primarily on the brainwave patterns of those who meditated. Austin and others now have tools like fMRI machines that allow them to focus in on specific areas of the brain that become active while a person is meditating, or praying.[1] What impressed me the most about *Zen and the Brain* was the number of naturally occurring chemicals in the brain, chemicals like nicotine. That's right! Nicotine occurs naturally in the brain, and in sufficient quantities it causes a release of dopamine into the brain. Dopamine is a chemical associated with feelings of euphoria. In other words, we feel happy and relaxed when nicotine causes dopamine to be released into our brains. Now you know why those cigarettes are so addicting.

Chemistry, though, is not the only factor that prompts the brain to respond to perceived dangers. There is also a physiological component, in particular a section of the brain called the *amygdala*, which researchers have found reacts specifically to threatening situations. This part of the brain is hard wired (to use the parlance of computer science) to an ancient system of the brain called the *limbic system*, and this area is the most ancient part of our modern brains, an evolutionary holdover from a very distant age. It controls not only our response to threatening situations but appears to have a lot do with our emotional state as well. Sorry, folks, it might not be love; it might just be an overactive amygdala.

I first learned about the limbic system when I read Carl Sagan's book *Broca's Brain: Reflections on the Romance of Science* (1979). The first chapter of this book is devoted to Paul Broca, who postulated during the nineteenth century that the brain was a compartmentalized system. Because of this he suggested the brain could be studied to show which parts control which functions. Of course, we take this idea for granted today. What I found most interesting about this chapter is how Sagan described the evolutionary development of the brain. He said that the limbic system was an ancient part of the brain that we share with all animals, that it controlled most of our autonomic functions, and that it was the core around which the *superior* human brain had developed. The implications here are clear: humans literally have two brains. This is a central concept in brain theory, but the point to be made here is that fear operates at this basic level of human anatomy, in the limbic system, where physiology and chemicals do all the talking.

Because raw fear is so closely tied to our biology there is little we can do to get rid of it. We can try to compensate for it with the more rational part of our brain, but the battle will always be lopsided in favor of the unconscious mind. It is a *condition* with which we must all learn to live and, as mentioned above, without it we might stand a little less chance of survival in certain situations. For example, imagine you are a woman in a big city at night. You have just gotten out of a cab, alone, and someone starts to follow you. You grow a little nervous because it is only you and the person behind you on the street. Then, you pass by a coffee shop where a crowd of people sit. Do you duck into it or ignore the alarm bells going off in your head? Maybe you are just being silly, but your limbic system has been trained over millions of years to react to this situation. When it is dark and you are all alone, and someone or something unknown to you approaches, you either turn to fight or you run away.[2]

Fear and *anxiety* are often used synonymously, but the former has an immediacy the latter lacks, which is why we should now insist on a distinction. The reason for this should be apparent when talking about the culture of fear, since anxiety usually does not prompt to action but fear usually does. In this respect we will find that what we have been calling "the culture of fear" would probably be more accurately termed "the culture of anxiety," since few people in modern societies act on these anxieties. They just learn to live with them, or take drugs so they can ignore them. That is why I have said that the culture of fear (or *anxiety*) paralyzes and infantilizes.

Most professional researchers make a distinction between the terms *fear* and *anxiety*, although it is unclear where the line should be drawn. In general, *fear* is caused by objective and immediate threats to our well-being while *anxiety* is "objectless" and in some distant future. If we view these two states along a continuum, then anxiety might be just to the left of zero. Zero would represent a calm repose. As we move left of zero we grow more anxious until, faced with an immediate threat, we enter into a state of fear. However, a fear does not have to be real. We can believe that we face an imminent threat even when we do not. Maybe you are wondering what happens if we move to the right of zero? Well, that is not the subject of this book, but I can assure you there is no end of books devoted to this rightward move into *perfect serenity*. Just spend a few hours in the self-help section of your local bookstore to see how many books claim to have all the answers.

There are many reasons why we might fear things that in reality are not threats to our safety and well-being. For instance, some researchers believe that a perceived loss of control in certain situations might lead to an increase in anxiety. These situations could lead us to believe we have few options, that we are being boxed in. This inability to cope with certain situations might derive from our inability to assess both the situation and our own strengths and weaknesses. On the flip side of this is the person who can do a proper assessment of both the situation and himself. This person is able to respond quickly to changes because they have prepared for likely contingencies and have accepted that planning will not always work. We read about examples of this in Joanna Bourke's book, presented in previous chapter.

The biological evidence suggests that people exist on a continuum somewhere between excessive caution and the complete inability to properly measure risk. Where you fall on this continuum will have a lot to do with biology, but as we get older psychology begins to play an even greater role in establishing our primary fears and our assessment of risk. Evolutionary biologists have begun to theorize about the relationship between fear and larger brain capacities in humans. Our brains appear to be sophisticated devices able to detect complex patterns within systems that have thousands of data points. That same brain also serves as a biologically-based simulator. It allows us to run all kinds of sophisticated scenarios about what could happen next in particular situations. However, these systems are not always accurate, because sometimes we connect events that are not really connected, and sometimes we run scenarios that have no objective basis in reality.

Why is this? Why is it that our brains sometimes seem so inadequate when it comes to dealing with the world around us? Why is science now starting to tell us to distrust what we see, hear, and feel?[3] The first clue can be found in evolutionary theory, in how we believe the brain developed through a series of kludge-like steps that culminated in the human prefrontal cortex. Please remember as we discuss human evolution below that we cannot predict what effect a single biological adaptation may have on other aspects of development, or even on the ability to survive in a particular environment. For example, Richard Dawkins suggests that symbolism and abstract thinking were possibly a direct result of the development of language, which as we learn below might have resulted from bipedalism. However, none of this could have been predicted beforehand. We only know it in hindsight. This becomes an important point when we begin to discuss culture, because it is hard to imagine human culture without language, symbolism, and abstract thought.[4] However, there was no way to predict whether bipedalism would lead to such a thing, and the evidence is that it did not always lead to such a thing. Evolution seems to proceed by starts and stops in complex environments, which is why it is difficult to predict what any one adaptation will yield. For ninety percent of the known species now catalogued their adaptations have meant extinction.

***

The most accessible description of human evolution can be found in Desmond Morris's *The Naked Ape* (1967). However, it is not a good starting point for those who want an accurate, up-to-date introduction to evolution. In an attempt to demystify—and maybe even sex-up—evolution, Morris also presented several controversial theories about gender development and pair-bonding. Still, except for these controversial theories and a now outdated evolutionary timeline, it is an interesting introduction to the science of evolution and human culture. Morris's final description of the naked ape as a "vertical, hunting, weapon-toting, territorial, neotenous, brainy" species, who is a "...primate by ancestry and a carnivore by adoption, ready to conquer the world" seems as apropos today as it did fifty thousand years ago.[5]

It took millions of years for the process of evolution to produce an ape-like creature that served as the basis for modern man and his primate cousins. The timeline presented by Morris has changed somewhat the last few decades, and this may confuse the general reader were he to pick up a later treatment by Wilson, Mayr, Gould, or Dawkins. For example, Morris writes that around fifteen million years ago the ancestral species of what would become modern man diverged from a common ancestor that he shares with the other major primates, i.e., chimpanzees, gorillas, and orangutans. It is now thought that this occurred some seven million years ago. Morris also says that bipedalism developed only in the last million years while modern researchers believe this happened as long ago as six or seven millions years ago. This is important because the question of bipedalism is related to the development of the human brain.

Craig Stanford addresses this question in his book *Upright: The Evolutionary Key to Becoming Human* (2003). According to Stanford, bipedalism should be seen a necessary precursor to the development of the modern human brain, a development which most likely began in earnest around five million years ago. Walking upright affects the way we breathe and the way blood flows to the brain. Walking upright would have given our early ancestors the ability to modulate their voices, and possibly even speak. Meat eating, as Morris also points out, would have been an important dietary change because it would have led to larger brain sizes. The question of why bipedalism would develop at all is still a bit of a mystery since evolutionary theory demands that any adaptive quality must contribute to survival, if it is to be useful. So, there is a cost-benefit issue associated with every biological adaptation, although with natural selection theory this cost-benefit analysis can never occur beforehand.[6]

One adaptation that may help to explain both bipedalism and our larger brains is the *vertebral plexus*, a system that drains blood from the brain when we stand up, and which may serve as a cooling system. The brain is very sensitive to heat, which is why fevers are so dangerous and why doctors make them a priority in the treatment of illness. Is it possible that standing benefitted the brain's development? Of course, then the question has to be asked, "Why did we stand up in the first place?" The answer is still, "We don't know." However, we can eliminate the possibility that it had anything to do with someone thinking beforehand about how it would directly benefit the development of the brain. So, it was more likely a food gathering strategy, a mating strategy, or a defensive strategy, that caused our ancestors to stand up. Over a long period of time this erect posture morphed from a part-time necessity into full-time bipedalism. What we do know is that it happened about five to seven million years ago, it came and went with several species, and this development is one of the main reasons our own species took off like a rocket about 300,000 years ago.[7]

It should be pointed out again that none of this was destined to be. The law of natural selection could have easily kept us living side-by-side with our ape-like ancestors: the chimpanzee, the gorilla, and the orangutan. As Stanford writes,

> Bipeds rose early and quickly in human origins and almost certainly included not only those that eventually led to modern humanity but many others barely known or yet undiscovered. All evidence points to a form of bipedalism in which natural selection tinkered and toyed but never tried to create "the perfect biped."[8]

Another reason for the rapid development of hominids, according to Morris, may have had to do with something that happened around seven million years ago (*Morris said fifteen million years ago in his original book*).[9] It was around this time that the forests in which these species dwelt began to diminish in size, so some were forced out of the forests and into competition with the already well-developed predators on the plains.[10] One of the initial problems with this was that primates tend to be less socially cohesive because their diet does not require the kind of coordination and effort that carnivores require. In other words, if most of what you eat comes from the ground, or from picking fruit from a plant or tree, you tend to have less call for social coordination.[11]

It is generally agreed by evolutionary biologists that walking upright was a very important development, because it meant an amazing increase in the size of hominid cranial capacity. The human brain is six times the size it should be for a mammal our size.[12] The reason this is so important is because it eventually set modern man on the path to creating the cultural patterns that have so dramatically influenced the way we live today. The true revolution in human development began about 50,000 years ago when human culture began to dominate human existence; however, this would not have been possible without the millions of years of biological development that preceded it. Human cultural development can be seen as a response to natural selection since it largely tries to free us from the harsh environment with which our ancestors had to struggle for millions of years. Prior to the development of culture and civilization we were at the mercy of natural forces, only cooperating in limited ways when engaged in predatory activities. With the development of culture and civilization we have, in many respects, created our own environment, an environment less susceptible to the vicissitudes of the natural world. In other words, where we formerly had only the option of adapting to nature we can now envision a world where we adapt nature to ourselves.[13]

How does all this relate to our discussion of the culture of fear? The answer to that question may have best been answered by Desmond Morris when he wrote, "Cultural developments have given us more and more impressive technological advances, but wherever these clash with our basic biological properties they meet strong resistance." This is because no matter how strong the tug of our cultural environment "a complex beast" always "stirs within us."[14] Freud would have agreed, as evidenced in his essay *Civilization and Its Discontents* (1930). This is why we must look under the hood, so to speak. In order to understand the culture of fear, we must start with a basic knowledge of the human brain, which always leads us back to the story of evolution. This, however, is freighted with controversy because it forces us to consider the cultural implications of evolutionary theory, and this often results in a debate about nature versus nurture.[15]

For the moment, though, let us leave the cultural debate and talk about what we actually know and do not know about the brain. To do this we have to talk a little about the biology of the brain, which will later help us to understand how fears are formed in the brain. The next few pages will give us a short overview of the makeup of the brain. This, of course, does not do justice to the complexity of the human brain. The general reader may feel a little overwhelmed by the next couple of pages, but do not worry since there will be no test at the end.

***

The brain as a whole is made up of five basic areas: the brain stem, the cerebellum, the diencephalon, the limbic system, and the cerebral cortex. The brain stem, sometimes called the "reptilian brain," has three parts: the medulla oblongata, pons (bridge), and the midbrain. The medulla oblongata controls involuntary activity like breathing and digestion, the pons is a "bridge" serving as a communications gateway, and the midbrain controls sensory and motor control like that associated with the movement of the eye.

The cerebellum is the central processing area for movement and balance control. It is interesting to note that this area makes up only a tenth of the whole volume of the brain, yet it contains fifty percent of all the neurons in the brain. This may indicate how important motor control and movement has been in our evolutionary development. Neuroscientist Daniel Wolpert recently gave a TED talk, arguing that the brain's primary function has largely been getting us from point A to point B.[16] That fifty percent of our neurons are devoted to this activity would seem to support this claim.

The diencephalon is made up of two sub-systems: the thalamus and hypothalamus. The thalamus works like a central processing unit, deciding where signals get sent when they come into the brain. The hypothalamus is associated with motivation. It regulates things like sex drive, enjoying music, the maternal instinct, etc. It also establishes the Circadian Rhythm, which regulates the twenty-four hour schedule of biological, chemical, and physiological functions, and which often responds to environmental cues.

The limbic system has three sub-systems: the basal ganglia, the amygdala, and the hippocampus. The first is concerned with fine motor control, the second controls our emotional responses, and the last is intricately involved in our memory system. There are lots of other sub-systems in this area of the brain but these are the three major ones.

Finally, we have the cerebral cortex, which is comprised of the two hemispheres: the left hemisphere where language is processed and the right hemisphere where most of our spatial awareness resides. We know this because certain areas of the brain have been identified as essential to certain functions of the body. For example, in the left hemisphere there are two areas of the brain that control how we speak and how we understand speech. The section called Broca's Area controls our ability to speak. If it is damaged we cannot speak properly, or at all, although we can still understand the speech of others. Another section in the left hemisphere is called Wernicke's area. If this area is damaged our speech becomes nonsensical. All of these areas were beginning to be identified by the end of the nineteenth century as individuals like Paul Broca, David Ferrier, Gustav Fritsch, and Eduard Hitzig started mapping them. These individuals quickly learned that the frontal cortex controlled voluntary movements while the prefrontal cortex was linked to personality and behavior, damage to the latter caused major changes in personality and behavior.

The cerebral cortex also has four lobes: the frontal, parietal, occipital, and temporal. The first controls our ability to pay attention and to plan. The second controls our spatial processing. Think of it as a built in GPS system. The third, the occipital lobe, controls our vision. Lastly, the temporal lobe controls the processing of sound and language. This area is also connected somehow to the hippocampus, so it may have some effect on how we form and store memories.[17]

We have only scratched the surface here when it comes to the complex biological structures of the human brain. That is why it is difficult for us to understand how the brain works as a whole. We are like the early cartographers of the planet, mapping out areas and peoples about which we know little. We do know one thing, though; the brain often takes raw data and fills in the gaps. Whether this addition of remembered data yields an accurate picture of the world is dependent on how good our memories are, and our memories have been shown to be *not that great*. This helps us to understand why the brain works the way it does when it comes to fear. Believe it or not your brain does not really care what you think; it knows danger when it sees or senses it, and this is one of the reasons fear is a problem in a modern society.

In his book *Fear Itself* (1998), Rush W. Dozier maintains that fear is a pervasive experience intersecting with the most mundane aspects of our life and determining in large part the structures of society. He writes,

> Somewhere between these opposite poles of torment and utter painlessness most of us live our lives, our minds filled with an ever-changing hierarchy of pain-inspired fears.[18]

The challenge for human beings is to face those fears and make choices that are good for us in the long run. Most of us can adjust to the normal fears of everyday existence. We even have the ability to adjust our lives to situations where there is a persistent risk of danger, as evidenced by civilians going about their daily business in bombed-out urban landscapes. However, there are limits and those who live in perpetual and mortal fear, whether real of imagined, eventually become psychically exhausted.[19] Therefore, it is imperative that we understand the processes that make fear such a pervasive experience.

One way we can conceptualize our biologically-based fear system is by splitting it into three main subsystems. The first subsystem of fear is exemplified in the primitive *fight-or-flight* response, which we have mentioned previously. This system has been proven to kick in a tenth of a second before we are conscious of what is going on. This is why when we see something that looks like a snake crawling on the ground we instinctively jump away from it. This is because we have an instinctual fear of noise, spiders, and snakes—a fear we share with our primate cousins. This fear even extends to pictures of spiders and snakes flashed on a screen too fast for our conscious minds to process. Subjects have reported feeling uneasy or scared when subliminal pictures of spiders and snakes are mixed with a variety of innocuous material on a computer screen. This proves that our brain sees these pictures without our conscious knowledge and it tries to warn us before the danger becomes apparent. However, the fact that this subsystem can be activated by pictures and not real dangers shows that it responds to dangers whether real or imagined, which means we probably have little chance of eliminating this primitive subsystem of fear response.[20]

This primitive subsystem makes decisions that are primarily irrational, especially when placed in the context of a complex, stable society. It tends to make decisions based on generic "rules of thumb," or intuition. For example, many stopped taking planes just after September 11, 2001. This might have been a rational decision for a week or a month but it lasted far longer than that, and according to one statistical study done by Gerd Gingerenser, a psychologist at the Max Planck Institute in Berlin, 1,595 more people died in auto accidents than should have in the year following the September 11th attacks. This is because people began driving more, and driving is statistically more dangerous than flying. This behavior was caused by what is called the *example rule*, which states that people will assume that when they observe something happening in the world that they are at greater risk of it happening to them, even if that event is completely random and happens thousands of miles away. We encountered this idea earlier but called it the *availability heuristic*. So, most decisions are made at the gut level, using the primitive subsystem, and this is particularly true when decisions have to be made quickly.[21] That is why we must make an effort to use the second subsystem talked about in Dozier's book. This will help us to make better decisions, although there is no guarantee of being right all the time, or even most of the time.

The second subsystem of fear takes charge after we are initially frightened and then processes the events after the fact. This system is associated with that part of the cerebral cortex responsible for how attentive we are and how well we plan things. This is the part of our brain that helps us to avoid painful situations in the future. One of the things this system relies on is our memories, and it has been shown that memories are strengthened if formed during times when we are highly emotional. So fear episodes tend to be remembered with clarity. One of the side-effects of this system is that our ability to anticipate pain could heighten our consciousness of fear, even when there is no rational reason to be scared. For example, the discovery of fire unleashed mankind's potential in his struggle with the environment, but it also sowed the fear of our annihilation at our own hands. We can also get addicted to fear because of the chemical reward that comes with surviving a life or death situation. In situations where the flight-or-fight response kicks in, the body releases *noradrenaline*. After that sudden rush of noradrenaline the body releases "opiatelike neurochemicals" into the brain. This gives us a post-exhilaration high to which many people can become addicted.[22] This explains why roller coasters and parachuting are so popular.

This second biological subsystem of fear began to develop several hundred thousand years ago. It has been the focus of research for decades and has given rise to what Paul Slovic and Daniel Kahneman have called the "affect heuristic." The theory behind this is based on the observed increase in the size of the human brain, which most likely led directly to the development of language, symbolism, and abstraction. This was mentioned earlier when we talked about the prefrontal cortex. This second subsystem is more analytical in its approach to the stimuli it receives from the outside world; however, the news is not all good because even this subsystem can be faulty and highly biased. For example, the *anchoring rule* proves that we are heavily influenced by numbers we have encountered prior to making later calculations. We know this because researchers have asked subjects to write down the last two digits of their Social Security number at the top of a bid list and then they asked them to place a silent bid on a bottle of wine. What they found is that there is an amazing statistical correlation between the two numbers, even though they are totally unrelated to one another. This experiment has also been done with judges passing down sentences. Judges are asked to roll a die before making sentencing decisions. If the number on the die is lower the sentence will be shorter while higher numbers on the die will yield longer sentences. This is what psychologists have termed "priming," and it is a widely observed behavior.[23] It is also why corporations and politicians run their ads several times a day when they want you to buy what they are selling.

In the end we must admit, along with Herbert Simon, that we are rational, but only to a point. We engage in what Simon calls "bounded rationality," which, among other things, proves the lie of the *rational economic man*. Even with all our statistical analysis we still tend to make decisions based on anecdote and the gut. For example, the controversy over silicone breast implants and their relationship to women getting sick has still to be proven. There is no statistical correlation between the two, yet Dow Chemical was forced into bankruptcy because some women got sick years after their surgeries. We just assume that B follows A in a narrative fashion, regardless of the statistical evidence. Ellen Peters at Decision Research has suggested that better and more widespread training in mathematics would ameliorate this problem; however, as we will see in a future chapter, even experts with extensive backgrounds in mathematics are subject to the *example rule* and the *anchoring rule*. This probably has a lot to do with another phenomenon that has been observed. In experiments where people are surrounded by others claiming something completely opposite of what they know to be true the subject is 75% more likely to go with the crowd and against his better judgment.[24] This has profound implications for those who work in groups. Science and other academic pursuits are collective efforts where mainstream ideas are sought to be proven, not challenged,[25] so what does this mean for knowledge and decision-making if the group has it wrong?

Daniel Gardner said it best when he wrote, "Rational risk regulation is a slow, careful, and thoughtful examination of the dangers and costs in particular cases."[26] When this statement is measured against what we are learning about things like the *example rule* and the *anchoring rule*, we begin to see the shortcomings of both in a modern, complex, and stable society. Living by anecdote on the African plains 200,000 years ago might have worked most of the time but today it is a bad way of not only surviving but of thriving.

***

The spectrum that runs from constantly fearful to the stupidly fearless is a consequence of genes and brain development. The body, according to Rush Dozier, must be viewed as a single complex unit, which we can term *consciousness*, or *mind*. This term is meant to be a catchall for what happens when each individual's limbic system, left prefrontal cortex, and frontal cortex work in concert—not always well.[27] Dozier claims that consciousness serves as an arbiter between our primitive and rational fear systems; however, it is this last claim where Dozier may have gone astray in his analysis. Michael Shermer and others have made the convincing case that *mind* is only an intellectual construct, that it does not exist apart from the constituent biological parts that make up the human thinking process.[28] One way to retrieve Dozier's view from its reductionist fate is to see the mind as a product of human culture, something that can be stored, modified, and retrieved collectively, and in various ways. For example, the fear of death has not only been used by religion to cajole and prod into submission but it has also been used to habituate ourselves to the knowledge of our own inevitable demise as living creatures.[29]

Dozier suggests that both individuals and societies can experience fear, and that "a society's attitude toward fear profoundly shapes its response to issues of individual liberty, change, and personal security."[30] It may be more accurate to say that individual human beings are the only ones who can directly experience fear, since fear is a momentary construct that results from the human brain's response to outside stimuli. However, a society could be said to experience fear vicariously through human culture. Viewing the *mind* from this perspective makes it partly a reflection of our collective selves, manifested as human culture, and if viewed this way it is another way to explain the phenomenon we call *the culture of fear*.

Chapter Four

The Psychology of Fear

Men fear death, as children fear to go in the dark; and as that natural fear in children is increased with tales, so is the other.

Sir Francis Bacon, 1561-1626

Up until now we have dealt primarily with the question, "Why are we so afraid?" We have touched a few times on the issue of those who head into danger rather than away from it, and this would seem to argue against the idea that all are motivated each day by a degree of fear. For example, how do we explain those who choose to go into situations where death is the only certain and logical outcome? How do we explain an individual's ability to dampen millions of years of survival instinct for a cause they see as greater than themselves? Why does simple human pride often win out over the rational choice for survival? The explanation, again, becomes clear when we turn to biology and the chemical reward that follows any challenge to the limits of our mortality. However, beyond this merely biological explanation there is yet another factor that contributes to our fascination with what Sigmund Freud called the "death instinct." This idea is difficult to understand in clinical terms but it becomes more resonant when found in literature and film.

For instance, at the end of Aldous Huxley's novel *Brave New World* (1932) John Savage realizes he has become a prisoner in a world that he does not understand and that he does not want to understand. Huxley paints for us a near perfect portrait of pathos as John, this man of the wild desert, explains why he cannot enjoy peace without conflict, or life without the expectation of death, or even pleasure without the possibility of pain. Self-slaughter becomes the only answer for this man whose *freedom to suffer* has been stripped away. This romantic notion has a germ of truth in it. We may consciously reject it, but we feel it as we watch Mel Gibson's portrayal of William Wallace in *Braveheart* (1995), especially as he rallies the troops against the English with his call for freedom or death, a conviction he reinforces while being drawn and quartered at the end of the film. When we hear Wallace's cry of "Freedom!"—as every joint in his body is pulled apart—we cannot help but be enthralled by his faith to the cause.[1] We wish for a moment to have such conviction in our own lives, a conviction that provides us with the same certitude and purpose. We can only imagine that the same feeling overwhelms the earnest Christian as he views Mel Gibson's later film *The Passion of the Christ* (2004). Both stories reinforce the notion of redemption and new life, a state that can only be attained through the blood of another, a proxy sacrificed for our sins. Redemption is a ubiquitous message in film and literature, but it is a theme sometimes subtle or so often repeated that we hardly notice it anymore.

So, what would encourage such behavior in the face of certain death? Again, the answer can be found in biology, but with a twist since the psychology of bravery and self-sacrifice can be traced back to the fight-or-flight response. How do we know this? Because, we see it in the study of what has been called "terror management theory," a theory that got its start with the work of Ernest Becker whose book *The Denial of Death* (1973) was completed as the author was dying of cancer.

Ernest Becker postulated that heroism exemplifies our fear of death since it is an attempt to overcome death through great acts of sacrifice. The hero may die but he lives on through his deeds. His deeds are made sacred through the memory of society. For example, Socrates and Jesus are immortal because of the actions they took in life, because of the words attributed to them, and because of their conspicuous deaths. This would be true of the latter even if had never been physically resurrected. We remember them for their wisdom, their lives, and the way they met death. This idea of achieving immortality through one's death to a higher purpose is ultimately rooted in humanity's narcissistic tendencies, the inability to see the world from any perspective but our own. Where religion once pandered to this narcissism, culture now serves as a substitute. It is no longer the Church we look to for cosmological answers. We more often look to society and culture. In fact, our societies have taken the place of the heroes we have long forgotten, and of the ones we will soon forget.

"Man has elevated animal courage into a cult," which is why fear and death are always present with us even though we are not always conscious of it. This cult begins when the child is completely dependent on the parent and achieves a level of power that will fade to nothing in adulthood. While young every whimper of discomfort is somehow magically answered by the parent, and this breeds a sense of power in the mind of the child. One is reminded of the Buddha, whose father did not want the "real world" to intrude into the life of his son for fear Siddhartha would abandon life and his role as a prince, as a prophecy had once foretold. What happens in adulthood is that we seek to reassert the power we had as a child by living "more fully," but no amount of extreme sports or fetishistic pursuits will eliminate our knowledge and fear of death. No individual initiative can ever restore that unlimited power we once thought we had as children. That is why we turn to the collective. Only in others can we retrieve the power and eternal youth we once had as children.[2]

Humans are symbolically-oriented creatures. It is this way of viewing the world that is the source of our frustration and fears. Culture drapes us in a cloth meant to hide our physicality. Culture becomes a rejection of the body, a trap in which, ironically, even the hedonist can be snared. Culture reveals the general repulsion that most human beings have for their own bodies, and for the little talked about functions of those bodies.[3] While the symbolic world represents freedom from limitations, the body reminds us continually of the limitations against

which we struggle. This is why society and culture become such powerful forces in our lives. Society and culture are not constrained by the
same limitations as the individual. Kill a member of society and the society continues to live on, because it is theoretically immortal. This is the
attraction of society and groups; they make individuals vicariously more
than they can be on their own.[4] Of course, there is a trade-off. What we
give to society may not be given back with equal measure, since most
societies fail to equally distribute the fruits of collective action.

Life is big. We only learn this when we go out into the world and
learn how small we are in comparison to it. Some, like Jean Paul Sartre,
might talk about the *ineffability* of life, the inability to encapsulate the
sum total of the human experience, or to fully circumscribe the world
around us into mathematical formulas and scientific theorems. This is
ultimately the question of *being*, as theologians and philosophers have
defined it for centuries. We are intimately concerned about the incom-
prehensibility of ourselves, the universe, and what most term *God*. In
other words, to our limited senses the world might as well be infinite,
even if it is not in reality. From a psychological perspective, our only
choice upon realizing this truth is to limit or narrow our vision of the
world, and one consequence of this limiting process is the creation of
what has been called the "grand illusion." What is meant here by the
term "grand illusion" is human society and culture itself,[5] and if we try
to escape from the illusion of society and culture we are exposed to the
raw reality of death, terror, and despair, in other words: *the absurdity of
the universe.*[6]

Probably no one understood the fear of losing touch with the *grand
illusion* better than the theologian and philosopher Søren Kierkegaard
(1813-1855). To lose touch with that grand illusion was to enter the
realm of existential despair. On this topic Kierkegaard presaged both
Freud and the neo-Freudians. He suggested that the attempt to dispel
the fear of death through the symbolism of culture and character would
always end in failure, because these symbolic structures can never truly

dispel the fear of death. Man attempts to wrap himself in a cloak of denial that he calls "character," but this is simply just another illusion, the illusion of being free from the limitations of the body. Those who reject society make a conscious choice to free themselves from the trap of culture and character. Aristotle said much the same thing when he wrote that a man who does not need society is either a beast or a god.[7] For Kierkegaard this meant that man had to look for a more sure way of addressing the terror and despair of death's inevitability, once the symbols of culture and character had been stripped away. For Kierkegaard that meant turning to God in our despair. For the modern psychologist it means honestly confronting death without any real weapons against it.[8]

Freud originally got it wrong because he believed that sexuality, not the fear of death, was the key source of neurosis. Freud later introduced the life and death "instincts" into his theories; however, he saw these instincts as extensions of his earlier "pleasure principle." Freud suggested that we all naturally seek to create *ex nihilo*, i.e., from nothing, those symbols that best reflect our desire for power and immortality. We soon realize unconsciously, if not consciously, that we can only achieve this power and immortality through others. So, in Freud's view, coming to terms with our limitations serves as the only means by which we can make a breakthrough when it comes to neurosis. Unlike Kierkegaard, Freud thought that merely being honest about the man-made symbolic structures of society would be enough to address our fear of death. In other words, Freud's solution for neurosis consisted of a stoic acceptance of the inevitable fate of all men, and a nominal assent to the conventions of society.[9]

Is this enough, though? One is here reminded of the distrust with which Young Goodman Brown eyed his fellow villagers upon learning that they were all in league with Lucifer. If you are unfamiliar with this short story, written by Nathaniel Hawthorne, it is about a young villager named Goodman Brown who goes into the forest to make a pact with the Devil because he has fallen on hard times. Arriving at the designated site he learns that the whole town has already given itself over to Satan, something he decides not to do at the last moment. However, to his horror he finds that even his new wife is among those celebrating the Black Mass. So, he wakes the next morning not knowing whether what he saw was real or not, but that uncertainty cannot stop him from living the rest of his life with a jaundiced eye fixed on all those around him.[10] This story relates several truths. The first is that our hearts and minds tend to cloud the world around us, for good or ill. A second truth is that there is something the human heart finds repulsive about those who live their lives in hypocrisy. The desire for faithfulness and authenticity is uniquely human, and it goes beyond mere religious sentiment.

In answer to the question above: "No, this is not enough." The reason it is not enough to *just be honest* is that we all desire the psychological satisfaction that comes with hero-worship, which is really just an attempt to share in the glory of the hero-object. Think for a moment about the passing of a celebrity and how many people feel obliged to take part in the grief of someone they never knew. Some might even feel entitled to participate in the grief along with the family. Attaching ourselves to greatness, in whatever form it takes, gives us a sense of power and helps us to forget that we are weak and decaying creatures. One way in which this connection between the hero and his followers can be achieved is for the hero to initiate a certain code of behavior for his followers. The followers can then ape the hero's actions without judgment. The moral code of the hero allows him to act through his followers, and it relieves the followers from the full responsibility of their actions, since they act on behalf of the hero. Moral codes are the chief way in which we enlarge ourselves and our egos. These moral codes also protect us since nothing bad can or should happen to those who are "good"—as defined by the hero-object. Even if something bad does happen to an individual follower they live on in the collective, through the memory of the group. This transference of the self to another object helps us to step outside ourselves; it is the penultimate act of death-denial, a fetishistic attempt to abandon our weak physical bodies.[11] As Becker writes,

> This is the logical fate for the utterly helpless person: the more you fear death and the emptier you are, the more you people your world with omnipotent father-figures, extra-magical helpers.[12]

Once we intimately attach ourselves to the hero-object and his symbols, we become naturally aggressive toward those who oppose the hero-object and his symbols. Remember, it is not an attack on the hero-object and his symbols that are the true source of aggression but the fact that the hero-object and his symbols have freed us from our fear of death. So, attempts to kill the hero-object or to malign the symbols that represent him are direct assaults on the *death-denying ideology* we have adopted.[13]

There are only four responses to those who would challenge our *death-denying ideology*: *derogation, assimilation, accommodation*, and, when all else fails, *annihilation*. The response of a death-denying culture, *which most cultures are*, will depend on the circumstances. A strong, healthy culture, not immediately threatened by outside influence or differences, will be tolerant. They will likely choose accommodation and assimilation. However, a culture rife with division and competing claims to dominance will be more prone to violence and to marginalizing those who are different. They will likely seek an "other" upon which to focus all the animus of society. The most well-known, modern example of this type of scapegoating is that perpetrated by Nazi Germany. The Holocaust was an acute manifestation of an already existing European animus toward the Jewish people. Before the rise of Nazi Germany the Jewish people had experienced frequent *pogroms* against their communities. Christians heading off to the crusades between the eleventh and thirteenth centuries would often baptize their swords in the blood of the local Jewish population, before heading off to the Holy Land to shed an even greater amount of Saracen blood.[14]

Europe was not the only society to have preyed on the weak and the different in order to maintain its social cohesion through a defense of its cultural symbols. American's have gone through several periods in which an animus toward "the other" was very pronounced. This lack of tolerance showed itself as soon as the English colonists arrived in the early seventeenth century and began fighting with the Native Americans. Once the Native Americans were perceived as ineducable and uncivilizable the slaughter began. By the first half of the nineteenth century the Native Americans had been effectively corralled on reservations or "civilized." Throughout American history the government has used a variety of the cultural responses mentioned above. In isolated cases the American government has even engaged in "annihilation" when they thought it necessary.[15] The U.S. has not been historically alone in this, since Spain, Portugal, England (Britain), and others have all, at some point or another, treated the native inhabitants of other lands with complete disregard for their humanity.

Culture is largely the product of symbols we hold sacred. When the world fails us we cling with even more earnestness to these symbols in hopes it will diminish our anxiety. Wealth is one symbol we use to challenge the power of death. We are prone to believe this symbol can be used to buy our way out of our mortal fate. We believe this so wholeheartedly that we see a lack of wealth as a type of "social death," which may eventually lead to the real thing. Lacking wealth in our society, a society where the accumulation of material goods has become the *raison d'être* of everyday activity, makes us feel especially vulnerable. So, when we cannot easily access *money*, the prevalent symbol of power in our society, we cling even more to those symbols we still have access to: God, hedonism, or a non-material aesthetic of some kind. Lacking all of these symbols our personal world grows empty, it becomes a life "red in tooth and claw."[16] For, there is no symbolism where the Darwinian struggle is concerned.

Another phenomenon that occurs in modern society is that we are often deprived of traditional hero-objects—usually tied to religion. When this happens we attempt to substitute an "other" as the complete object of our love, the storehouse of all that is infinite. This too fails, though, because the romantic experience ultimately reminds us of our "creatureliness." As Becker writes, "If your partner is your 'ALL' then any shortcoming in him becomes a major threat to you."[17] This gets us to a question that theologians, philosophers, and psychologists, have given much thought to, why do human beings need objects outside themselves in order to have meaning? In seeking an answer to this the psychologist Otto Rank claimed that man is a naturally theological being because he is forced by circumstance to look beyond the physical world for a self-centering experience. This seems like a modern-day confirmation of Kierkegaard's view,[18] and this idea has much in common with the work of the psychologist Carl Jung and the literary scholar Joseph Campbell, who both saw the human experience as naturally geared toward the pursuit of meaning through symbols. More recently Karen Armstrong in her book *The Case for God* (2009) argues for a more broad conception of the term God. In fact, she argues that religions have often encouraged followers to avoid conceptualizing God at all, since to do so is to limit God. So, Armstrong agrees, humans have need of God, but she asks, "Which one?"[19] We will discuss this in a later chapter.

For Otto Rank a neurosis is the continuation of a historical process in which the great question of death is inadequately addressed by modern psychoanalysis. Neurosis is, in short, the breakdown of the illusions we have about life, a breakdown that reveals the truth about our creatureliness and death. Another way to put this is that we try to take too much of life in at one time rather than narrowing our focus as most "normal" people do. So, a healthy mental state requires buying fully into the illusion of culture, and neurosis results from peeking behind the curtain, so to speak. This is particularly true when it comes to the search for meaning. That is why the therapist, once she has reduced the patient to a product of their childhood often becomes the object of hero-worship, or *transference*. The breakdown of the illusions with which we live our lives naturally leads to hyper-individuation, which is at the root of what Kierkegaard would have called *sin* and what Rank would have called *neurosis*. No matter what it is called, both can be traced back to the creatureliness about which we are always in despair.[20]

***

Human beings are not by nature idle creatures, and there appears to be a relationship between depression and inaction. Loss of purpose can be fatal for our species. As the proverbist once wrote, "Where there is no vision, the people perish." (Proverbs 29:18) This is a truth we know from experience; we must act or pay the consequences. When examining the myriad number of mental illnesses that plague modern society we see indications that the fear of death is operating within each of them. The schizophrenic is repulsed by his physicality and attempts to make everything an abstraction; however, most of these folks do not possess the ability to communicate the abstractions they see. For this reason their vision frequently collapses in on itself like a psychotic singularity. Perversion and fetishism, another way of rebelling against our fear of death, is an attempt to assert our individuality, to increase our own status as the hero-object. Sado-masochism works to opposite effect. It subsumes the individual within the relationship between the dominator and the dominated. It is still, no less, a response to the terror of death. In the sado-masochistic relationship giving and receiving pain is a way of testing the boundaries of life without actually crossing over the line into death itself.[21] In this light, the real problem most neurotics are dealing with is freedom, and by extension the fear of death,[22] a theme fleshed out in the works of Jean Paul Sartre and Albert Camus, among others.[23]

Most psychological theories fall short because they presuppose that the human mind was "designed" to achieve stasis. It is believed that if certain personal and social conditions exist that a degree of psychological stasis can be achieved. The reality, however, is that evolution has thrust consciousness upon us with all its attendant horrors, rooted in our knowledge of impending death. It is for this reason we search for utopias and personal perfection—yet, in vain. For, it is enough that we simply learn to live as best as we can with our weaknesses, because as Becker writes, "Men are doomed to live in an overwhelmingly tragic and demonic world."[24] This is the truth from which we must start if we are to create cultural symbols that give us strength without the excesses of a *death-denying ideology*.[25]

We can now see that *the culture of fear* is largely a consequence of the *riskless society*, which is really just another *death-denying ideology* rooted in the misguided pursuit of social or economic utopianism.[26] When you combine these social phenomena with our inherent biological and psychological proclivity to fear the unknown, and that which we cannot control, you begin to see how easy it has been for many of us to slide into the despair that is *the culture of fear*. In the next section of this book we will explore how that despair makes many of us easy prey for *the makers of fear*.

PART TWO

THE MAKERS OF FEAR

Chapter Five

Burning the Village to Save It

Civilization...grows more and more maudlin and hysterical; especially under democracy it tends to degenerate into a mere combat of crazes; the whole aim of practical politics is to keep the populace alarmed (and hence clamorous to be led to safety) by an endless series of hobgoblins, most of them imaginary.[1]

H. L. Mencken

As I write this chapter the world is still in the grip of a significant economic downturn—a once in a century event fueled by excessive public and private debt.[2] Portentous events, possibly related to this economic downturn, are occurring all around the world in places like Egypt, Libya, Syria, and even the UK.[3] A lack of bread, more than political repression, has always been a more effective driver of revolution. That is why it is no coincidence the crowd was moved to crown Jesus a king after he had fed the five thousand with just five loaves of bread and a couple of fish. (Matthew 14:13-21)

Today, the West seems surrounded by forces that threaten to change forever the way we live, at least that is what politicians want us to believe. The latest bogeyman is the Iranian state which is clearly intent on developing nuclear weapons. For this sin, the United States says it will consider a pre-emptive sacrifice of American lives and treasure in order to stop Iran's entrance into the nuclear club. Politicians elevate the Iranian state to an existential threat, even though our allies in Pakistan already have nuclear weapons, and are ruled by a far less stable Islamic government that is baldly influenced by anti-U.S. elements in Central Asia. H. L. Mencken's words seem, in the modern context, prophetic.

Global warming—maybe you prefer the term *climate change*—overpopulation, globalization, terrorism, super-viruses, super collider-induced black holes, environmental devastation, chemical science gone awry, earthquakes, volcanoes, hurricanes, gay marriage, Islam, China, taxes, economic stagnation, infertility, contraception, corporate greed, etc. The things people are told to fear are as numerous as the fevered brains manufacturing these *fears de jour*.[4]

Do not mistake this criticism of growing political fears as an argument that the world is not a dangerous place. In fact, a good argument could be made that nature itself is constantly trying to kill us—not consciously, of course, but because our planet is not really a place where humans can naturally thrive, at least not without any effort or organization.[5] This is evidenced by the millions of years we and our genetic ancestors struggled to survive until about 50,000 years ago. Along with every other species we were subject for millions of years to the vicissitudes of the planet's environment, and that environment proved it could change fast enough to destroy 90% of all the known species that have ever existed on this planet. It was only with the "great leap forward" that mankind found he was able to fight back, to shape the planet's environment in unprecedented ways to meet his own needs.

This social, and eventually political, organization most likely began with large extended families coordinating food gathering, hunting, and defense. Alliances between these small, isolated clans would come next, until someone saw the need for even greater organizational scale. At this point you would have seen large villages and the first cities appear. For example, the city of Çatalhöyük, in present-day Turkey, is one of the largest and oldest known cities. It dates back to possibly 7500 BCE and its population averaged five thousand. These early cities would have been a direct by-product of the Neolithic Revolution which was occurring around the same time. The Neolithic Revolution is most closely associated with the move from a hunter-gatherer society to an agricultural society. At some point prior to 8000 BCE men had learned to cultivate the earth rather than just gather fruit from naturally occurring plants and trees.

Ever since the first cities were built mankind has experienced a geometrical increase in social, political, and intellectual development—with a few hiccups along the way. Many have pointed to the discovery of fire, our first technology, as an axial event. Without fire we would not be able to divide early cultures into the bronze and iron ages. One thing is certain were it not for technology and complex human organization we would not have the civilizations we have today, and for all the complaining most would choose the world we have today over the life of the average peasant in 1000 CE. However, that does not mean we are stuck with the way things are. There are things we can do to move toward a more perfect society—at least within reasonable limits.

First, though, we need to understand how some people in our society use fear for their own gain. These people prey on our natural inclination to fear the unknown, or the complex. One type of person who uses fear is the politician. So, we will first examine the political class, an interesting group of people who get it into their head that they always know better than the rest of us, and then run for office to prove it. There is a widespread belief among this class that fear can often be used to good purpose. I aim to show in the following pages why this is not true.

***

If you live in the United States and are over the age of thirty you are probably familiar with existential fear, because for fifty years the world lived in terror of nuclear annihilation, resulting from a direct confrontation between the atheistic, totalitarian, and communist U.S.S.R. and a God-fearing, democratic, and capitalist United States. This "Cold War" was the product of many factors; however, one cannot ignore the role of early twentieth-century cultural chauvinism, as displayed in the attitude toward immigrants from Eastern Europe during the early twentieth century. It was at this time that many "native" Americans attempted to "Americanize" the new stream of immigrants from southern and Eastern Europe. This was merely the continuation of a long history of seeing those who were different in skin color, language, religion, food ways, etc., as too different from the white, Anglo-Saxon, Protestant ideal, and if these people would not assimilate they would be ostracized. This was nowhere more evident than when it came to politics and economics.

Thirty years before the Cold War there was the *Red Scare*. This anti-communist campaign got its start after Russia fell to the Bolsheviks in 1917. The Bolsheviks adhered to a particularly doctrinaire strain of Communism that would become known as Leninism. Due to all the labor agitation in the United States and the popularity of the Socialist Party, led by Eugene V. Debs, Americans began to see a Communist under every bed. Twenty years prior to that, it was the *anarchists* who had struck fear into the heart of the middle and upper classes. In 1938 the United States House of Representatives felt that Communist activity had become so rampant within the country that it was necessary to establish a committee to root out these "un-American activities." The House Un-American Activities Committee (HUAC) was concerned with subversive plots to violently overthrow the government. However, as these types of political witch hunts are often want to do, the mere association with Communist organizations became enough to ruin one's reputation, and possibly deprive one of a livelihood. This only got worse in the 1950s as the Cold War heated up. Men like Joseph McCarthy began to increase the rhetoric and stir the pot of fear.

It should be said that fear can sometimes be justified, and it is difficult to know whether we today would not have made the same decisions under similar circumstances. How could Americans know how strong or weak the Soviet Union was? Having taken over Eastern Europe, and having begun the systematic support of nationalist or socialist movements around the world, how were Americans to know whether the United States was not next on the Soviets' list? In short, we should not judge the people of the 1920s or 1950s too harshly since they acted largely out of fear, which is a predominantly irrational reaction to perceived existential danger.

When we read about the American reaction to the Soviets' launching of Sputnik on October 4, 1957, things become a little clearer. Americans clearly feared not only that their way of life would be taken away, but that someone else would become the dominant power in the world. After a decade of being the dominant political and military power in the world the United States was loath to give it up—a problem with which it still struggles. On September 2, 1958, in an attempt to match the technological feats of the Soviets, Dwight D. Eisenhower signed into law the National Defense Education Act. This dramatically increased the amount of funding being directed at basic scientific research, which was thought essential to beat the Soviets in the "space race." This was followed by John F. Kennedy's 1961 pledge to put a man on the moon before the decade was out, a pledge that was fulfilled on July 20, 1969.[6]

The external threat of a Communist Russia was not the only thing that worried Americans. There were domestic fears as well. In the late forties and throughout the 1950s a counter-culture was developing, a movement that challenged the materialism and corporatized organization of American society. This *Beatnik* movement would eventually morph into the Hippy-culture of the sixties and seventies, both meant to upend American society by simply not participating in it. However, this was not the only thing that middle class whites had to fear. There was also the growing discontent among the black community, which had largely been denied many educational, economic, and political opportunities in American society, even after slavery was constitutionally abolished.

All of these domestic fears exacerbated existing concerns about the United States' external enemies. It could be argued that in one respect the external enemy, in the form of the Soviet Union and Communist

China, forced Americans to deal with the internal contradictions of its political, economic, and social institutions. Black or white, some at the time might have argued to themselves, we are all Americans and must stand against the "Red Menace." Of course, this dynamic changed at the end of the 1960s and beginning of the 1970s. The demand for law and order that put Nixon in office, Nixon's détente with the Soviet Union and his opening up of Communist China, plus the loss of Vietnam, all exacted a terrible toll on the American psyche. It may also have made racial and gender equality seem less urgent because now everyone was affected by oil shortages, falling wages, and what appeared to be a growing nihilism among young adult baby boomers. The 1970s became the age of *identity politics*, a movement that turned every class of people into victims looking for a governmental validation of their *rights*, by which was meant their identity and power within society.

It is not much different today. People are still striving for political solutions that go beyond merely getting themselves included in the social and political process. They seek power for power's sake, often to the exclusion of others. This has never been a good way to build a social and political order, especially when those excluded become numerous and angry enough to strike back. In addition to the unworkable "politics of identity" we have replaced the Cold War with a new existential threat: *terrorism*. This has given rise to a great deal of fear and the adoption of extra-legal government activities, which are justified because they are seen as necessary for safety and security. However, this is where the whole idea of fear becomes a little paradoxical, because as irrational as it is we cannot completely escape from it through the use of reason. Some have even found fear an exhilarating experience, and believe it provides us with moral clarity. Political commentators as varied as David Brooks, Frank Rich, George Packer, and Christopher Hitchens all agreed after 9/11 that this horrible experience possessed a unifying power which the nation desperately needed at the time. They argued that it had the power to sweep away the enervating spirit commonly associated with too much materialism, cultural relativism, or whatever other moral malady one believes ails Western culture.[7] These men maintained that fear, like Gordon Gecko's "greed," could be used to cut through and clarify our moral world. In other words, there is nothing like staring death straight in the face to give one moral and existential certitude.

This is not a new idea. Men have used fear for millennia to achieve political goals, always believing that the end justifies the means, and maybe even that fear purifies the soul as fire purifies a precious metal. Thomas Hobbes (1588-1679) believed this when he penned his best-known work *Leviathan* (1651). Hobbes believed that men were naturally disquieted by the state of nature, which is chaotic and brutish, so they see government as a necessity in conquering this natural state. That is why people voluntarily submit to the law, order, and peace established and maintained by government. They trade their fear of the natural, chaotic state of nature for "the quiet life" of an organized and highly centralized government.[8] Hobbes argued that only a strong, centralized government could keep people obedient to the government, which is the only thing that stands between the people and a state of natural chaos. So, argued Hobbes, this made the use of fear a legitimate tool of government in order to sustain the original compact of men.

The philosopher Montesquieu (1689-1755) saw things differently. Montesquieu was French while Hobbes was English, and while Hobbes had watched his country descend into anarchy, civil war, and eventually regicide, Montesquieu had watched as Louis XIV accumulated enough power in France to make even an oriental despot blush. Montesquieu said as much in his *Persian Letters* (1721). Like Hobbes, Montesquieu believed men did have something to fear but it was not the state of nature; it was the despot—who was made possible by strong centralized government. Montesquieu's belief that the French crown had become despotic led him to put forth his own political solutions rooted in the belief that a government should be tolerant, have many mediating institutions, and that it should meet the needs of a pluralistic society.[9] If these

ideas sound familiar you probably heard about them in your high school
civics class when the instructor discussed the "checks and balances" of
the U.S. federal government. Still, Montesquieu's prescription for better
government is built on fear just as Hobbes' system was built on fear. The
object of fear was merely redirected from anarchy to despotism.

The problem with using fear to build a political order becomes even
more obvious when we begin to look at our own preferred system of
government: *democracy*. One would think modern democratic society
would be, for the most part, free of fear. However, as Alexis de Tocqueville pointed out in his famous study *Democracy in America* (1835
and 1840): *even democratic government has its demons*. Tocqueville
pointed out that once democracy is achieved the masses begin to experience an anxiety associated with the rapid social changes that ac-
company political enfranchisement. An overwhelming sense of anxiety
dominates the democratic populace, who eventually turn to political
repression to allay their concerns. Most of this repression tends to be
directed at marginalized groups, who rightly fear the "tyranny of the
majority" and want to establish a Montesqieuan system of widely distributed political power.[10] Of course, then we have come full circle to
the original problem addressed by Hobbes: how can we have law and
order without a strong, centralized government? On the other hand the
paradox faced by those who would like to reform society, politics, and
economics, is that federalism does not allow opposition to be directed
at a single source of repression, which makes political action under a
Montesqieuan system much less effective.[11]

Political fear manifests itself in one other way in the modern world:
the totalitarian state. We had a ready example of this kind of state in the
Soviet Union, prior to its collapse in 1991. Under this kind of government the state not only uses fear to keep all elements of society in check,
but in its most extreme form it even seeks to convince the politically
repressed that the fear is good for them.[12] This type of thinking was bril-
liantly illustrated by George Orwell in his novel *Nineteen Eighty-Four*

(1948). The protagonist Winston Smith is the object of an elaborate plot to reveal his most secret fear so that the state can then use it against him. O'Brien, a member of "The Party," pretends to befriend Winston and then turns out to be Winston's designated torturer. The goal of the torture is not only to get Winston to confess his faith in Big Brother but to make Winston think that he himself truly believes that he has faith in Big Brother. In a totalitarian state it is not enough that people accept the fear imposed on them; they must believe it is good for them; they must invite it.

There are more subtle ways in which fear can be used. In his book *The Paranoid Style in American Politics, and Other Essays* (1965) Richard Hofstadter profiles how some conservative political leaders use the existential fear of a world-wide conspiracy to achieve political unity among their followers. This method of organization is less about achieving anything politically concrete and more about exploring one's "identity, values, fears, and aspirations." It creates a world divorced from reality, a world in which a Manichean battle is constantly being fought between the forces of good and evil. This is clearly a legacy of America's religious history, since Christians see the world as a war zone, a constant battle between the forces of Satan and the forces of God, and in this battle we cannot always know who the enemy is; for, he often appears as an angel of light. (II Corinthians 11:13-15)

By the 1950s and 1960s the enemy had become godless communism exported to the rest of the world through the imperialistic machinations of the Soviet Union. However, even those within the United States could not always be trusted, which meant the only true patriots were those who exhibited unquestioning loyalty to the American Way and to American foreign policy objectives. Any accommodation to the enemy was seen as suspect, even if that accommodation took the form of criticizing suspect moral action taken by the United States or its surrogates around the world. This meant there was no way to effectively challenge the American "empire of bases," which grew more numerous every year in the 1950s and 1960s. Criticism of this empire is still largely avoided in today's political discussions.[13]

It is not that everyone who practices the paranoid style of politics is actually paranoid themselves. In fact, this is what makes this tactic so insidious. Those who use it do so cynically, for political gain, but in the process their "overheated, oversuspicious, overaggressive, grandiose, and apocalyptic" expressions create an environment of paranoia where individuals are allowed to vent their fears in the form of unattainable political desires. The paranoid style is used by "normal people" upon the normal electorate, tainting the whole political process. This is not a new phenomenon in American politics. As far back as 1798 New England conservatives like Jedidiah Morse warned Americans against the evils of Masonry, Catholicism, and the Illuminati. Timothy Dwight railed against the "disciples of Voltaire," the "dragoons of Marat," and the concubines of the Illuminati." As late as 1855 these same warnings were being issued in a major newspaper in Texas. The *Texas State Times* at that time warned the reader about the "minions of the Pope" who are "boldly insulting our Senators; reprimanding our Statesmen; *propagating the adulterous union of Church and state...*" (emphasis mine). Hofstadter writes,

> These writers illustrate the central preconception of the paranoid style—the existence of a vast, insidious, preternaturally effective international conspiratorial network designed to perpetrate acts of the most fiendish character.[14]

By the mid-twentieth century Communism had replaced the fear of an international conspiracy of Masons, Catholics, and Illuminati—although these bogeymen are often still trotted out in modern popular fiction.[15] Since this modern battle is fought between the forces of good and evil there is no middle ground to be found. Nothing but complete victory will suffice, and those who see things differently are viewed as virtual traitors when juxtaposed to the *superpatriot*. In the 1950s the superpatriot would have been a member of the John Birch Society. Today they might be a member of The Tea Party or someone who slavishly watches Fox News. One aspect of superpatriot thinking is the general disdain for facts. In the Manichean struggle between good and evil facts become irrelevant, and the superpatriot feels obliged—within the context of this struggle—not only to ignore facts but to make them up or distort them for the greater good of winning the battle. The superpatriot can do this because he has amassed all the evidence he needs to convince himself, deftly avoiding any data that does not confirm his preconceived notions. Like the prophets of old the superpatriot becomes "not a receiver" of truth but a "transmitter."[16]

It may seem unfair to focus largely on conservative voices. After all, was it not Hilary Clinton who in 1998 claimed that there was a "vast right-wing conspiracy" operating against her husband as he was being impeached for lying to Congress? Yes, this is true, but in general only the far left wing of the political spectrum believes that the right is engaged in a conscious and coordinated conspiracy. The left-wing community as a whole is more inclined to believe that those on the right—mainly businessmen—are all working toward their own selfish interests and their agendas just happen to intersect because wealth creation is the *raison d'être* for all of their political action. For all the talk of the one percent today, few on the left would agree that these folks are in cahoots. It is more likely that the rich are more often at war with one another since wealth creation tends to result in the clash of economic titans, although not always.

The conservative, or rather pseudo-conservative, is a strange bird. Unlike a true conservative the pseudo-conservative is animated first and foremost by the desire to destroy *present* traditions and institutions, traditions and institutions that make him feel "restless" and dissatisfied. This makes the pseudo-conservative a reactionary who longs for some bygone golden age that exists only in his child-like conception of the past. The pseudo-conservative uses the "rhetoric of conservatism" to argue against "fictitious dangers" while "consciously or unconsciously" aiming to abolish existing American traditions and institutions, hoping to substitute them with his own vision of a past and perfect world. Pseudo-conservative rhetoric, thanks to the growth of modern media, has become entertainment in the modern world, an entertainment that keeps "the mass man in an almost constant state of political mobilization." The constant buzz of pseudo-conservatism, which streams across the airwaves and finds its way into print, effectively uses the *paranoid style* of politics to "redefine treason to embrace not only persons trying to overthrow the government but also those trying to 'weaken' it...." "Hyper-patriotism" is the result. One must be fully, and unquestionably, committed to the capitalist ethos, and if not, one is seen as disloyal to the American way of life, which becomes measured only by economic success and social status.[17]

Since 1965 the "radical right" has been most closely associated with classical economics, and "the radical rightism of the 1960s" was "predominantly a movement of white Anglo-Saxon Protestant Republicans, with only a fringe of ethnic support." For them Keynesian economics and the welfare state became not only a different way of viewing the modern economy, it was a departure from long lost moral values. Having taken a beating in the first half of the twentieth century in their efforts to curtail the teaching of evolution and to contain the effects of the mass immigration of non-Anglo-Saxon and Protestant stock, the pseudo-conservative turned to an agenda in which they try "to prohibit, to prevent, to censor and censure, to discredit, and to punish" any behavior that does not fit within their moral conception of the world "as it should be." In short, the whole conservative movement after 1965 became a rearguard action, lacking any positive way forward. This movement began with the defeat of Barry Goldwater in 1964. Pseudo-conservatives saw Goldwater's defeat not as a mandate against their economic individualism and Manichean views but as evidence that the American electorate had become *unregenerate*. Goldwater's defeat fed the neurosis of pseudo-conservative political paranoia. Pseudo-conservatives continued to believe that their defeat was evidence of a large internal conspiracy directed against their agenda. The limits of their power over the electorate proved to them the righteousness of their cause, so they could now give full vent to their "wide ranging…agitational mind, with its paranoid suspicions, its impossible demands, and its millennial dreams of total victory."[18]

***

As you can see, fear can be used for a myriad of political purposes. In American society it is frequently used as the means to achieve both political and economic objectives. However, as Corey Robin points out, fear is not a good basis for government, even though some people view it as a means of political unity.[19] The reality is that political fear is generated by governments and groups, through intimidation and the collective fear of social decline, or via the highlighting of alleged existential threats.[20] Fear is used for political gain, but it can never really solve problems. In other words, the process is reversed. Rather than using political structures to work against fear we are made to see fear as a means to draw us together, after which we can then solve problems, usually by acting against the object of fear that has been used to unify us. However, the fears against which we are unified almost always turn out to be politically intractable and, too often, an illusion. So, the vicious process continues.[21] It is for this reason that the alliance between fear and politics ultimately makes modern American politics almost completely ineffective, because fear is

> … a political tool, an instrument of elite rule or insurgent advance, created and sustained by political leaders or activists who stand to gain something from it, either because fear helps them pursue a specific political goal, or because it reflects or lends support to their moral and political belief—or both.[22]

There are other, more subtle, ways to influence the behavior of others besides the use of raw fear. Intimidation is often used where direct threats no longer work, or have become socially unacceptable.[23] For example, fear and intimidation are still alive and well in the world of American business. In fact, it is the last place where naked fear is still seen as a legitimate tool.[24] Corey Robin has called the corporation the last bastion of *absolutism*, where property rights in nearly all cases have priority over the rights of workers. In the business world fear can be used outright, especially in high-paying jobs where machismo is still prized. Emblematic of this is the story of Andrew Grove, one of the founders of Intel. He once came to a meeting with a large stick, which he proceeded to wave around and slam on the table when people came in late.[25] One is reminded of Robert De Niro's portrayal of Al Capone in the 1984 film *The Untouchables*. That the head of a premiere multinational company is allowed to menace his employees in such a manner says much about the contradictory political and economic ideas that animate modern democratic capitalist society. What may be even more disturbing is that Andy Grove told this story in his own memoir and was heavily applauded for it because it showed his business pluck.

If the story told by Andrew Grove was the only example we have of employees being intimidated and berated by their employers we might be able to describe it as an anomaly, but Barbara Ehrenreich has chronicled in her book *Nickel and Dimed: On (Not) Getting By in America* (2001) what goes on in many low-wage, low-skill jobs. Ehrenreich, a highly educated Ph.D., spent a year working as a service worker in several different jobs. Her goal was to determine whether one could live on the wages that approximate the federal minimum wage. From waitressing in Florida, to housecleaning in Maine, and then to working as a clerk at a Wal-Mart in Minnesota, she learned that she was barely able to keep her head above water, no matter how frugal she lived. She was often forced to hold down two jobs just to make ends meet, and this usually meant working seven days a week. She worked hard, and she points out that the work she did was not only physically demanding but also mentally draining as well. In the end she says the most burdensome part of working the low-wage service industry was the cost of rent, which because this sector of the economy is largely driven by market forces favors those who can demand better wages. For those near minimum wage it means a choice between endangering your well-being by living in an impoverished and crime-ridden part of town, or living somewhere safe but going without some of life's essentials—like food and medicine.

The main problem says Ehrenreich is that rents are far more elastic than wages, so low-wage workers can easily be priced out of the housing market during boom times. During these boom times housing prices rise dramatically while wages remain stagnant.[26] These conditions exist for one clear reason. She writes,

> . . . if low-wage workers do not always behave in an economically rational way, that is, as free agents within a capitalist democracy, it is because they dwell in a place that is neither free nor in any way democratic.[27]

This is nowhere more apparent than the random drug testing of individuals, and all the other assorted invasions of privacy in which the employer can now engage. These activities are ostensibly used to keep the workplace safe and productive, but they are ultimately meant to keep workers "in their place," and even if these laws apply to only a few they are meant to intimidate everyone. These laws and practices have a chilling effect, sapping any sense of common cause among workers, which can only help the companies to divide and conquer when it comes to labor, especially in the effort to organize labor into unions.[28]

As Corey Robin concludes, "fear American-style" is primarily restricted to the workplace these days, and it is here where we see the greatest need to challenge the bald use of fear and intimidation.[29] We must confront the too-often held belief among businesses and their advocates that the only way to effectively manage a business is through fear and intimidation.[30] To do this requires a deeper understanding of how fear has been used in the past, and why it is not a valid means of political or social action in the modern world, but how can this be done when the essential lesson of political and social action is drowned out by fear? Until we come to understand that justice, not fear, is the only basis for modern political and social organization, we will continue to be plagued by the use of fear as a political tool.[31]

Chapter Six

If It Bleeds, It Leads

It is advertising and the logic of consumerism that governs the depiction of reality in the mass media.

                                                                Christopher Lasch

I first saw the film *Network* (1976) just a few years ago. Lacking any historical context one might mistake this film for a commentary on today's media. Of course, prior to seeing the movie I had been treated for years to that famous clip where Howard Beale—played consummately by Peter Finch—tells his viewers to go to their windows and yell, "I'm as mad as hell and I'm not going to take this anymore!"[1] Of course, the real fireworks in the film begin when Beale announces that he plans to commit suicide on live television the following week. What happens instead is that Howard Beale gets huge ratings and his own show. However, he moves from decrying civilization in general to criticizing a recent oil deal struck with the Saudis, which forces Arthur Jensen, the head of Beale's network, to step in. Jensen is there to explain to Beale how he has tangled with forces beyond his ken. The scene is best watched rather than read, but let me give you a taste.

The scene opens with Howard Beale told to sit at one end of a conference table. Arthur Jensen (played wonderfully by Ned Beatty) walks to the other end. He closes the curtains and the room is darkened except for a dozen and a half green lamps that light the long table. Jensen then steps into what appears to be a spotlight at the other end of the conference room. Jensen begins his corporate catechism in a booming voice while stabbing an accusing finger at Beale:

Arthur Jensen: You have meddled with the primal forces of nature,

Mr. Beale, and I won't have it! Is that clear? You think you've merely stopped a business deal. That is not the case! The Arabs have taken billions of dollars out of this country, and now they must put it back! It is ebb and flow, tidal gravity! It is ecological balance! You are an old man who thinks in terms of nations and peoples. There are no nations. There are no peoples. There are no Russians. There are no Arabs. There are no third worlds. There is no West. There is only one holistic system of systems, one vast and immane, interwoven, interacting, multivariate, multinational dominion of dollars. Petro-dollars, electro-dollars, multi-dollars, reichmarks, rins, rubles, pounds, and shekels. It is the international system of currency which determines the totality of life on this planet. That is the natural order of things today. That is the atomic and subatomic and galactic structure of things today! And YOU have meddled with the primal forces of nature, and YOU... WILL... ATONE! Am I getting through to you, Mr. Beale? You get up on your little twenty-one inch screen and howl about America and democracy. There is no America. There is no democracy. There is only IBM, and ITT, and AT&T, and DuPont, Dow, Union Carbide, and Exxon. Those are the nations of the world today. What do you think the Russians talk about in their councils of state, Karl Marx? They get out their linear programming charts, statistical decision theories, minimax solutions, and compute the price-cost probabilities of their transactions and investments, just like we do. We no longer live in a world of nations and ideologies, Mr. Beale. The world is a college of corporations, inexorably determined by the immutable bylaws of business. The world is a business, Mr. Beale. It has been since man crawled out of the slime. And our children will live, Mr. Beale, to see that... perfect world... in which there's no war or famine, oppression or brutality. One vast and ecumenical holding company, for whom all men will work to serve a common profit, in which all men will hold a share of stock. All necessities provided, all anxieties tranquilized, all boredom amused. And I have chosen you, Mr. Beale, to preach this evangel.

Howard Beale: Why me?

Arthur Jensen: Because you're on television, dummy. Sixty million people watch you every night of the week, Monday through Friday.

Howard Beale: I have seen the face of God.

That last line is delivered as Beale shakes with religious fervor. Again, nothing beats actually seeing the film itself.

In 1976 *Network*, although critically acclaimed, was seen as high theater by most, but this is not true anymore. Since that film was released we have seen a variety of changes in the media, largely the result of an increasing number of channels for our entertainment pleasure. These niches in the market were gladly filled by the growing corporate media monopolies. Soon there would be CNN, Morton Downey Jr., Jerry Springer, and then Fox News. It would be unfair to say that all of these media were of the same caliber, but there is no doubt that a shift toward entertainment over the news had occurred by the 1980s. The news would no longer be the purview of sober-minded journalists trained to objectively report what they had seen and heard. The emphasis would now be on the belligerent gasbag—today called "a pundit." Thanks to people like Hunter S. Thompson a whole generation would be raised on "gonzo journalism," a style of journalism that prized style over accuracy. One is reminded of a line in the movie *V for Vendetta* (2005) when Evey tells V, "Artists use lies to tell the truth, while politicians use them to cover the truth up."

We should not deceive ourselves into believing that journalism ever really had a golden age. From its inception the popular press has always been a partisan affair. Why would anyone print anything if not to put forth an idea or an agenda that they desired others to adopt. In the West the first thing printed on a modern printing press was the Bible, a collection of cultural and religious propaganda directed at a growing population of literate, middle-class individuals. So, if we wail and moan about the state of modern journalism because we think it too partisan then we are directing our righteous indignation at the wrong thing. Modern journalism is not as much plagued by partisanship as it is by three modern developments: 1) the monopolization of media companies, 2) the constant stream of information without context, and 3) the facile emphasis of style over substance.

Entertainment is not the problem—we all need a break from the humdrum of life—but when everything is forced into the narrow confines of entertainment we lose the ability to experience life at a deeper and more complex level. We begin to resent the "real world" because it does not live up to the simple fantasies we engage in on a regular basis when watching television or the big screen.[2]

***

The First Amendment to the Constitution was ratified in 1791. It reads,

> Congress shall make no law respecting an establishment of religion, or prohibiting the free exercise thereof; or abridging the freedom of speech, or of the press; or the right of the people peaceably to assemble, and to petition the Government for a redress of grievances.

That little part in the middle about no law being passed to abridge "the freedom of speech, or of the press" has played a crucial role in American political history. It has also allowed the fantastic growth of modern media companies, mainly because it has insulated them from the social and cultural blowback that has resulted from monopolization. Paul Starr has argued in his book *The Creation of the Media: The Political Origins of Modern Communications* (2004) that present-day American media companies would not exist today were it not for the First Amendment to the Constitution and the Constitution's early support of a communications infrastructure, which we find enumerated in Article I, Section 8. There Congress is given the power to establish "Post Offices and post Roads." Another portion of this same section protects the "exclusive right" of authors and inventors, which relates back to media companies because it touches on copyright law.

Of course, the original desire of some of the founding fathers was to establish a press that would have the high responsibility of keeping the public informed. As Jefferson wrote in a letter to Edward Carrington,

> The basis of our government being the opinion of the people, the very first object should be to keep that right; and were it left to me to decide whether we should have a government without newspapers or newspapers without a government, I should not hesitate a moment to prefer the latter.[3]

Alexander Hamilton did not share Jefferson's opinion, which is not surprising since they were on opposite ends of the political spectrum. Hamilton saw the establishment of the First Amendment as unnecessary. In fact, he viewed the establishment of any amendments to the Constitution as superfluous. As he argued in *Federalist* no. 84,

> On the subject of the liberty of the press, as much has been said, I cannot forbear adding a remark or two: In the first place, I observe that there is not a syllable concerning it in the constitution of this state, and in the next, I contend that whatever has been said about it in that of any other state, amounts to nothing. What signifies a declaration that "the liberty of the press shall be inviolably preserved?" What is the liberty of the press? Who can give it any definition which would not leave the utmost latitude for evasion? I hold it to be impracticable; and from this, I infer, that its security, whatever fine declarations may be inserted in any constitution respecting it, must altogether depend on public opinion, and on the general spirit of the people and of the government.

It is a little difficult to parse what Hamilton is saying here, but he seems to be arguing that the Constitution would not be able to infringe the right of the press because the specific power to regulate the press had not been given to Congress, or to the Executive and Judicial branches. He is making what we today would call a "strict constructionist" argument. However, we all know the history now. The First Amendment did not prevent the passage of the Alien and Sedition Acts (1798), which did not directly target Anti-Federalist newspapers but did have a chilling effect on both speech and the press because criticizing the Adams administration and other Federalists in office became tantamount to treason. One can only imagine how much more latitude the law would have had without a First Amendment.

So, as Paul Starr argues, the modern American press would not have been possible without the built-in protections and encouragements of the Constitution. However, this protection and encouragement came with a price since newspapers, and now other news media, have ceased to adequately meet the standard that Jefferson and others set for it long ago. The reason for this is that newspapers in the nineteenth century abandoned subscription fees and turned to advertisement for their primary source of revenue.[4] This would set us on the course of creating a media more homogenized, and far more responsive to advertisers than readers. Starr writes,

> The relationship between the commercial media and democracy has always had two sides. Commerce both distorts and enlarges the public sphere; the incentive to attract more readers, listeners, or viewers sometimes produces reckless sensationalism and sometimes engages new groups in public debate. In the nineteenth century, as newspapers became increasingly dependent on advertising, editors and publishers began to see their readers less as members of the polity and more as consumers; yet advertising revenue also enabled papers to field far more reporters and provide a wider range of news independent of political subsidy. Pulitzer's equation— "circulation means advertising, and advertising means money, and money means independence"—captured the potential relationship between commercial success and editorial autonomy. It was on this basis that journalism produced both the greatest muckraking and the worst jingoism.[5]

What has been the result of the monopolization of the media? What has been the result of the exponential growth of practically useless information? What has been the result of society's almost complete abandonment of itself to amusement as the only way to stave off the boredom of middle-class existence? It has resulted in a homogenized media product controlled by a handful of companies, responsive only to advertisers and avoiding any real criticism of the social, political, and economic structures of the United States. Arthur Jensen's vision, his "evangel," is being realized right before our eyes as each of us becomes convinced that the existing structures of American society will provide all our necessities, tranquilize all our anxieties, and deliver us from the ennui of modern life. It is largely the role of modern media to convince us of these propositions, and so far they have done an excellent job.

As we dig deeper into the story of modern media it becomes clear what has happened, and Ben Bagdikian has helped us to better understand this moment in time with his book *The New Media Monopoly* (2004). For example, we learn that in 1983 there were fifty major media companies in the world but by 2003 there were only five, and these were: Time Warner, The Walt Disney Company, News Corporation, Viacom, and Bertelsmann (Germany).[6] However, monopolization is not where the story ends since these five cartel-like organizations are involved in so many overlapping business ventures that they are virtually one huge corporation. They have so many inter-locking board directors and so many joint media ventures that it would be a mistake to view them as merely competitors in the same market. They are instead partners who engage in a kind of *corporate sibling rivalry*. To illustrate this point, in 2001 Bertelsmann's purchased $400 million of advertising from AOL/Time Warner, a purchase that was made solely for the purpose of pumping up AOL/Time Warner stock. In exchange for this AOL/Time Warner engaged in the quid pro quo of purchasing shares in a subsidiary company belonging to Bertelsmann.[7] This type of back-scratching is common in the corporate world, as it is in smaller communities.

The larger issue of this conglomeration is that the press ceases to function as expected. Even with a highly partisan press there is a good chance one will be exposed to enough information to form correct opinions about the world around them. However, one of the primary problems with consolidation is that the press is not just muzzled or hoodwinked by government officials or business leaders, they simply do not have the resources on the ground to figure out what is really going on, and this is a direct function of corporate consolidation of the media and the pursuit of a fatter bottom line.

There are many who think that the Internet has fundamentally changed how information is generated and distributed, but the largest and most commercially viable entities in newsgathering will survive the populist storm of blogs and Twitter feeds. There is a good argument to be made that the Internet will make the strong only stronger, at least once they master the new technologies and begin to establish industry standards. The battle for the control of content—information and entertainment—also proves another powerful point: *access to capital within our present corporatized environment will always overwhelm any grassroots movement of political, social, or economic action.* Many new media titans have been born during this early struggle to control the Internet, but they have quickly made common cause with a previous generation of media titans in order to protect their hard-earned intellectual property gains. The proof for this can be seen in the desire among large media companies to pass SOPA (the Stop Online Piracy Act). Dozens of well-known websites protested the passage of this law on January 18, 2012, but others like Facebook were conspicuously absent from the protest.[8]

In order to better understand what is happening here and why it is so important to challenge the entrenched power of the media we turn for a moment to what has been called the Herman/Chomsky "Propaganda Model." Although most of Edward Herman and Noam Chomsky's book, *Manufacturing Consent: The Political Economy of Mass Media* (1988), is directed at media in the United States, the model they propose could be theoretically extended to any country with a modern communications system of radio, television, books, and newspapers. According to Herman and Chomsky the *propaganda model* can be reduced to five "filtering" mechanisms that determine what information we will get disseminated and how that information will be framed.

The *first filter* comes in the form of *large media companies* held by large corporations that are controlled by a small group of wealthy investors. The corporate structure makes profit the primary goal of these media conglomerates, so content becomes irrelevant as long as it makes money and does not question the system by which that content is manufactured, marketed, and distributed. Because these corporations are primarily concerned with bottom-line profit statements, there is a *second filter* that develops: media companies become almost completely beholden to *advertisers* rather than their readers, listeners, or watchers. Sometimes these advertisers can even dictate content themselves. A *third filter* affects those in the newsgathering business, where there is an almost complete dependence on the "*official line*" which comes directly from press releases sent out by government officials, business leaders, and "experts." A *fourth filter* to ensure the media does not sway too far from its propaganda role, is the use of "*flak*" against less-disciplined members of the media. This "flak" could be as direct as being fired for violating corporate policy or as subtle as being assigned to lesser tasks as punishment for certain reportorial indiscretions.

All of these things, combined with a *fifth filter*: an *overarching narrative theme of national purpose*, keeps major media subservient to the cause of elites. This last filter works effectively because it plays the role of a quasi-national religion and control mechanism.[9] There is nothing better than the charge of heresy or blasphemy to keep your critics quiet. When Herman and Chomsky first wrote their book the national narrative took the form of a struggle between capitalism and communism, what we used to call the Cold War. Today, after the demise of the Soviet Union in 1991, the national narrative is more likely viewed as an existential struggle against Islamic-based terrorism, or the desire to spread American-style freedom and democracy to the rest of the world.

One of the most egregious examples of the press's failure in recent history is the lack of pushback the Bush administration received when they claimed that an invasion of Iraq had to be immediately approved to prevent weapons of mass destruction from falling into the hands of terrorists. This was an example of how the media tends to tow the line when it comes to the dominant national narrative, and how reporters tend to rely far too much on official channels for their raw information. There is very little investigative reporting done these days, and you can count on one hand the number of news outlets that challenged the

Bush administration's official line. This has everything to do with the monopolization of media sources since the first thing to go when corporations gobble up smaller news agencies is the reporter in the field. This is particularly true of foreign correspondents, the lack of which has a direct correlation with the ignorance of the American people about the world and what kind of things the U.S. government gets up to in other countries. For example, most of the money shipped overseas in the form of U.S. foreign aid is thought to go to peaceful programs like food and medical assistance. The reality is that most of this money comes back to the United States in the form of arms purchases made from U.S. military contractors. These weapons are then often used on the very people who now hate the United States, along with their local oppressors. This situation was repeated time and again during the Cold War, but while most Americans viewed these efforts as attempts to liberate these oppressed, third-world countries the local people viewed U.S. involvement as support for their own repressive regimes. This is the problem of a foreign policy built solely on the rule that the enemy of my enemy is my friend. It is not always that clear.[10]

The major metropolitan areas of the United States are now host to only a few behemoth newspapers—often only one newspaper in some major cities, and they are often part of a national corporate chain. Compare this with major cities in Europe where dozens of newspapers exist and are owned by independent entities. They are not heavily influenced by the filter of a national narrative or driven by concern for stock prices. In the United States Gannett is a perfect example of what has happened in the United States over the last fifty years. Small, local newspapers have been gobbled up, their news staffs slashed, and their editors' salaries raised to encourage them to tow the corporate line. This has been done while Gannett has continued to spew out a log-cabin mythology to explain the origins of their corporate brand, one that has become synonymous with American patriotism. The greatest lie that Gannett feeds its readership is that local newspapers will continue to address regional concerns and interests. Instead, these newspapers tend to become carbon copies of Gannett's flagship publication *USA Today*, a publication that is best described as "superficial, materialistic, bland, and escapist."[11]

One of the reasons Gannett and other corporations target reporters when they acquire a local newspaper or television station is because they see reporters as naturally antagonistic to corporations. They feel, and maybe with just cause, that reporters are always trying to expose the failings of corporations and their executives. This is why corporations that acquire newspapers, and television and radio stations, immediately begin to intimidate and muzzle the professionally-trained journalist. Ultimately, these corporations want to be viewed as the heroes, not the villains, of American society. Reporters, whether for career advancement or out of an ideological desire to achieve social justice, see corporations and concentrated power as naturally evil and in need of a beat down.[12]

All the facts above expose the lie of the liberally-biased, mainstream media. That this is a myth is evidenced by the criticism Bill Clinton leveled against the media during the 1990s. Of course, he had reason to feel put upon by the media when the salacious details of his Oval Office tryst with a female intern came to light. Yet, even conservatives like James Baker, Patrick Buchanan, and William Kristol agreed that the Republicans got a fair hearing from the mainstream press during the 1996 presidential race. They also agreed that the mainstream press did not possess any more influence than more conservative voices in radio, television, and print. This was a rather honest admission from which many have backtracked over the years, especially since the introduction of the Fox News Channel in October of 1996. The reality, as Eric Alterman maintains, is that "conservatives are extremely well represented in every facet of the media," but they "work the ref" and "mau-mau" the opposition by claiming that there is a liberal bias in the "mainstream media."[13]

If we compare the U.S. press corps with that of the Europeans, it is decidedly right of center, and there is a simple reason for this, as touched on above. It is the mega-media corporations who dictate the content their companies put out. For example, economics reporters are nearly unanimous in their support for free trade and globalization. They ignore nearly all the disadvantages to the poor and working classes, because they are not allowed to question the fundamental proposition that trade and globalization is good for all involved. Reporters do not interview Bangladeshi or Chinese workers—even if they could—so American consumers have only one means by which to judge the value of trade and globalization: the prices they pay at the store. This compliance of reporters does not happen by magic. Companies ensure through their corporate structure an adherence to their chief agenda: making money. Those working in the news services of these large media corporations quickly learn that their jobs are on the line if they do not comply. For this reason most reporters and editors do not have to be directly in-structed about which stories to pursue or how to present them, they end up censoring themselves—which as we learn in *Nineteen Eighty-Four* is the best way to censor those who are part of a corporate body. As Alterman writes, "Reporters could be the most liberal people on earth. But…they simply do not 'make' the news." Daniel Gardner, a newspaper reporter from Ontario, makes the same observation when he says that most news stories tend to be about what concerns an editor, and the things editors care about are part and parcel associated with the con-cerns they have about their own way of life.[14]

Only when we look at what has been called the "punditocracy" can we see a clear bias in the media, and that bias is in favor of the conser-vative or reactionary point of view, not the liberal or radical view. The punditocracy is dominated by the conservative voice, which is well-fi-nanced and well-organized. Television proves to be the perfect medium for conservative ideas since conservative—or rather pseudo-conser-vative—views tend to be uncomplicated and can be readily reduced to quick, simple messages that are easily digested by the viewer. Conserva-tives make much of *commonsense*, and the popularity of this pabulum-style television commentary is why Bill O'Reilly, Sean Hannity, and

Chris Matthews—who is barely a centrist—can command seven-figure salaries. In the last decade only the now defrocked host of *Countdown with Keith Olbermann* has gotten close to the style of the conservative, in-your-face pundits featured on Fox News. Olbermann's evening replacements on MSNBC: Ed "Psychotalk" Schultz, Rachel Maddow, Al Sharpton, and Lawrence O'Donnell, cannot collectively raise the same amount of conservative ire that Olbermann's "Worst Person in the World" once did each night. According to Alterman, in order to have an equally bellicose left-leaning show among today's punditocracy we would have to invite the likes of Noam Chomsky, Alexander Cockburn, Vanessa Redgrave, and Fidel Castro to participate.[15]

The dominance of the conservative or center-right voice in television came after decades of effort on the part of conservative think tanks to create a façade of intellectual heft through organizations like The Heritage Foundation, The Cato Institute, and the American Enterprise Institute. These well-financed organizations got their starts in the 1970s as conservatives struggled to regain their footing after the political and moral losses of 1964 and the Watergate scandal, which drove Richard Nixon from office. The primary goal of these *propaganda mills* is to provide right-wing Republicans with talking points, not to expand the corpus of human knowledge and understanding. Their only goal is to make the right-wing conservative viewpoint appear more within the mainstream. One of the best examples of this is the way in which non-peer-reviewed "scholarship" has been marketed by these organizations, as though it were properly vetted academic work. A specific example of this was the 1994 publication of Richard Herrnstein and Charles Murray's *The Bell Curve: Intelligence and Class Structure in American Life*, a book that essentially argued against social programs to equalize educational outcomes because I.Q. is not a socially malleable quality. One of the most controversial aspects of the book was the suggestion that low I.Q.'s measured among African-Americans might be the product of genetics rather than socio-economic conditions, a view that accords with the general Social Darwinist streak within the right-wing, "conserva-tive" movement.[16]

It should be pointed out that *The Bell Curve* probably got more criticism than it deserved for its racialist undertones. The brunt of the criticism should have been directed at Herrnstein and Murray's conclu-sion that *all* racial groups were being imperiled by a growing number of children born to cognitively inferior individuals. The goal of their research was to prove that social programs for this ever-growing group of *parasitic dullards*, regardless of race, was a pointless waste of resourc-es, a standard refrain among the libertarian community. As Stephen J. Gould and others pointed out this was a smack in the face of anyone who had been taught that all native intelligence could be enhanced by hard work and diligence in education. The argument also assumed that an I.Q. can accurately assess the intelligence of an individual, a subject itself of much controversy.[17]

Manufactured conservative controversies like the one above, com-bined with the FCC's decision to eliminate the "fairness doctrine" in 1987, have helped conservatives take over virtually all of AM talk radio. A "recalibration" had already been occurring in radio during the 1980s, just as it had previously occurred in print media. The end of the fair-ness doctrine completed this recalibration in radio while in print *faux liberals* like David Broder and faux-liberal magazines like *The New Re-public* made anyone on the "real" left appear as part of the lunatic fringe. Individuals like Rush Limbaugh and Sean Hannity have only pushed the right-left political line further to the right by making the moniker of "liberal" almost as hated as that of "pedophile." The important point here is that there are no comparable radio voices on the left side of the political spectrum. Self-described liberals like Stephanie Miller, Thom Hartmann, and Randi Rhodes, all have their own radio shows but are virtually unknown to most Americans. However, even those who do not count themselves among faithful "ditto-heads" have heard of the inimi-table Rush Limbaugh.[18]

You might be apt to think that Alterman, Herman, Chomsky, and Bagdikian have exaggerated the effects of monopolization on the modern press. Maybe you still think the mainstream media is dominated by liberals. If so, how would it be possible for someone like Ann Coulter, a leading "intellectual" conservative to get airtime on CNN, MSNBC, and other liberal venues? For example, Coulter's 2006 book *Godless: The Church of Liberalism* is a ridiculous screed against those she calls liberals, but those she calls liberals might better be described as sociopaths. She writes things like "Liberalism is a comprehensive belief system denying the Christian belief in man's immortal soul." Doubling down on this animadversion she writes,

> No liberal cause is defended with more dishonesty than abortion. No matter what else they pretend to care about from time to time— undermining national security, aiding terrorists, oppressing the middle class, freeing violent criminals—the single most important item on the Democrats' agenda is abortion.

What legitimate *liberal* news organization would let a person like this anywhere near a studio camera and microphone? Fortunately, her appearances in the "mainstream liberal media" have become rare of late. In fact, appearances by this bedeviler of moderates and so-called liberals have gone down dramatically as she has gotten more strident. Her latest work, *Demonic: How the Liberal Mob Is Endangering America* (2011) merely reiterates her particular brand of anti-intellectual Christian faith, a hodgepodge of neo-con foreign policy and economic libertarianism. According to an article in *The Washington Post* Coulter may be losing her audience since her last book only debuted at number three and does not appear to have any staying power.[19] Is it possible she has gone too far, or that the political pendulum has begun to swing the other way? Only time will tell.

Were Coulter the only example of right-wing conservatives using religious invective against the would-be phantom of liberalism we could just ignore her, the way people ignored the John Birch Society after 1960. However, Coulter is in good company. The male version of Coulter can be found in the person of Dinesh D'Souza the author of *The Enemy at Home: The Cultural Left and Its Responsibility for 9/11* (2007) and *The Roots of Obama's Rage* (2010). The latter book argues that Obama is attempting to implement his father's Kenyan socialist policies because of his anger at having been abandoned as a child. The absurdity of all these ideas are made a little more respectable by more mainstream pundits like Sean Hannity, whose books *Deliver Us From Evil: Defeating Terrorism, Despotism, and Liberalism* (2004) and *Conservative Victory: Defeating Obama's Radical Agenda* (2010) explore the same memes as Coulter and D'Souza, only in the more coded language of patriotism.

Pundits seem to be everywhere these days. Everyone wants to be one, and we do not seem to be able to stop listening to them on our TVs and radios. Their views have come to dominate the dialogue of American politics.[20] The reason I mention them here is because I believe this phenomenon relates to the central concern of this book: *the culture of fear*. It is clear that fear is a tool often used by "conservative" pundits, who are really at heart the same pseudo-conservatives we talked about in the last chapter, the ones who warned us of worldwide communist conspiracies against our lives and liberty. By a series of *ad hoc* events that have occurred since 1970 the pseudo-conservative voice, which once cried alone in the wilderness, has now been given a megaphone. They now command the eyes and ears of tens of millions, and are even able to create their own political movements almost *ex nihilo* and without the need for any grassroots work.[21] None of this would have been possible without the growing monopolization of media companies and the press, which has always had as its anonymously attributed creed: *if it bleeds, it leads.*

In those five words is summed up the mindset of modern American media in general and, more specifically, the American press corps. It does not matter whether we are talking about the so-called liberal mainstream media's five o'clock news show, the ones that feature the latest school shooting or the latest warning by so-called experts about what not to eat; it does not matter whether it is the right-wing conservative pundit spewing his or her fear-based patriotism; it does not even matter whether it is the newest police drama that exposes us psychologically to a level of crime that most of us will never encounter in our own life. What matters is that we are already afraid, and for reasons we often do not understand. We are looking for answers, and none can be found in modern media because the goal of its corporate owners is to use your fear against you, even if it is only to sell you a little deodorant or tooth-paste.[22]

We have talked about the use of fear in politics and the media. It is now time to move on to a third group of uncoordinated fear-mongering: "expertise." I put this word in quotes to distinguish real expertise from the celebrity-type expertise we are exposed to in the media. We should strive to know the difference, and I hope the next chapter will help you begin that task. If there is one lesson to be learned it is that we should have respect for the true expert who has proven herself, but that we should take with a grain of salt the pronouncements of those self-proclaimed experts we encounter most of the time in modern media.

It is possible to live life without the constant advice of "experts," and we should trust a little more in your own modest abilities while working toward social and political institutions that are more responsive to our needs and wants. However, the latter cannot be achieved as long as we continue to be paralyzed by fear and infantilized by those who think they always know best.

In the next chapter we will profile the last of the *fear makers*, those who call themselves *experts*, those who try to convince us that if we do not heed their advice we are surely doomed. As we pull back the curtain on these so-called experts we will ironically learn that it is better to trust those who question themselves and their ideas. For, it is the self-examiner who turns out to be more flexible, better able to adjust their thinking to the facts, and ultimately more pragmatic. It is only the *fear maker* who is certain of all he says and does.

Chapter Seven

Stand Aside...I'm an Expert!

Even when the experts all agree, they may well be mistaken.

Bertrand Russell

No event in history better illustrates how experts can get things wrong than does the financial crash of 2008. The financial community's casino-style betting on complex mathematical formulas that were built on the foundation of subprime mortgages, derivatives, and credit default swaps, shows how sometimes the smartest people in the room are not the ones with the most common sense.

In Nassim Nicholas Taleb's 2007 book *The Black Swan: The Impact of the Highly Improbable* we are introduced to the staggering uncertainty inherent in a complex market, a market that theoretically has no limits to the upside or downside. Anyone who has ever played craps in a casino has experienced this in microcosm. They know how fast money can accumulate and disappear as bets are placed on certain rolls of the dice, for or against the point, and for or against the pass line. Taleb experienced this first hand while working as a "quant" on Wall Street, back in 1987. It was at that time he became financially independent by making the right bets on the market. He did this by *shorting the market*—betting that it would go down, which he did again in 2007 and 2008. Taleb's advice is simple and traditional: "don't put all your eggs in one basket." In order to effectively manage risk, he says, you are better off investing in ten things with a huge potential upside. This type of investing also means that you have a greater chance of losing all your money in one particular transaction since the risk-reward ratio is high, but it is also more likely that one of the ten bets will pay off and cover your losses. If you get lucky one bet will not only cover your losses but will make you even more money. Unfortunately, there is no way to predict which investments will take off and which ones will decline. Either of these events is what Taleb calls "black swans," unpredictable events in the market that lead to huge profits or heavy losses.

One way to understand what happens when people use *leverage* (debt) to place their bets in the financial markets is to imagine a situation in which someone works at McDonald's for minimum wage and gets the opportunity to buy an $80,000 house with only $2,000 down. They do not have $2,000 so they borrow that money using $200 worth of collateral that they have in a savings account in order to get yet more financing to buy the house. They think they will soon be able to sell the house for $100,000, a 9000% return on their initial investment of $200![1]

The house is purchased but in addition to the income from their job they have to keep borrowing each month to keep up with the difference between their wages and the monthly payments on their mortgage and the loan they took out for the initial down payment. Then, one day the person lending them money each month decides to stop. Maybe they heard that the person lost their job at McDonald's? Now, not only is their $200 in collateral gone but they are stuck with a mortgage that is over five times their previous annual income, and they still owe someone for the $2000 that was lent to them at the beginning of the transaction.

This is clearly an oversimplified analogy since Lehman Brothers, Bear Stearns and others were engaged in thousands of similar transactions to keep the "house of cards" standing, and they thought their downside risk was covered by a type of *insurance* called *credit default swaps*, but this gives us a sense of how much risk was being taken on by these companies, and with little thought for the downside. These companies were thinking no differently than the guy who walks into a Las Vegas casino thinking he can *break the bank*.

Why can't we trust everyone who claims to be an expert in their field? Why should we tune out those who speak with such certitude about markets, social issues, government policy, national security, or a myriad number of things they claim should animate us to action?

Fortunately, several journalists and researchers have already made good attempts to answer these questions for us. One of them is David H. Freeman. His book *Wrong: Why Experts* Keep Failing Us—and How to Know When Not to Trust Them* (2010) helps us to understand the limits of expertise.[2] Much of Freeman's book focuses on the work of John Ioannidis, a medical mathematician who examines the long-term statistical accuracy of research and peer-reviewed literature. What he has found is disturbing. If Ioannidis is correct nearly two-thirds of all medical findings published in prestigious journals are later proven wrong by subsequent studies. This can only lead to one conclusion, "...expert wisdom usually turns out to be at best highly contested and ephemeral, and at worst flat-out wrong."[3]

Expertise is always limited, and experts will not always get it right for one reason or another, but there are a few rules to help us navigate the world of good and bad advice.[4] Bias and corruption—more prevalent among informal, self-appointed experts—is a common reason for why experts get things wrong. That is not to say formal experts are always right, they are just more right, more often. However, as we mentioned above, that may only mean being right 30% of the time, which is less than the odds of tossing a coin in the air and having it land on heads. There are other reasons as well. There are some who claim to be experts on a certain aspect of life but who have merely created a coherent but irrational system of belief that *allegedly* helps us to navigate the world, and to get us what we want. A good example of a seemingly coherent system that defies commonsense would be *The Secret* (2006), a system which claims that if people simply visualize what they want the universe will somehow respond to their wants or needs. One is hard pressed to understand how this would differ from the Christian's belief that prayer can do the same, a contention that has been disproved time and time again in blind studies.[5]

Often an expert is simply a demagogue, someone who says what they know the audience wants to hear. We touched on this in the last chapter when we talked about pundits, who are inveterate demagogues, and who too often believe their own hype. Ineptitude can also be a widespread problem amongst both formal and informal experts. Again, the former cannot be as intellectually lazy as the latter, but it still happens. This brings us to an important point that distinguishes the informal from the formal expert. The latter usually is associated with a community that prevents them from making outrageous claims in their area of expertise. Sometimes this works, but too often it fails. An example of success was the claim made by Stanley Pons and Martin Fleischmann in 1989 that they had observed cold fusion in the laboratory. This "discovery" received much media hype, but the scientific community quickly showed that the results could not be replicated and were therefore bogus.[6] Unfortunately, the case of Andrew Wakefield's study of the MMR (Mumps-Measles-Rubella) vaccine and its possible connection to autism made it into the prestigious scientific journal *Lancet* in 1998, before it could be repudiated by the larger scientific community. Not only was the study itself flawed, because Wakefield used only twelve subjects to achieve his results, it also violated two rules that Freeman says should set off bells and whistles in our heads: *it purported to be a "groundbreaking" study and it was a study based on a single dataset.* Most good expert advice is based on years of observation and study. *Longitudinal studies* are the best ones because they measure statistical correlations between two events using numerous studies done over a period of many years.

Another problem in the expert world is that most research tends to focus on a particularly narrow subject which tends to create a type of intellectual tunnel-vision. The researcher begins to see everything within the paradigm in which they work every day. This is why lawyers tend to view all problems as legal issues that can be chopped up into separate issues where each point has a differing level of relevance. Economists might also view everything as a question of value, substitution, or supply and demand. This type of intellectual tunnel-vision has been called the *hedgehog effect*. Intellectual hedgehogs tend to shoehorn all data into an overarching intellectual framework, they ignore or explain away anomalous data, they prize simplicity over complexity, and they categorically reject all views that do not support their claims. The hedgehog's counterpart is the *fox*. Intellectual foxes tend to think outside the box, do not try to fit everything into their overarching intellectual framework, they emphasize complexity over simplicity, and they are tolerant of views that qualify their own.[7]

Freeman calls the hedgehog phenomenon "automaticity," which is the idea that experts tend to accept things that sound like stuff they think they already know. They do this without analyzing the situation to see if there is some reason it is different. One of the reasons people respond so positively to these type of experts is that they usually speak with such "clear cut, actionable, universal, and palatable" advice that it is hard for us to resist them.[8] Freeman calls this the "certainty principle." We all like confidence and feel uneasy with those who qualify their opinions too much. Malcolm Gladwell points this out in his book *Blink: The Power of Thinking Without Thinking* (2008). Many reject the advice of those who do not "look" or "sound" like they know what they are talking about.[9] Gladwell tells the story of two doctors, one who gives a single diagnosis and treatment protocol and another who suggests it could be a couple of things, and that there are several ways to proceed to find out what is wrong. The former was seen as knowledgeable and decisive while the latter was seen as ineffective, yet when the statistical results of their diagnoses were put side-by-side the less certain of the two doctors proved to be a far more effective diagnostician, and he was better liked. Deep down we do not really like *know-it-alls*, even we may defer to them.

The problem here is that humans tend to make most of their decisions using what Daniel Kahneman has called "system one" of the brain.

This is that part of the brain that works largely at an unconscious or intuitive level. This is the system that provides us with our gut instinct, which works fine most of the time but often it is not enough in a complex world. Kahneman uses the example of multiplying two numbers to explain how and when *system one* and *system two* kick in. If we are asked to solve for 2 x 2 we will immediately answer *four*. We will give this answer as though we did not even have to think about it. This is system one at its best. However, if we are asked to solve for 27 x 56 our brains shift to system two in order to complete the task. In the latter situation we are far more conscious of our effort and the reason may have a lot to do with how our brain stores memories. In other words, if it were possible to memorize a multiplication table that went up to 120 times 120 then the second problem in the example above would be as easy to answer as the first problem. It is the same reason we know immediately that a man with an upper-class English accent who claims to have tattoos all up and down his back is an anomaly, but we cannot figure out what the price of oil should be.[10]

With such an unreliable system of decision-making it is no wonder we look to experts to help us navigate the complicated world, and this is okay as long as we are careful. So, do not lose hope. Here are a few rules of thumb, courtesy of David Freeman, to help us navigate the world of expert advice. They might protect you against bad advice, and also help you to discriminate between good and bad experts. The first thing that should set off bells in your head is if the expert maintains that his advice is simple, universal, and definitive. Often an expert will preface what they say with "It's simple...." After hearing that phrase, you should listen real close and assume that what you are about to hear is *complete bullshit*. It is also very likely the expert will contradict himself within sixty seconds, especially if pressed hard. He will eventually admit that the subject under consideration is not so simple, but that his "simple answer" is a major factor in addressing the subject. One of the reasons experts believe things are more simple than they are is because their views are largely based on a single study or murky anecdotes, and these studies usually turn out to be incorrect or grossly overstated, or "ground-breaking." Two other ways in which you can identify bad expert advice is that the individual pushing the advice stands to benefit directly from you believing him, and his solutions tend to be an attempt to lock the barn after the horse has already escaped.[11] Always look for the straw man. He will inevitably be found in the details.

So, if you hear some advice and it sounds right but you cannot explain why, then ignore it. A good expert will be able to explain why they believe what they do and include all the necessary qualifiers and exceptions that come with his advice. If it is controversial, it is most likely a marketing ploy and you can ignore it too. Most good advice is the result of a long process of research and wrangling among experts who come to generally accepted conclusions, even if they disagree about some particulars. If it has mass appeal and everyone rushes to it at the same time, wait a little while to see if it pans out—particularly true if all the experts are in immediate agreement. A good expert will point out possible flaws in methodologies and conclusions when a new idea is presented. They will show a certain amount of skepticism, even with their own claims. If the only argument for it is that it has appeared in a prestigious journal or is supported by someone with sterling credentials, take it all with a grain of salt. That is not to say experts should never be heeded. It just means preferring the long-term consensus of multiple experts who have proven themselves free of hype and unbiased by notions of a universal panacea.[12]

Keep in mind that experts are susceptible to the same social, economic, and political pressures as the rest of us. The desire to conform makes working in groups difficult because people tend to agree with one another to keep group cohesion from breaking down. The best work is usually done independently of the group, or where the group is organized as a loose confederation. The loose confederation, or committee-style work, also differs from what some have called the "wisdom of crowds." The "wisdom of crowds" is a statistical phenomenon that sometimes works with large groups of people who have no deep, personal, social, or political affiliation. The susceptibility of experts to all these social and political pressures means they are no less likely than the average person to engage in sensational stories put out by the media. Sensationalism in American society has a direct relationship with social and economic success. We should always keep this in mind when trying to determine who to trust.[13]

Why is it so important that we be able to navigate the world of expert advice? Because, we live in a complicated world of our own making called "civilization," a world and an age in which we now measure life in seconds—no longer moons. Our gut instinct, which is fine for operating in the everyday world of family and work, is a much less effective tool when we try to cope with the array of uncertainty that surrounds us in the modern world. There are people who know we possess this inherent weakness in our way of thinking, and they are willing to take advantage of it. They do everything in their power to convince us they have answers that will protect us from dangers we ourselves cannot fully understand. However, to do that they are forced to muddy the distinction between likely and unlikely dangers. They create a world in which everything becomes a danger, even our continued existence.

In the late 1960s Paul Ehrlich, an American biologist, won worldwide fame when he published *The Population Bomb* (1968). The thesis of his book was *simple*. Aha! Ehrlich claimed that the population was growing faster than the world's food supply. Ehrlich claimed that it was a mathematical certainty that hundreds of millions of people would starve to death in the 1970s. If you were around in the 1970s you might remember watching a movie called *Soylent Green* (1973). The film explored the idea of what would happen if we had to deal with an exploding and starving population in the near future. The movie starred Charlton Heston, who played a cop investigating the murder of a wealthy businessman. He eventually traces the murder back to the government and learns that they are motivated by the desire to hide a secret about the world's food supply, which has been adversely affected by pollution, overpopulation, and the greenhouse effect. The final few scenes of the movie reveal the horrific secret the government has been trying to hide, and as Heston is carried away at the end of the movie, shot and bleeding, he yells over and over again, "Soylent Green is people! It's people!" This movie was based on a 1966 novel, *Make Room! Make Room!,* written by Harry Harrison. It is difficult to know here whether fiction was influencing "fact" or the other way around since Ehrlich's book came out in 1968.

This is just one example that illustrates how experts can be used to put forth unsubstantiated ideas that serve only the purpose of making people more afraid and passive to those in authority. However, most experts are not of the same ilk as Paul Ehrlich. Most tend to be more parochial in their influence. Two more examples will hopefully suffice.

In 1997, a year that coincided with the general fear that violent crime was rising, Gavin de Becker published a book entitled *The Gift of Fear and Other Survival Signals That Protect Us From Violence.* Here we have an example of a professional security expert—who usually protects A-list celebrities trying to create a larger market for his techniques and services. The book becomes immediately relevant if one assumes, as did the Oprah show, that the security needs of an average middle-class family living in Des Moines, Iowa, are the same as an A-list celebrity.

The best way to convince people that this is the way of the world is to tell them anecdotes about women being raped in their apartments by strange men who have offered to help them carry in the groceries, or to relate stories about near misses. One story of a near miss is told by de Becker at the beginning of the book. A young woman allegedly escapes a potentially violent situation because of her mother's fear and intuition about the situation. The young woman's roommate is eventually kidnapped by her disturbed boyfriend after the young woman moves out, proving that had the young woman not listened to her mother's inner voice she might have ended up hurt or dead.

De Becker argues that we are all born with the natural ability to assess dangerous situations but that we need to hone them using his techniques, most of which are common sense. De Becker is right. We are a species with a particularly sensitive apparatus for detecting danger, and encouraging people to be cautious is not wrong, but to overstate the probability of stranger-on-stranger violence is to misinform people. That is what de Becker is doing, ignoring the fact that most violence in the United States is committed by someone we know: a spouse, a parent, a child, a significant other, or another trusted member of the community. According to the FBI, in 2009 there were 13, 636 homicides in the United States. Less than thirteen percent of these homicides were committed by complete strangers. Of the homicides solved that year, 5,974 were committed by individuals designated as "acquaintances" or "family members." Of course, these statistics do not tell the whole story since 43% of the 13, 636 murders remain unsolved.[14]

If *stranger danger* is not your concern there are plenty of fears left to choose from. There are experts on every fear, waiting to provide you with detailed advice on how to "survive." It does not matter whether you will be surviving the victimization of a stranger or the collapse of the entire world system of finance, trade, and government.

If you are afraid that civilization is not as stable as you think it should be, then you might want to pick up James Wesley Rawles's *How to Survive the End of the World As We Know It: Tactics, Techniques, and Technologies for Uncertain Times* (2009). This nationally best-selling book encourages the reader to develop a GOOD (Get Out Of Dodge) strategy for surviving what the author believes is the inevitable crumbling of U.S. society, most likely initiated by a pandemic of influenza that will cause a cascading disruption of energy and the food supply.[15] Mr. Rawles encourages his readers to live all year round at their "retreat," but he sympathetically understands that most people are not able to do this. So, the best strategy is to keep a vehicle ready, along with a properly-mapped route of escape, and to make sure your retreat is properly stocked with food, ammo, and, of course, gold—because money will soon be worthless. Rawles writes early in his book, "Suffice it to say, we live in an increasingly dangerous world, with a fragile and highly interdependent infrastructure."[16] If you believe this, and have little trust in those who are running things, then it is easy to accept the notion that things could come crashing down any moment.[17]

You may have noticed an apparent contradiction above. How, you might ask, can we distrust experts while at the same time trusting those same people to run a complex system like our civilization? Is Rawles right, should we not be worried? The answer is *yes* and *no*. The reason we can trust those who control our complex system is that most of them are not experts. They are merely cogs in a large machine that no one really controls. Experts might have a greater degree of power and control but it is not unlimited, and it is always subject to collective assent. No expert has unlimited power. Their bailiwicks are rather circumscribed, which is what makes them an annoyance when it comes to "the culture of fear," but in the end they are merely one contributor among many to the milieu of fear that is built up by politicians, pundits, and other purveyors of pandemonium.

Daniel Gardner, again, sums it up nicely in his book *The Science of Fear*. He writes, "Rational risk regulation is a slow, careful, and thoughtful examination of the dangers and costs in particular cases."[18] This is not something Gavin de Becker or John Wesley Rawles have done. The fear-based scenarios these *so-called experts* have created are based on a belief that one needs to assess the danger and cost of nearly impossible "particular cases." As Frank Furedi has written, if we continue to manufacture theoretical fear after theoretical fear we will quickly find that there is no end to the number of dangers by which we can annihilate ourselves and this will eventually paralyze from doing anything.

We should end here with a note of caution. To say that we should not *always* blindly follow experts is not an argument against having experts. Andrew Keen has addressed the problem we get into when we do not trust any expert advice. His book *The Cult of the Amateur: How Today's Internet Is Killing Our Culture* (2007) will probably be seen by many as an elitist screed against the common-sense of the average Joe. In one respect this type of elitism permeates the book, especially when he says that the popular fascination with the internet is allowing the "takeover of the monkey" and "mob rule." Although he uses the internet extensively himself, Keen sees it as ultimately a destroyer of expert opinion and destructive of that class he calls "the cultural gatekeepers," which is why Keen harbors a distinct contempt for Wikipedia.

The problem, he says, is twofold: 1) the internet allows for too much anonymous misinformation to be disseminated and 2) it robs professionals in the "gate-keeping" business of income. So, Craigslist destroys the newspapers because want ads cease to be a chief means of revenue for printed dailies. Wikipedia makes it difficult for Britannica to compete, since Britannica has to pay for its content while Wikipedia gets it for free.

Another example Keen uses is a Frito-Lay sponsored marketing ploy. The company offered a $10,000 prize to each of the top five people who could create a thirty-second TV-ready commercial for their product. This meant a savings of $331,000 for Frito-Lay's advertising campaign since a professional ad usually costs an average of $381,000, but it also meant lost revenue for a professional advertising agency.[19]

The Luddite complaint that technology destroys jobs is an old saw, and there is a lot of truth to it.[20] However, this wailing and moaning about loss of income rings a little hollow coming from a privileged member of the *cogniti*. A more salient criticism offered by Keen is that the internet is creating "less culture, less reliable news, and a chaos of useless information." Even worse, it contributes to a society where people *seem* to have access to unlimited information but where they actually only have stronger opinions reinforced by the shared ignorance of their online echo chambers.[21] So, "experts" are only trusted and respected when they agree with what we already believe. It is a view that even infiltrates scientific debate, which becomes by necessity politicized and then fixed into simplistic binary categories from which it is nearly impossible to escape.[22]

One of the reasons for this may be found in the cultural critic Neil Postman's suggestion that losing our connection to the past has impoverished us socially and intellectually. While the eighteenth-century Enlightenment attempted to accurately map reality by bringing clarity, logic, and rigor to language, we do exactly the opposite in the modern age.[23] There is irony running throughout this situation, since we live in a society that desires a type of language which allows us a great deal of flexibility, but we also long for certainty. In the end we get neither, unless we turn to traditional religion or the simplistic bromides of politics, or unless we reject the only language that provides us with any real *clarity*, *logic*, and *rigor*: mathematics.[24] This is not to say that teaching mathematics to children would solve all our problems, but it might be better than building up their self-esteem so much that even the slightest disappointment in life leads to emotional devastation.

Training people to do math would help but what is even more important is training people to place things in context, which goes against our modern notion that everything can be explained in five minutes or less, and that understanding does not require connecting each module of learning to another. As Postman writes,

> The process of making meaning from a text involves as much withholding meanings as adding them, and knowing the rules that govern when it is appropriate to do either is at the core of reasonable interpretation.[25]

What Postman was calling for here was a holistic approach to knowledge and wisdom, without which we become merely a technocratic society, expert in maintaining the machines but unable to discuss why they exist in the first place. More importantly, those left at the mercy of the machines, and the technicians that run them, have no understanding about how they work and are perpetually afraid that the machines will someday cease and they will be forced to survive on their own. This gives them an incentive not to rock the boat socially or economically, because they fear they might somehow be responsible for the destruction of this great machine, which *meets all their needs and tranquilizes all their anxieties.*

***

In the next section of this book we will explore the human fascination with storytelling. The story of cosmos (*order*) and chaos is an age-old one. It is a story that continues to permeate the modern human mind, whether the source of those stories are our religious inculcation, our exposure to movies and literature, or even our political education.

We all desire *identity*, *place*, and *a predictable moral universe* in which we can learn to both survive and thrive. The story of cosmos and chaos allows us to vicariously participate in the great universal drama. It makes us all actors on a intergalactic stage that has as its ultimate purpose the consummation of mankind with its divine potential. However, this pervasive belief in human progress and perfection, when robbed of its means or threatened by all manner of self-destructive tendencies, yields a dystopian vision from which many believe we cannot escape.

The next section begins with an introduction to this dystopian vision, and subsequent chapters help to explain the origins of this dour temperament. By the time you get to the end of the next section you will hopefully understand why American society has become today effectively dysfunctional when it comes to politics, foreign policy, and social and economic justice, issues we will address in the final section of this book.

In a nutshell, the dysfunction of our social, political, and economic system is the direct result of *the culture of fear* and its closed cousin, *the apocalyptic mind,* which we cannot combat without a renewed social dialogue on morality and a renewed commitment to democratic action, especially as it relates to social and economic justice.

PART THREE

COSMOS, CHAOS, AND TOMORROW

Chapter Eight

The Dystopian Vision

I am the Nightrider. I'm a fuel-injected suicide machine. I am the rocker, I am the roller, I am the out-of-controller.

Maniac driver in opening scene of *Mad Max* (1979)

Up until now we have been directly concerned with *the culture of fear*. We have focused on how our evolutionary development, and the willingness of some in society to take advantage of that evolutionary development, explains how the culture of fear exists. However, there is another way of explaining the culture of fear, which is ultimately rooted in the prophetic tradition of the Christian faith. It is this prophetic tradition that predicts a final, universal battle between good and evil followed by the institution of a utopian community of true believers. It is this idea that must precede all dystopian thought. For, only smashed hopes and broken dreams can yield the kind of dystopian nightmares that make the culture of fear all too real for far too many.

In the early days of Christianity these prophetic ideas used to be specific to small communities of believers, even though the prophetic themes within each community were similar to the others. There came a time, roughly 500 to 1500 CE, when this prophetic tradition began to dominate Western society. This was when the Roman Catholic Church, in league with the Germanic states, began to hold religious sway over all of Europe, and pushed what was called an *amillennial* interpretation of the coming kingdom of God. The Protestant Reformation broke up this religious monopoly in the sixteenth century but it did not diminish the

Christian interest in a future where all would be part of the same believing community, and where the kingdom of God would be finally realized here on earth. Of course, these prophetic interpretations became far more varied, yielding, as we will see below, very interesting social and political consequences.

Today these Christian themes have become universal and secular, especially in the form of the *death-denying ideologies* of free-market capitalism and, now moribund, communism.[1] In the next few chapters we focus on how Christian prophetic tradition has helped to define the character of the American nation, and why so many still believe that the United States stands as a beacon of hope to the rest of the world. For the most part Christian prophetic tradition, which has dominated the western world, promoted an extremely sanguine view of the future, even if that future might be preceded in some scenarios by terrible calamities.

What happened, though, when the promise of science and technology, animated in large part by Christian prophetic traditions, was deprived not only of moral inhibitions but of human hope? What was the result when we were left with the *machine of material progress* but ceased to have any way of assessing its rhyme or reason? What happened was that men begin to imagine all sorts of bad things, even as I began to imagine bad things at an early age.

***

In the summer of 1980 my family and I moved to Cedar Rapids, Iowa. Taking a break from house-hunting we went to see a double-feature at the local drive-in theater. For those of you too young to remember, people used to watch movies from their cars in large parking lots with a gigantic screen at each end of the lot. I still remember bringing our own jug of Kool-Aid and a paper grocery bag full of popcorn so we could avoid the outrageous prices at the snack bar. The movie I was most eager to see that night was George Miller's *Mad Max* (1979), which starred a young, not-yet-famous, Mel Gibson. This was the latest in a series of movies I had enjoyed during my childhood in the 1970s, movies that had scared the crap out of me, in much the same way a roller coaster does. Prior to seeing *Mad Max*, one of my favorite apocalyptic movies was called *Damnation Alley* (1977). The movie follows a rough-and-tumble group of post-nuclear war survivors who build a specially-rigged post-apocalyptic vehicle in order to search for others who can help them rebuild society. The irony in many of these movies is that they often combine dystopianism with humanity's abiding faith in the power of technology. The same science and technology that wreaked havoc on the planet is now used by the survivors to live and to re-build the world they once knew.

Mad Max was not much different when it came to technology. Cars and motorcycles play a major role in the film. They were used not only to pursue but to kill. In the first half of the movie Max Rockatansky's wife and child are run down by a gang seeking revenge for one of their comrades, a maniac who in the opening scene of the movie is killed while being pursued by the police. In the second film these pursuit vehicles are referred to as the "last of the V-8 interceptors," because it is clear by the second film that Max lives in a post-apocalyptic world where these machines are no longer being produced. Each movie gets more technologically backward, so much so that in the opening scene of *Mad Max Beyond Thunderdome* (1985) Max's car is being pulled by camels across a desert. The second movie, *Mad Max 2: The Road Warrior* (1981), had focused on the lack of gasoline, needed to keep the remaining machines running. By the third movie the issue was not only gas but keeping the machines themselves going.

These iconic films represent a general strain of thought that flourished in the 1970s and 1980s. These types of films encouraged a dark view of the future, a vision of ecological and biological destruction that we discussed in the first part of this book. In modern American society many are now predisposed to view the future in decidedly dystopian terms, the kind of terms that were previously limited to the religious world but which have now become completely secularized. We will touch below on only a small segment of the literature and film that has been produced using these themes. I have purposely limited this discussion to books and movies that I have read and seen because it is difficult to capture the messages and nuances of popular art using the observations of others.

I've already mentioned four movies, and I have to admit that until I was a teenager I did not do much reading. So, my view of the world was largely shaped by numerous films and TV shows. Of course, I grew up watching the *Star Trek* series, which gave me a particular fondness for science, technology, and Vulcan logic. *Star Trek* is one of those cultural influences that simply cannot be ignored. With this series Gene Roddenberry created a "new frontier" thesis.[2] The narrative at the beginning of each episode says it all:

> Space, the final frontier. These are the voyages of the Starship Enterprise. Its five-year mission: to explore strange new worlds, to seek out new life and new civilizations, to boldly go where no man has gone before.

Gene Roddenberry was not a technophile. He was as an explorer of the human condition. In Roddenberry's view technology did not fundamentally alter what it meant to be human. Roddenberry's stories were about good and evil, about the moral choices we make, and how those choices define us. For Roddenberry the technology was just a prop, since the true purpose of the *Star Trek* series was to explore ourselves through others. The recent redux of the film series by J. J. Abrams, *Star Trek* (2009), continues that tradition, which for all its world-ending excitement is still just a story about two people, Spock and Kirk, and how they dramatically affect the course of one another's lives, and how in the process they affect the fate of the world. Yes, in many respects this series is the ultimate "buddy story," which differs little from one of our earliest known tales of friendship and loss, the *Epic of Gilgamesh*.

Gilgamesh was a Sumerian king who reigned sometime around 2500 BCE, in the area we now know as southern Iraq. Like many kings at the time Gilgamesh was believed to be a demigod, the offspring of a human and a god. These larger-than-life figures often inspired larger-than-life stories, tales that grew with time. The *Epic of Gilgamesh* was one of those stories. The main plot of the story centers around the question of immortality, but it all begins when the gods create Enkidu, a brutish man sent to be Gilgamesh's companion. Gilgamesh had been oppressing his people and the gods thought Enkidu might distract Gilgamesh from such bad behavior. At first the plan was successful. Gilgamesh and Enkidu engage in all kinds of manly pursuits, like the killing the monster Humbaba in the Cedar Mountains. However, the two go too far when they kill the prized Bull of Heaven. This angers the goddess Ishtar, so much so that she demands the death of Enkidu. She gets her wish and Enkidu's death sends Gilgamesh into a great funk. It also sets him on a quest for immortality. What is the point of life, asks Gilgamesh, if it can be taken away so quickly, and one can be so easily forgotten?

Gilgamesh first seeks the immortal flood hero Utnapishtim (possibly an early version of the biblical Noah). He hopes to learn how he can achieve immortality. However, Utnapishtim has only bad news for Gilgamesh: the gods have reserved immortality for themselves. Utnapishtim is ready to send Gilgamesh on his way empty-handed until his wife encourages him to give our hero a fighting chance to obtain his prize. So, Utnapishtim tells Gilgamesh of a plant that grows at the bottom of a sea, the same sea that Gilgamesh had crossed in search of the flood hero. Gilgamesh is told that the plant is similar to a boxthorn plant, and if he retrieves and eats it he will become immortal. In high hopes Gilgamesh travels to the middle of the sea and attaches stones to his feet. He dives deep and finds the plant. Returning to the boat he continues to make for home, planning to first try the plant on someone much older than himself. However, he stops to bathe and a serpent steals the plant. It is at this point that our hero weeps for all his lost labor and finally accepts that immortality is only for the gods.

At the end of the epic the god Enlil reveals the moral of Gilgamesh's story. He says it is meant to illustrate the futility that men encounter when seeking physical immortality. If a man wishes to live beyond his natural life, says Enlil, then let it be through his deeds or great works of architecture. That we still talk about Gilgamesh seems to prove Enlil's counsel, made still truer by pyramids, the historical renown of great generals, and that we still honor the memory of great minds long extinguished. The story of Gilgamesh intersects with the story of modern technology in that technology has now become the chief means by which mankind hopes to eliminate his physical limitations.[3] However, the paradox is that technology has also within it the seeds of human destruction. Will we someday weep as Gilgamesh did?

Later we will talk about Mary Shelley's *Frankenstein*. This story is an example of overweening scientific enthusiasm in the pursuit of eternal life, a tale which leads to personal destruction. What happens, though, when the monster that escapes from a lab does not limit itself to killing a few? What happens when that monster has no mind of its own and kills indiscriminately and without conscious intent?

In the summer of 1991 a friend and I decided to take several weeks and travel the United States. We were going to drive from Toledo, Ohio, to Los Angeles, California. We rented a Pontiac Grand Am and set off on our adventure. One of our chief goals was to drive as much as possible along old Route 66, which we would connect with in St. Louis. On that trip I decided to read Stephen King's *The Stand*, which had just been re-released in 1990. It had originally been published in 1978. We spent nearly two weeks on the road and I completed the book as we traveled back to Toledo from LA via Las Vegas, an interesting coincidence since a fair amount of the novel took place in Las Vegas.

If you are unfamiliar with the book it starts with the escape of a deadly virus from an Army base in the Southwest. Soon the virus is spreading, creating a pandemic that ends up killing nearly all human beings and domesticated animals. Two competing survivor societies are then established, one in Boulder, Colorado, and another in Las Vegas, Nevada. The former is led by a centenarian visionary named "Mother Abigail" Freemantle who sees a great evil rising in the west. The rising evil in the west is led by Randall Flagg, a malevolent fellow with no apparent past and what appear to be occult powers. Flagg's power becomes apparent when he somehow survives the detonation of a nuclear weapon in Las Vegas and finds himself in another part of the world.

I mention Stephen King's work because it serves as an example of how the dystopian nightmare is effectively disseminated through literature. As for those who could not get through all 1100 pages of the novel, ABC produced an 8-hour miniseries in 1994. The movie captured most of the book's horror, and continued the twentieth-century tradition of presenting mankind with various scenarios in which the secular apocalypse might occur. For example, King has said that he was influenced by George R. Stewart's *Earth Abides* (1949), another novel in which nearly all of mankind is destroyed by some type of biological contagion. Aldous Huxley contributed to this genre in 1948 with his *Ape and Essence*, a dark vision of post-nuclear war society where infanticide is regularly practiced, Satan is an object of worship, and reproduction is limited to a two-week annual period that starts on Belial's Day Eve (Belial = Devil).

Again, in all of these novels we are asked to deal with the contradictory benefits of science and technology. In *The Stand* the earthy, egalitarian, and democratic community of Boulder is set against the technically-proficient and despotic government of Las Vegas. The implied message here is that technology somehow corrupts the soul. That same vivid message permeates Aldous Huxley's *Ape and Essence*, and we find it in more subtle form in his earlier dystopian novel *Brave New World* (1932). Walter Miller's *A Canticle for Leibowitz* (1959) takes us far into the future but deals with the same theme: mankind cannot be trusted with technology and will always end up destroying himself with it.

Physicist Brian Clegg addresses this issue in his book *Armageddon Science: The Science of Mass Destruction* (2010). The title is a little misleading since Clegg argues *for* science, not against it. His point is that we should be *cautiously optimistic* when it comes to science. Fears about black holes created by the Large Hadron Collider or the connection between inoculations and autism are overwrought. Yes, there are risks in science and technology, but there are also gains, and we have to measure one against the other as we do in many areas of life. Clegg is addressing a perennial question associated with science and technology, just as the Greeks did with their story of Icarus. However, another problem with science and technology is raised by Lewis Mumford and Neil Postman. These authors were concerned that mankind could be easily consumed by technology, even if it did not destroy them. We lose, they argue, something fundamentally human when we allow technology to take the lead rather than directing it to our own ends.

Lewis Mumford began writing about this possibility as early as 1934 in his book *Technics and Civilization*. Mumford splits technical history into three phases: *eotechnic*, *paleotechnic*, and *neotechnic*. The first is introduced by the clock, which revolutionized our view of time.[4] The second phase is dominated by what we generally term the "industrial revolution," a time when brute force was used to lay the foundation for the mass-consumption culture of the early twentieth century. The final phase was inaugurated when electricity and information became major commodities. This inaugurated the age of the scientist as opposed to the age of the technician. This was a dramatic swing in intellectual emphasis when viewed from a sociocultural perspective. Mumford's concern was that science and technology were getting ahead of us, that we were forgetting who was supposed to serve whom. He made this very clear in a later two-volume work, both of which were subtitled *The Myth of the Machine* (1967 and 1970). The latter volume was entitled *Pentagon of Power* and dealt with how western culture had fused scientific, technological, and political power into what Mumford called a *mega-machine*.

Mumford warned that we were in danger of being overcome by this machine.

Two decades later the cultural critic Neil Postman issued the same warning in his book *Technopoly: The Surrender of Culture to Technology* (1992). The problem, in Postman's view, was that technology had become deified, and the sociocultural effect was that technological progress was pursued for the sake of technological progress. The problem with this is that it encourages the "rapid dissolution of much that is associated with traditional beliefs."[5] The obsession with always adopting the latest technology creates an almost priestly class of technicians controlled by political and economic elites, who convince us that we cannot live without their expertise and ever-new products.[6] Postman was not anti-science or anti-technology. He was a Luddite in the original meaning of the word. He believed technology should benefit men rather than rob them of their ability to make a living or to achieve purpose in life.

For Postman "scientism"—the general belief that everything can be quantified—does not allow us to understand science's limitations. Science must by necessity limit itself when it comes to areas it cannot quantify.[7] Postman believed that this was the chief reason science and technology could not provide mankind with existential meaning, and that it was good to maintain a distinction between biological beings and their mechanical counterparts. Only by maintaining the tension that exists between the biological and mechanical worlds would we be able to judge the true benefits of technology.[8] Postman's whole argument is summarized in a single powerful paragraph:

> Into this void comes the Technopoly story, with its emphasis on progress without limits, rights without responsibilities, and technology without cost. The Technopoly story is without a moral center. It promises heaven on earth through the conveniences of technological progress. It casts aside all traditional narratives and symbols that suggest stability and orderliness, and tells, instead, of a life of skills, technical expertise, and the ecstasy of consumption. Its purpose is to produce functionaries for an ongoing Technopoly. It answers Bloom by saying that the story of Western civilization

is irrelevant; it answers the political left by saying there is indeed a common culture whose name is Technopoly and whose key symbol is now the computer, toward which there must be neither irreverence nor blasphemy. It even answers Hirsch by saying that there are items on his list that, if thought about too deeply and taken too seriously, will interfere with the progress of technology.[9]

Again, Postman did not stand against science but rather argued for more balance. Echoing Goethe's comment about art and science Postman writes, "…we must join art and science. But we must also join the past and the present, for the ascent of humanity is above all a continuous story."[10] To abandon that continuum of history is to expose ourselves to a great danger, the danger of creating a society where nothing is connected to anything else and where we are encouraged everyday to simply "amuse ourselves to death."[11] This is a powerful critique of a society where "friending" and constant cell phone use replaces, rather than augments, human interaction. It is an argument against shortened, disconnected episodes of digital interaction, and an encouragement to engage in longer, more fluid interactions, the type that prove in the long-run richer and more satisfying.

Here are a few titles that have recently boosted—possibly out of all proportion—the role that science and technology will play in the near future. The first two were written by the well-known physicist Michio Kaku. *Physics of the Future: How Science Will Shape Human Destiny and Our Daily Lives by the Year 2100* (2011) is really just an updated version of Kaku's earlier book *Visions: How Science Will Revolutionize the 21st Century* (1997). Both tout the future potential benefits of genetics, information technology, and material science. That these things might happen is not the objection of critics of "technology for technology's sake." The real criticism is in the idea that we should abandon ourselves to complete faith in scientists, some of whom claim they can conquer many of our most intransigent problems. Some of these folks argue that new sources of energy, the ability to create heretofore unknown industrial materials, data-mining, etc., will all contribute to the establishment of a scientifically-based utopia in the not so distant future. However, one has to ask only two simple questions, "What happens if we establish such a world but many cannot participate in its bounty?" and "Doesn't the stigma of being an *unproductive member of society* mitigate against a system that makes it impossible for a large minority of the population to participate in the productive economy?" It would seem that the scientific *vision* of Michio Kaku would have to be accompanied by a different way of structuring society.

Another title that once promised more short-term gains from technology is Bob Davis and David Wessel's *Prosperity: The Coming Twenty-Year Boom and What It Means to You* (1998). This book would appeal to anyone who has an unquestioning faith in technology because it argues that digital systems are becoming so simple that they will revolutionize the workplace by creating so much productivity that everyone will begin to share in the benefits. Of course, this Pollyanna-like faith in technology ignores three historical facts: 1) most of the profits from productivity go to income earners at the top while middle class wages remain stagnant or declining, 2) these smarter systems are masking the larger cognitive problem of not training citizens and workers to think for themselves, and 3) most of the jobs lost to technology exceed the number of jobs created as a result of this *creative destruction*—there is always a net loss of jobs. For some reason I am reminded of the horrific and symbiotic relationship between the Eloi and Morlocks in H. G. Wells's *The Time Machine* (1895).

This is just a sampling of the boosterish spirit of popular science literature. There are whole industries built around the assumption that technology is an unmitigated boon for business and society. That this assumption goes largely unquestioned in the scientific community is proof that Mumford, Postman, and others are right. We have given our society over to the notion that technological development is in and of itself always a good thing. It is this unquestioning faith in technological progress that creates an environment in which people outside the scientific or creative community begin to imagine all sorts of dire consequences should things go wrong. This is particularly true among those who perceive themselves as the victims of technological progress, or what some euphemistically call "creative destruction."

The only acceptable voices of dissent have become those found in literature and film, and they tend to create a vicious feedback loop in which people begin to not only imagine but accept the inevitable demise of humanity, usually at the hand of science and technology but also sometimes as a result of natural disaster. Films like the recent—poorly written and directed—*Book of Eli* (2010) tell us not to bother. The future is not about thriving; it is about surviving. Max Brooks's novel *World War Z: An Oral History of the Zombie War* (2006) is set to be released as a film in 2013, and continues the film tradition of George A. Romero's *Night of the Living Dead* (1968). Of course, re-animating the dead is not the only way science can bring about the apocalypse. Richard Matheson's *I Am Legend* (1954) may have inspired Romero, but it was not necessarily about zombies-proper. In this book, and the many movie-adaptations that followed, humanity is turned into a sentient, vampire-like race. The recent movie *Daybreakers* (2009) turns the whole vampire genre on its head by proposing a future in which society is controlled by vampires and humans are kept around merely to serve as a food supply.

It would be redundant to continue listing the books and films that have been written in these genres. If you are even a casual reader and movie viewer you will know how prevalent these types of books and films have become and the point will be made: *literature and film are the two chief ways in which "technopoly" and the "mega-machine" are criticized*. Yet, when we leave the theater the first thing we do is turn on our cell phones. If we have a digital phone we might immediately check our Facebook accounts. After all, our fellow zombies need to know exactly where we are every minute of the day.

***

The whole point of the next few chapters will be to show that modern dystopianism is a legacy of religious apocalyptic belief, passed down from generation to generation in many different forms. It is nearly impossible to see how modern secular dystopianism could have developed without the influence of Christianity on western society. There was no apparent dystopian distemper among the Greeks or Romans, and it was only the influence of Zoroastrianism via the Jewish sect of Christianity that made religious utopian thinking possible. Yes, Plato conceived of a utopian society founded on reason. Yes, the Romans, as exemplified in the work of Virgil, believed that the Roman Republic played a special role in human history. However, there was to be no struggle between the forces of light and darkness. Instead, Rome would rule the world because it was the will of the gods and because Roman law was the most perfect legal system ever devised, not by the gods but by men who rested their political faith on republicanism.

As we will see in the next few chapters, it was only with the legalization of Christianity in the early fourth century that apocalypticism made inroads into western thought. Christianity was soon made the official religion of the Empire and for centuries dominated the political, social, and intellectual landscape of Europe. The weakening of the Church through its many battles with the states of Europe enabled secularism and the Scientific Revolution to set western society on a whole new trajectory. However, faith in the coming kingdom of God was not easy to set aside with the doctrine of the Church. Men began to imagine that through reason and science they could achieve what had been previously thought possible only through divine intervention.

The last century has challenged man's faith in reason and science, and it is the argument of this book that *the culture of fear*, which we detailed in the last two sections of this book, is a direct result of that loss of faith. It is also one of the reasons we have seen breakdowns in other areas of human endeavor. We have lost faith not only in reason and science but in democracy. Losing our faith in the power of reason and science has forced us to turn to other ways of asserting power over our lives. Since the 1960s we have turned to identity politics, which isolates group after group from one another, making it nearly impossible to address the fundamental disparities in the distribution of economic income and social justice. We sacrifice community-centered competence for the credentialed professional's advice, which is often legislated into power. In desperation we turn to the unexamined benefits of technology without any knowledge of the science behind it, or any appreciation for its sociocultural effects. As will become clear in the last section of this book, *this is not good*. For, it merely allows the elites in society to remain in power while keeping us in a perpetual state of social, political, and economic paralysis and infantilism.

Utopian thought is a prerequisite for the dystopian mind. Dystopianism requires utopianism just as death requires birth, and just as renewal requires rebirth. What golden age could be discerned in a world that has never changed? How could we look forward to a better world if we first did not view the present as somehow lacking? That is the central theme of all utopian thought: that we do not now measure up but we will *someday*.

Conversely, the central theme of dystopianism is that we have come so far that is only inevitable we will eventually visit destruction on ourselves. For some this might be a permanent condition visited on us. It might even lead to extinction for the human race. For others, it is just the prelude to an even more glorious future that requires the burnishing fire of technological self-immolation.

I believe the true road to human success lies somewhere in between these extremes and by the end of this book I hope you agree.

Chapter Nine

In The Beginning: The Origins of Cosmos

To the dumb question "Why me?" the cosmos barely bothers to return a reply: why not?

Christopher Hitchens

In this first chapter we will focus on origin stories and how they serve as the foundation for the development of apocalyptic thought. There are some very basic and universal questions that we humans ask as we grow more and more conscious of ourselves and the world around us. *Who am I? Where did I come from? Where am I going?* These are perennial questions that seem somehow hard wired into the human brain. Each one of us eventually asks these questions, but in time most of us grow inured to them, especially when they take the shape of insoluble cosmological mysteries like *if God created the universe what created him?* Why try to solve such academic questions when "real life" presses in hard on each of us as we grow older? Aren't these questions for children, philosophers, and theologians?

Emotional and mental maturity eventually brings about a practical abandonment of these "silly" cosmological queries. Yet, even the inured cannot completely escape the emotional and existential angst these cosmological questions engender deep within the soul. That is why we turn to more parochial concerns to establish *identity*, *place*, and a *moral universe* within which we can safely operate. However, even these parochial pursuits seem impossible to many, and they are constantly under assault if they are ever achieved. Proof of this can be found on any modern metropolitan street. Go ahead, look for the afraid and existentially unmoored; they are not hard to find. They are usually the frenetic ones, those afraid of slowing down and self-reflecting. They are those terrified of what they might discover if they engaged in just one moment of introspection. What they may fear even more is finding nothing at all, because they seem to know intuitively that such moments of deep reflection might only provoke an encounter with the existential abyss that always stands ready to swallow them whole.

What is all this? What is all this talk of *fear, self-reflection, existential abysses*, and *being swallowed whole*? To the ear of a modern person it sounds like a bunch of hooey because modern people have lost touch with age old ideas about cosmos and chaos. We are products of the modern intellectual conviction that order (*cosmos*) is the norm while chaos is an external force that must be introduced into our universal system of natural order. This has not always been the case and the main topic of this book, *the culture of fear*, reveals that deep down we do not always believe in that universal and natural cosmic order. Like the ancient Egyptians, Mesopotamians, and Vedic Indians, we believe in our heart of hearts that the battle between cosmos and chaos is a continuous one, and we are never quite sure who is going to win in the end.

Saying that these cosmological questions relate to our personal and everyday experience might seem like a stretch, but that is only because we do not look deeper into our own experiences, into the roots of our desire for identity, place, and a moral universe. We want to know who and what we are, we want to know our place in the scheme of it all, and we want to assure ourselves that there are rules by which we can conduct ourselves in what appears to be a contingent universe. That is why, when the great cosmological questions prove themselves impossible to answer, or only lead to absurdity, we turn to the more parochial task of "tracing our roots" in order to find some solid ground on which to build our lives. The popularity of genealogy research during the last several decades bears witness to this need for reference, as do recent television shows like *Who Do You Think You Are?* and *Faces of America with Henry*

Louis Gates Jr. In addition, there are Websites like *Ancestry.Com* that help everyday people trace their family trees, an activity once confined to royalty, and other succession-obsessed nobility, but now the means by which the common man attempts to connect with his past and own identity.

Most of us eventually make a full transition from pure cosmological worry to the practical concerns of everyday life. Most will make this transition early in life, but this will depend on the individual's temperament and native social ability. Some will make only a partial transition, and some will not transition at all. Those who do not make the transition will have a difficult time operating in society. They will be convinced that social structures are irrelevant, and that their participation is pointless. They will tend to place themselves, and others, in a cosmological struggle between the forces of good and evil because they see a world made up of only two people: *us* and *them*. This dichotomy is not always seen by the cosmologically-oriented as a spiritual battle but it most often takes that form. Again, most people transition away from these cosmological worries, but the underlying concerns are still there, even as they morph into concerns about pair-bonding, child-rearing, genealogy, etc. How many do you know with spouses, children, and jobs who are also concerned on a daily basis about questions of cosmology? There is simply no time to worry about such things, yet the emotional and psychological need for these cosmological answers does not disappear. The need is merely redirected into more parochial concerns.

This is largely a practical matter since the societies in which we operate have established all sorts of rules and conventions by which people are judged. These social conventions and rules are often rooted in our view of the immediate past. In a modern society family, wealth, status, choices made about education, and social pursuits, largely determine how we view ourselves and how others perceive us. Yes, we are largely the product of genetics and the environment, but mankind has worked hard the last 50,000 years to reduce the influence of *unkempt nature*. The chief creation of men is civilization, from which all other intellectual, technical, and social advancements have proceeded over the last ten thousand years. By the term *civilization* we mean the development of cities and all the benefits that accrue to those who take part in the urban experience. For millennia the city was seen as a kind of "world navel," the place from which all life and order sprang. This is why Jerusalem and other cities are still held in such esteem by the ancient religions of Judaism, Christianity, and Islam. In the ancient world cities held a particularly important place because they were not just centers of commerce like they are today. Cities were bastions of *cosmos* (order), established to keep *chaos* at bay. They were all home to one chief god or another who, it was said, had a hand in establishing the ordered world, a world set apart from primal and universal chaos. This is why the city temple or church—not so long ago—was a representation of heavenly order and would have dominated each city. Today city halls, courts of justice, and stadiums have that high honor.

The role the city played in ancient life was intimately connected to creation myth. These violent and fascinating stories of warring gods who created earth, heaven, and mankind were told at festivals and celebrated with all manner of rituals, and these rituals were not empty ceremonies. These rituals were very important to the inhabitants of these ancient cities. The peoples' faithfulness to the gods protected the city from the ire of the gods themselves. It also strengthened their gods as protectors against other competing cities and gods. This is an important point. It is a point that should be kept in mind as we talk about the early relationship between the Christian church and the state. For, when Christians are sporadically persecuted during the first few centuries of the current era it is because many Romans saw the Christians as treasonous. Christians refused to give respect to the Roman pantheon and it was thought that this imperiled the empire. This is an argument that many Romans made against the Christians and it was one of the chief reasons Augustine wrote his book *The City of God* (c. 410 CE), to put forth a counter-argument against those who were blaming Christians for the sack of Rome that year. In a later chapter we will reexamine this idea because many American Christians believe that the abandonment of traditional faith and morality has imperiled their nation's future.

Joseph Campbell writes that "ancient cities" were "built like temples, having their portals to the four directions, while in the central place" stood "the major shrine of the divine city founder." We still have examples of this today in the form of St. Peter's in Rome, the Kaaba in Mecca, and the ruins of the Hebrew temple at Jerusalem. However, in the modern world the "holy place" has been replaced, in many minds, by a far more pantheistic view of God's presence. In other words, now "the World Navel" has become "ubiquitous."[1] So, it can no longer be encompassed by a geographical space.

***

Creation myths tell us a lot about the societies in which they developed, and in the following pages we will learn that they can still teach us about ourselves in many ways, because creation myths are ultimately about establishing three primary psychological objectives: *identity*, *place*, and a *moral universe*. The curse of modern society—in the minds of many—is that these three fundamental psychological needs can now be anything we want them to be. People are often told, "You can be anything you want to be!"—as if by sheer intellectual fiat and force of will we can change ourselves and the world around us. It is not surprising that most of us in modern society have adopted this view. It is an empowering view, made largely possible by the promise of modern science and technology.[2] However, some of us often find ourselves simply not up to the task of modern life, which is why we turn to traditional religious faith.

All traditional faith, though, proves inadequate in the modern world. Those who adhere to traditional faith spend most of their time trying to restrain the modern world, to place the city back into its ancient role of "world navel." Those possessing traditional faith tend to see the modern metropolis, modern capitalism, and modern science as evils that have been unleashed upon the world. These modern developments are more often associated with chaos than order, and traditional faith argues that we should fear them and bind them with the coils of traditional moral restrictions.[3]

The believer's view is that traditional creation myth is under assault. If it is not science telling us we are cousins to the apes, and a biological accident in the grand scheme of things, then it is philosophers and satirists trying to "take the piss out of us." A good example of this is a skit in Monty Python's *The Meaning of Life* (1983). Two men arrive at a man's door and proceed to take his liver out because he has agreed to donate it. He protests, because as he says, "I'm using it!" This does not stop them, though, and one of the men ends up in the kitchen trying to convince the man's wife to give up her liver as well. To convince her to donate her liver Eric Idle performs a musical number which in part goes like this:

> The universe itself keeps on expanding and expanding
> In all of the directions it can whizz
> As fast as it can go, at the speed of light, you know,
> Twelve million miles a minute, and that's the fastest speed there is.
> So remember, when you're feeling very small and insecure,
> How amazingly unlikely is your birth,
> And pray that there's intelligent life somewhere up in space,
> 'Cause there's bugger all down here on Earth.

This gives you a good idea about the theme of the movie; however, the opening song, also sung by Eric Idle, packs even more punch as it ponders whether we are merely "spiraling coils of self-replicating DNA." This idea of contingent existence, which got its real start with Darwinism in the mid-nineteenth century, is what truly scares people. There is something disconcerting about the idea that we merely evolved from single-celled organisms beginning several billion years ago. The reason this is so upsetting for the human psyche is that it seems to leave very little room for the idea that mankind is special and therefore entitled to some higher moral consideration. We will return often to the theme of morality since I believe it is an integral part of explaining why *the culture of fear* exists.

As for the traditional religionists and their protestations, the reality is that the "war" on traditional creation myth is largely manufactured by those who do not understand why creation myths exist in the first place. These religious enthusiasts have overcompensated for the last century and a half against the nineteenth century's "higher criticism" of the Bible. The traditional religionist believes that faith cannot exist when one does not swallow whole all of scripture. There may be some truth to this, but the reason is far more complicated, and often rooted in past controversies between religion and science.[4] We now know that the idea of an earth-centered universe is dishearteningly wrong, and that truth leaves little room for stroking the human ego. Darwinism also deflates the human ego in that it shows us to be just another biological adaptation to the environment. So, the real problem with the traditional religionist's view is that we cannot go backward. We are propelled forward by science, and traditional ideas are put in jeopardy by this movement forward.

Still, we cannot get away from the question of our origins, no matter what form it takes. The question plagues us like death because our origins help us to lay claim to *identity*, *place*, and a *moral universe*. Whether through biology or social indoctrination we are all generally convinced of the *right of first possession*. If this were not true no Native American could lay claim to anything on the North American continent. So, we are constantly tracing a way back to the past, attempting to establish our claim in the here and now, or trying to delegitimize the claims of others. One of the many examples of this is the lengths to which royalty and no- bility used to go in order to trace their origins back to some great king— the idea being that if one were descended from a great king then that greatness would also flow in one's own veins.[5] The famous Hapsburg dynasty attempted to trace their lineage all the way back to King David and Aeneas. The latter had escaped his own fire-ravaged city of Troy to found the "eternal city" of Rome.[6] The same Hapsburgs wanted to connect the ancient past to the reconstituted Roman Empire, which had been established on Christmas Day, 800 CE. Establishing this direct line would have given the Hapsburgs political legitimacy and the power to rule over the empire by *divine right*. In the race to co-opt ancient heroes even Jason the Argonaut did not escape. Jason's legend was used as a model for Philip of Burgundy's Order of the Golden Fleece, established in 1429 CE. The members of this organization were knights, crusaders committed to retaking the Holy Land, which in this case might be seen metaphorically as the Golden Fleece itself.[7]

All of this illustrates how important we believe the past to be when establishing present claims of legitimacy. Our origins are important to us, and for a variety of reasons. Although we may not believe any longer in *divine-right succession*, we still cannot rid ourselves of the general conviction that older is better, that it is somehow purer and truer. There is an Old Testament injunction that says, "Remove not the ancient landmark, which thy fathers have set." (Proverbs 22:28) In this sentiment is evinced the human desire for a permanent connection with the past. This is why when we talk about human origins we look to the ancient past to see what has been said about our origins. We are mesmerized by tales of *golden ages*, idyllic times to which we wish we could return.

The astrophysicist can now look further back into the past than any of our ancient ancestors could ever have imagined. We can now envision the birth of chaos itself in our mathematical models and test those models in huge particle accelerators. However, the ability to peer back nearly 14 billion years ago, to the birth of the universe itself, brings no satisfaction to the soul. We are still left with an ethical and existential angst that science cannot alleviate. So, we look to creation myths and their dramas. There we find not only purpose but moral understanding. Life itself has meaning in the context of a myth in which we play a central role. However, these myths and dramas are challenged each day by the clear evidence of science, which argues that the universe is a contingent place in which biological existence is possible only because of the sheer vastness of the universe.

Against this what is a creation myth to do? Well, it could simply serve its original function, which is to be a moral tale of how order is needed to battle chaos for the good of mankind. Creation myths are man's first attempts to explain his origins but that is not their primary function. Creation myths exist to help mankind understand his *place* within the cosmos, a very different thing than merely explaining *how* things happened. This is where people get tripped up. Creation myths are not attempts to explain what actually happened but to explain why the *moral universe* exists, and why that moral universe is constantly pitted against the primal forces of chaos. These stories also explain mankind's role (*identity*) in helping to maintain the cosmos through good relations with the gods.

However, in the modern age it is difficult to see much benefit in these stories. Cosmic battles between the gods of order and chaos seem meaningless to the scientifically-oriented mind. This is because most of us tend to view the universe as highly organized and chaos as something that is fundamentally difficult to introduce into an ordered system. Most ancient accounts of creation involve some kind of violent battle which sets the gods of *cosmos* against the gods of *chaos*. The ensuing battle ends with the victory of those who protect cosmos, and who often use the bodies of the defeated to form heaven and earth, or living creatures. So, cosmos is formed from the very material that once existed as primal and universal chaos, and this chaos continues to exist outside of the divinely established order. Cosmos and chaos stand eternally opposed to one another, ever jockeying for position. Yet, chaos is older, the source material for all order.

This ancient view of creation myth is not known to most modern religious people, especially in the United States. The truth is that American Christians do not even have a firm grasp of their own creation myth. Most do not know there are actually two short accounts of creation at the beginning of Genesis. They also cannot begin to explain why there are two accounts, or why they are at odds. For example, the first account, in chapter one, says that God created plant life on the third day while man was created on the sixth day; however, in the second chapter of Genesis (2:5) it says that no plants had yet sprung up before the creation of man. God creates man and then creates the Garden of Eden. Yes, this is a small point to most of us, but should not an inerrant book at least be consistent?

If American Christians do read these short chapters in Genesis, they read them as history, not myth, which is why they persist in remaining ignorant of modern astrophysics, geology, and evolution. Additional confusion is introduced by these folks into the United States educational system because biblical literalists have engaged in an anti-evolution campaign for the last several decades, muddying the intellectual waters with so-called "creation science" and now "intelligent design"—two strains of thought that differ very little in substance. If modern American Christians simply stopped trying to read the first two chapters of Genesis as a literal account of how the universe and the earth were formed, it would solve a lot of problems, including their own issue with modern-day moral relativism. What the evangelical zealot does not realize is that by placing the account in Genesis on par with scientific theories he forces this creation myth into being a scientific theory. This creates two problems for the evangelical literalist. The first problem is that a literalist must now defend the myth of creation using the tools of the scientific method, which just cannot be done. Anyone with a nodding acquaintance of modern evolutionary evidence and theory understands this. The second problem is that literalism reduces myth to mere facts, so they cease to be a means by which we can learn about the human condition—which is the purpose of all good literature.

Let us spend a few pages exploring the idea that a creation myth's primary goal is to instruct us about the *moral universe*, not the physical universe. We will do this by comparing three ancient myths: the Hebrew account in Genesis, the Babylonian version called the *Enuma Elish*, and the Greek account found in Hesiod's *Theogony*. We begin with Genesis because it is probably the most familiar to Americans.

In the Genesis account, which we find in the first two chapters of the book, creation is a far more peaceful act than we find in the Babylonian or Greek accounts. There are no great battles. God merely speaks and it is done. The book begins with a simple statement, "In the beginning God created the heaven and the earth." It continues,

> ²And the earth was without form, and void; and darkness was upon the face of the deep. And the Spirit of God moved upon the face of the waters. ³And God said, Let there be light: and there was light. ⁴And God saw the light, that it was good: and God divided the light from the darkness. ⁵And God called the light Day, and the darkness he called Night. And the evening and the morning were the first day.

The closest we get to a mention of chaos here is when verse two says that "the earth was without form, and void." The first two chapters of Genesis tell different creation stories but they are both equally peaceful accounts of a god unhurried and unharassed in his creative work. This tells us a lot about the God who inhabited the mind of the writer.

It is now believed by biblical scholars that the account we read in Genesis, along with the other four books of the Pentateuch, was written by more than one author—not Moses. The latest additions to these creation stories were added just before it was made part of the canon of accepted Hebrew scripture, probably around the middle of the fifth century BCE. By this time the idea of a universal creator without limits to his power would have been commonly accepted by the Hebrews who lived throughout the post-exilic Middle East. It is believed that prior to the Babylonian captivity, which occurred between 587 and 538 BCE, the Hebrews did not worship just one god. They may have viewed Yahweh, though, as a chief god and deserving of more honor than the other gods. So, the Hebrews may have been well within the traditional polytheistic tradition prior to being taken into captivity and exposed to the idea of monotheism. Later this lack of faithfulness to one god, Yahweh, would become one of the chief explanations the Hebrew prophets would give for why the Hebrews were sent into exile in the first place. As it says in Second Kings 24:20: "It was because of the LORD's anger that all this happened to Jerusalem and Judah, and in the end he thrust them from his presence."

Historians believe that the Hebrew exiles were exposed to the monotheistic tradition in Babylon when they encountered Zoroastrianism. From this Persian tradition the Hebrews adopted their own strong monotheism, which they displayed upon returning to Jerusalem and while rebuilding the temple in the sixth and fifth centuries BCE. Much of this story is related in the books of *Ezra* and *Nehemiah*, written decades after the events, sometime around the end of the fifth century and beginning of the fourth century BCE. Some of these post-exilic Hebrews also carried back to Palestine the apocalyptic (prophetic) ideas of Zoroastrianism. However, these ideas would play no large role in Hebrew identity until they were passed on to Christianity, which must be seen in its early history as a small sect of Judaism. While rebuilding the temple some priests claimed they had found ancient documents detailing the early Mosaic traditions of the Hebrew people, and it was these restored traditions of the sixth and fifth centuries that served as the foundation for modern Judaism.[8]

The Hebrew creation myth was not by any means the oldest. The Babylonian creation myth, found in a book called the *Enuma Elish*, dates from around 2000 BCE. It tells a fantastic story of power, intrigue, patricide, matricide, and the making of a great king over the gods. The main character is Marduk who is forced to take up arms against Tiamat, the mother of the gods. What brings this whole incident to a head is the plan of Tiamat's husband, Apsu, to kill all his children because they are making too much noise. The story of Noah found in Genesis 6 bears too many similarities here to be a coincidence, so this was clearly a common theme in Middle Eastern religious myth. The only difference was the motivation for the slaughter. In Genesis it was because of the "wickedness" of mankind while in the Babylonian account it was because "they troubled the mood of Tiamat by their hilarity in the Abode of Heaven." The latter seems capricious by comparison to the Genesis account, but they are likely separated by 1500 years so it is not hard to imagine how man's view of the gods could have changed over this time.

Of course, where the God of Genesis succeeds in his plan Apsu is not so lucky. Apsu is slain by another god named Ea-Nuddimud. In what smacks of a Shakespearean tragedy Tiamat then takes as her husband Kingu, of whom the younger gods roundly disapprove. This creates a whole new source of conflict that eventually leads to Tiamat trying to do to her children what she had discouraged Apsu from doing: killing them. This sets the stage for one of the greatest Mesopotamian heroes, Marduk. This war god agrees to go against Tiamat if all the other gods will bow down to him. In doing this there is the implication that they are focusing in him all their collective power, which will be needed to subdue the great Tiamat.

With all manner of godly aids, such as the "gift of Anu," Imhullu (the whirlwind), the four horses that pull his chariot (Killer, Pitiless, Trampler, and Haste), and another aide-de-camp simply known as "the Batterer," Marduk goes out to meet Tiamat on the field of battle. Tiamat is enraged that the gods would even consider coming up against her. Who are they to question her ancient authority, or her choice of royal consort? After some choice repartee Tiamat is quickly dispatched by Marduk, who manhandles all of Tiamat's allies and makes Kingu "the usurper" a god of the dead—not a choice position. He then looks upon Tiamat's corpse, pondering what to do with it. He decides to cut her in half and use the pieces to create his own *cosmos*. With one half of her body he fashions the "arc of the sky" and with the other half he places a boundary between *cosmos* and the domain of Apsu, understood here to be primal chaos.[9] It is only in the fifth tablet of the *Enuma Elish* that mankind is created using the blood of Kingu, which is apropos since in Mesopotamian myth men were to serve as slaves to the gods. We will continue this story in the next chapter, but for now let us move on to Hesiod's *Theogony*, which is in many respects similar to the Babylonian account.

Hesiod's *Theogony* is thought to have been written in the eighth century BCE. It is decidedly less cryptic than the other tales, as when in line 116 it says, "Verily at the first Chaos came to be, but next wide-bosomed Earth, the ever-sure foundations of all the deathless ones who hold the peaks of snowy Olympus…." From this point on there is a litany of gods birthed by Chaos and Earth, both capitalized because they are not just things but personalities. Earth is said to give birth to Heaven with whom she later couples to bring forth Oceanus, Coeus, Crius, Hyperion, and Iapetus. Last, but definitely not least, Earth gives birth to Cronos, who early on shows an *oedipal* hatred for his father. As in the tale told by the Babylonians, the ogre-father, Heaven, begins to mistreat some of his children, so Cronos volunteers to punish his "sinful father." Cronos waits until Heaven comes to lay with Earth and then springs upon his father, decapitating him using a "great long sickle with jagged teeth." His father's blood falls to Earth, bringing forth giants, nymphs, and other assorted divine creatures. Heaven's severed body parts are cast into the sea, and one part forms into the goddess Aphrodite, who is honored by all the gods for her beauty.

The intrigue does not stop there, though, because Cronos becomes, like his father, an ogre. He takes Rhea as his wife and bears many gods, including "wise Zeus." However, Cronos is haunted by a prophecy that he will eventually be overthrown by one of his children, so he begins to eat them whole. Zeus escapes, hidden by his mother Rhea and with the help of Earth. This ruse is accomplished by having Cronos swallow a large rock that he is told is his latest born. After many years Zeus grows strong enough to face his father and forces him to vomit up his brothers and sisters who are so grateful they make him the king of all the gods and of man.

Take a step back. Do not attempt to place all these stories parallel to one another. Yes, they all tell the same general story but they tell them differently. The themes are cosmos, order, conflict, power, retribution, reward for service, justice, etc. Again, these creation myths are meant to instill within us a certain moral sense, and they are surprisingly illuminating when it comes to the subject of intergenerational conflict. Did Marduk really cut his grandmother in half? Did Cronos really cut his father's head off and segment his body? Did God really drown all mankind because of its wickedness? To ask these questions means one has not gotten the point of these stories. These stories are not meant as real histories. They are a means by which we can examine ourselves within the context of a moral order established by the gods.[10]

In the following chapter we will continue to build on the foundation laid in this chapter. We will explore how ancient creation myths are integral to understanding the subsequent cosmologies of combat myths and apocalypticism. What has a beginning must also have an end; however, one's perspective on this truth differs dramatically depending on whether one subscribes to a cyclical or linear view of history. The shift to a linear view of history, which occurred about 2500 years ago, proved to have a major influence on world history, and even now continues to influence our world.

Chapter Ten

The Birth of the Hero

Where have all good men gone
And where are all the gods?
Where's the street-wise Hercules
To fight the rising odds?

Bonnie Tyler, *I Need a Hero*

As we saw in the last chapter the act of creation gives the creator a special status. By establishing *cosmos* (order) a deity acquires the right to dictate the behavior of others, not only the behavior of men but of other gods. However, this power does not come without its challenges, or challengers. Each myth of cosmic genesis is accompanied by an equally potent myth regarding the perpetual interplay between cosmos and chaos. For millennia those of the Middle East, Central Asia, and Europe subscribed to the general belief that chaos was biding its time, waiting to exploit any weakness that appeared in the cosmic order.[1] That was why the relationship between the gods and mankind was so important, because the growing contempt of mankind was understood to weaken the gods and allow the primal forces of chaos to overwhelm the guardians of cosmos. Hesiod's five ages of man illustrates how some Greeks viewed the inevitable decline of creation from a golden age to that of iron, an age exemplified by the breakdown of common familial bonds, the quick corruption of the body, a general state of war, and the gods' abandonment of men—and once the gods abandon men, Hesiod writes, "there will be no help against evil."

Nothing is said by Hesiod about how this last age will end, but if Hesiod accepted the general view at the time he most likely believed that the age would end with destruction and that the "eternal cycle" would begin again. However, before the golden age can be re-inaugurated the "great" or "perfect" year must pass. This "great" or "perfect" year would involve widespread destruction, likely the result of some alignment of the stars and planets. This was a common motif in religions from India to Greece, even Plato spoke of it in his classic work *Timaeus* (360 BCE). The reason for the "great" or "perfect" year is to purify mankind prior to being reconciled to the gods and prior to the birth of a new golden age.[2]

The theme of death preceding birth is a universal theme. American Christians might be most familiar with the concept if they have read the Gospel of John where Jesus says, "Verily, verily, I say unto you, Except a corn of wheat fall into the ground and die, it abideth alone: but if it die, it bringeth forth much fruit." (John 12:24) The ritual of baptism can also be seen as a symbolic form of death: dying to the old and coming alive to the new. This is what Christians mean when they talk about being "born again." The microcosmic experience of the individual Christian believer as they go through the conversion process will also be accomplished at the macrocosmic level when the new heaven and new earth replace the old. (Revelation 21:1) This too is a common theme, but not one found in all ancient religions; in fact, few ancient religions see the future in such a linear fashion.

The idea that life is renewed through death is a common theme in all religions. This renewal or rebirth might come through the sacrifice of an animal or, as some religions teach, by dying to the self—in other words, one's own ego. The latter has wider existential ramifications be-cause once one is "renewed" they begin to see life aright for the first time. What that means is that they begin to see that the world is divided into physical and spiritual worlds, and the former becomes a mere shadow of true reality where the forces of cosmos and chaos are constantly battling for dominance. This motif derives directly from ancient creation myth. In the stories of cosmic origins are sown the seeds of conflict which will later contribute to commonly held *combat myths*, and eventually that theme would result in Christian apocalypticism. As we saw in the previous chapter great battles often precede the establishment of *cosmos*, but the war does not end there since *chaos* must be constantly beaten back through the efforts of both gods and men.

One of the chief ways in which this can be accomplished is by appointing someone king, a divine representative of the city's deity—one who is possibly divine himself. This king is a law giver and dispenser of justice, as well as the chief protector of the city. Probably one of the best examples of this, and one that you might have read about in high school, is the king Hammurabi, c. 1792-1750 BCE. You may have heard about his famous "code," one of the earliest codifications of legal pronouncements and the procedures by which those laws would be carried out. The code, which may have been written c. 1772 BCE, begins with a very interesting introduction which is pertinent to our discussion. It reads,

> When Anu the Sublime, King of the Anunaki, and Bel, the lord of Heaven and earth, who decreed the fate of the land, assigned to Marduk, the over-ruling son of Ea, God of righteousness, dominion over earthly man, and made him great among the Igigi, they called Babylon by his illustrious name, made it great on earth, and founded an everlasting kingdom in it, whose foundations are laid so solidly as those of heaven and earth; then Anu and Bel called by name me, Hammurabi, the exalted prince, who feared God, to bring about the rule of righteousness in the land, to destroy the wicked and the evil-doers; so that the strong should not harm the weak; so that I should rule over the black-headed people like Shamash, and enlighten the land, to further the well-being of mankind.

Let's focus for a moment on two things here. First, notice that Hammurabi makes reference to several gods in the Babylonian pantheon. Anu, Bel (Enlil), and Ea are three major gods in the Babylonian pantheon. It is they who gave Marduk, the son of Ea, complete control over the gods (Igigi) and mankind. This was touched on in the last chapter, in the story where Marduk killed Tiamat. Babylon, referred to here as a male, is the city of Babylon which like heaven and earth is to be an everlasting kingdom. So, the first half of this introduction establishes the hierarchy and why the city of Babylon exists at all. It is because the gods established the city. The city is one of those "world navels" that we mentioned in the last chapter.[3] Then, Hammurabi begins to explain why he should be taken seriously as a lawgiver and judge. Put simply, he says, because Anu and Bel say so. Notice Hammurabi does not invoke Marduk as the one who has given him his divine mission of establishing "righteousness in the land." As far as Hammurabi is concerned he and Marduk are equals when it comes to maintaining the divine order. Hammurabi and Marduk are on the front lines battling chaos by maintaining the divine order established at Babylon. So, it is in creation myth and divinely established cities that combat myth begins to dominate the intellectual landscape of the Middle East. For, what else could one think as he looked beyond the fortified walls of his city-state into the chaos of the desert? What else but "Here in this city is order. Here I am safe."

Although chaos was believed to have always threatened the divinely established order there was still a general sense among Middle Eastern culture that life possessed a largely "immutable" quality. The world had not been shaped by gods who had themselves existed forever; the only thing which had always existed was chaos. If anything what was unchanging was the battle between the forces of cosmos and chaos, a battle that would never end. This can be seen in three Middle Eastern religious traditions, that of the Egyptians, Mesopotamians, and Vedic Indians.

In Egypt chaos was a "boundless ocean" known by the name of Nun. It had existed before all the gods and was thought of as their father. However, Nun was no longer an active force in the world; that was left to the younger gods. The *demiurge*, or supreme god, was the one attributed with creating the organized world out of chaos. He is "the One," as the Egyptians would have put it, "who makes himself into millions."[4] The Egyptians believed this demiurge to be Ra, the sun god. He is said to have created the world through an act of masturbation or spitting, and he was omniscient and all powerful, unlike the other gods.

The Egyptian idea of world order was encapsulated in the term *ma'at*. This force, similar to notions of *karma* in the East, allowed humans to envision a world in which a moral order permeated the universe and their own lives. However, this order was always seen as existing within a larger, more primal universe of chaos. *Ma'at* emphasized notions of harmony and regularity, the defying of which would bring retribution in either this life or the next. Sometimes *Ma'at* refers to a deity, believed to be a daughter of Ra. If you have ever seen Lady Justice at a courthouse you have already been exposed to this motif. The statue of a lady holding a scale in one hand, a sword in the other, and blindfolded, symbolizes justice equitably dispensed to all. This is a recurring motif, as is seen in the Egyptian Book of the Dead where Ma'at's head-feather is used by Anubis to determine whether someone should be let into the "Field of Reeds," the Egyptian version of Heaven. Anubis takes the heart of the dead and places it on one side of a scale then places the feather on the other. If the feather should sink the scale to its side, too bad for this poor soul, otherwise "Welcome!"[5]

Ma'at does not exist alone. *Isfet* was a force in the universe that ran counter to it. *Isfet* was often associated with "a gigantic, dragon-like serpent" and is sometimes embodied in the god Apophis, also known as Apep. The existence of these two forces meant that a "gigantic unceasing struggle at the cosmic level between Ra and Apophis, order and disorder" would always exist, and that this struggle "had its counterpart in the vicissitudes of individual lives." Everyday people were part of the cosmic drama because the Egyptian temple that stood in every major city was a microcosm of the order that had been established, and it was a major bulwark against chaos. However, Egyptians believed that time stretched on "endlessly and changelessly" and that there would be cycles in which order and chaos might get the best of one another from time to time. Even so, time stretched on so long into the future that there was no immediate concern it would end anytime soon. This is not to say that the Egyptians did not subscribe to the notion that the world would end someday. They just believed this end to be so far in the future that it was not a practical concern.[6] Of more concern was that which awaited one after death.

The "Field of Reeds" was mentioned above. It was the Egyptian analog to the Christian Heaven, an "unending fertile paradise." By the time of the Middle Kingdom (c. 2055-1650 BCE) all Egyptians were thought to be eligible for this paradise if they worshipped Osiris and maintained their lives in accordance with *ma'at*. As also mentioned above, "judgment day" was described in the *Book of the Dead*. If one had lived life according to *isfet* instead of *ma'at* they would not gain entrance into paradise. So, for the Egyptians there would never be a final conflagration. Their only hope was to live their lives according to *ma'at* and reap the reward of the afterlife.

There are some similarities between Egyptian and Mesopotamian conceptions of order and chaos, but due to geography and topography there were some dramatic differences in how they viewed their gods and their relationship to those gods, primarily because the Mesopotamians lived a harsher, more uncertain existence than did the Egyptians. In Mesopotamian culture Anu was the corollary of Egyptian Ra. It was Anu who created the original order out of chaos, and, as we saw in the creation story contained in the *Enuma Elish*, it was Marduk who was set over this order with the approval of Anu. Marduk's chief city was Babylon, which served as the symbolic center of the struggle of order against chaos. The Mesopotamians used the Akkadian words *kettu* and *mesharu* to designate their ideas about order and justice. It was the chief task of the gods to maintain these things and the task was heavily divided. Mankind had been created for the sole purpose of serving the gods, as we learned about in the story of Kingu. So, the chief task of men was not to challenge the immutable order of the world. To do otherwise was to challenge *kettu* and *mesharu*, and for this there would be consequences.[7]

Mesopotamian kings were not often seen as divine themselves, but they were definitely seen as divinely appointed. The reason the gods did this was to keep the rather "stupid race of men" on the straight and narrow—in other words, properly serving the gods. Because of this arrangement the well-being of the kingdom was seen as totally dependent on the king. Of course, this could work the opposite way as well. If the kingdom began collapsing this would be seen as a sign that the king had been abandoned by his divine helper. In the Mesopotamian scheme of things social justice was paramount, so any type of disorder, no matter how small, was feared.[8] We see here now why the Code of Hammurabi turned out to be such a great political tool. Law and order is always an effective way of getting the populace to support a politician.

There was nothing more effective than success in war to prove one's divine *bona fides*, especially when it came to the political control of Mesopotamian society. So, when Babylon was threatened by others it was seen as a trial of the king's mandate. Would the gods be with him in battle or abandon him? From this perspective *cosmos* was never safe, because it can be threatened. It is always precarious. A defeat during wartime could often be a sign that chaos was gaining an advantage over cosmos. It should also be remembered that because Mesopotamians viewed themselves as slaves to the gods, cosmos was not seen as having been established for their sole benefit. That is why humans were always subject to attack by demons and other spiritual forces, and the afterlife was no better than this one since it was merely a continuation of life's harsh battles. So, as far as the Mesopotamians are concerned the war between chaos and cosmos would never end.[9]

There are some stark contrasts between the cosmological ideas of Egyptians and Mesopotamians. For example, the Mesopotamians did not possess any corollary to the Egyptian "Field of Reeds." The Mesopotamian cosmology was also more warlike, because they view order as more precarious than the Egyptians. They were constantly on alert and ready for battle. It has been suggested that the major reason for this difference was that Egypt was naturally defended by deserts to the east and west, mountains to the south, and a sea to the north. Invasion was difficult—but not impossible. This is not to say that the Egyptians did not know how to fight; it is only to point out that Mesopotamian culture, because of its harsher environment and proximity to invading forces, was far more prepared to go to war at any moment. Such a society yielded what we call a *warrior culture*, which would of necessity influence Mesopotamian cosmology. Geography and topology was a major determinate in how pervasive the *combat myth* would become. The seed of this war-like cosmological view was planted in every creation myth, but it flowered into a full combat myth because of the cultural soils into which it was planted. This was also true of the Vedic Indian tradition, which we consider next.

Much of what we know about Vedic Indian tradition we find in the *Rig Veda*. These sacred writings were written down as early as 600 BCE but may have existed as oral traditions as long ago as 1200 BCE. In the Vedic tradition the *cosmos* was always viewed as imperfect and "constantly threatened by destructive forces." This, according to Vedic tradition, would never change. Indra was the chief god of the Vedic pantheon, the one who established order out of primal chaos. Order was designated by the Vedic word *rita*, and its opposite was *anrita*, or primordial chaos. Two other words played an important role in the cosmology of the Vedic Indians: *Sat* and *Asat*. The words respectively denoted existence and non-existence, and it was Indra who separated them at the same time the world was created.[10]

All the creator gods (Ra, Marduk, and Indra) represent the development of a new and fertile regime that replaces the sterile and static regimes of older gods like Tiamat or Vritra, the latter a Vedic god. As Norman Cohn writes,

> In one form or another the myth [the combat myth] flourished over vast areas of the ancient world. And what it says in all its forms is the same: that cosmos has always been threatened by chaos and always will be, yet has always survived and always will.

In the Vedic tradition the myth of Mitra represents this new regime. Mitra, like Ra, is often identified as the god of the day or the sun. He is a close associate of the Vedic god Varuna. Mitra is seen as the defender of order in the never ending cosmic battle. As in the other traditions of the Middle East sacrifice was seen as the chief means by which the gods were strengthened in their tasks, and the king's sacrifice was of particular importance. Chaos, sometimes viewed in more concrete terms as the wilderness or uncultivated land, was personified by the god Rudra. For the folks of this time and place being outside order, outside the city, meant being surrounded by danger, uncertainty, and fear.[11]

From creation myths to myths regarding the maintenance of a precarious cosmic order, we are given the central motif from which nearly all great literature has been drawn: the *hero*. It is the myth of the hero that serves as the basis for all combat myth, since without some heroic intent the hero would be merely a marauder or a villain. One of the best treatments of the hero motif is contained in Joseph Campbell's classic 1949 work *The Hero With a Thousand Faces*. In it we learn of "monomyth," which is defined as a three-step process through which every hero must work in order to achieve some type of wisdom, self-knowledge, or boon, which he can then bring back to the profane world of his birth. These three steps generally begin with *separation*, that is followed by *initiation*, and then, of course, the *return*. Each step in this process can be generalized for all hero mythology, although the details of each myth might differ greatly.

Campbell writes that

> ...the symbols of mythology are not manufactured; they cannot be ordered, invented, or permanently suppressed....

> ...the heroes, and the deeds of myth survive into modern times. In the absence of an effective general mythology, each of us has his private, unrecognized, rudimentary, yet secretly potent pantheon of dreams.[12]

This monomyth is clearly evident in modern hero-stories: Luke Skywalker in *Star Wars*, Harry Potter in the J. K. Rowling series, and Bilbo and Frodo Baggins in the popular tales of J. R. R. Tolkien. In all of these stories the hero is separated from the life he has known, discovers resources he did not know he had, and returns to his former life with a great boon or to fight a great battle in which he serves as the catalyst for victory. Each stage: separation, initiation, and return, is achieved in one way or another.

There are many nuances in this three-step process. The separation begins with a call to adventure, which can initially be rejected. However, most heroes have no choice and through the aid of a mystical figure the hero begins his journey by crossing over some threshold, which can take the form of a doorway, or of being swallowed up by some great force like a giant fish. Initiation occurs along the road as the hero faces trials of varying degree. There are helps along the way. The hero may meet a goddess, a symbol of the *magna mater*, an encounter that symbolizes the beginning of the hero's process of rebirth. However, other female encounters might involve a temptress, whom the hero must resist. There can also be oedipal encounters which will ultimately require atonement with a father figure. The ultimate goal is the "apotheosis" (transformation) of the hero and the acquisition of an "Ultimate Boon," which the hero must then decide whether to share with the rest of the world. This is where the final stage of the hero's journey begins. Some heroes may refuse the initial call to return to their former world but most do not, and many have to engage in a "Magic Flight" or be rescued from without in order to once again cross over the threshold into their former world. Once the return has been completed the hero becomes the master of two worlds, an example to all of how to live in true freedom. As Campbell writes, "The composite hero of the monomyth is a personage of exceptional gifts. Frequently he is honored by his society, frequently unrecognized or disdained." The hero exists because some kind of symbolic deficiency plagues either the hero himself or his society. So, the hero's journey is of paramount interest because it is meant to restore or redeem a fallen world through the reclamation of symbols without which people cannot live.[13]

In the modern age the hero is no longer seen as one in a series of heroes who defend order against chaos. The hero has become, within a linear context, one who will for all time end the threat of chaos. The shift from a cyclical view of history to that of "time's arrow" transforms the role of the hero in a dramatic way. In fact, without this change in temporal perspective the hero of Christian apocalyptic myth, which we consider in the next chapter, might not have been possible. However, even with this transformation of our historical and temporal perspective the hero continues to conform to the three-step process of Campbell's monomyth. The transformation of humanity's general temporal view, especially amongst the three monotheistic traditions of Judaism, Christianity, and Islam, makes it possible for us to envision what some have called an "omega point," the end of the world. It is our ability to imagine such an end-point that allows us to believe not only in utopian schemes of unlimited progress but also dystopian schemes of never-ending terror. This imaginative ability is central to understanding one of the main threads of this book: *the culture of fear*, but our journey into apocalyptic tradition is not yet complete. So, let us continue to explore how ancient combat myth was transformed millennia ago into an often familiar apocalyptic theme, which has heavily influenced our popular literature and film, and which has also served for several thousand years as the central promise of the Christian religion.

＊＊＊

In our search for the origins of modern apocalyptic thought we must turn to an ancient Persian religion known as Zoroastrianism. The reason we have to focus on this religion in our pursuit of the story of apocalypticism is because there is strong evidence that Zoroastrian eschatology was passed on to a small group of heterodox Jews sometime in the fifth century BCE, and that these heterodox views were later passed on to those who called themselves Christians.

The first advocate of this religion, from whom the religion got its name, was Zoroaster, and he can be counted among the first of the *millenarians*, those who believe that time will soon come to an end after a cosmic battle that will forever free the ordered world from the threat of chaos (evil). Like Egyptian, Mesopotamian, and Vedic creation myth, Zoroastrianism conceived of a world carved from chaos by the chief god of the Zoroastrian pantheon, Ahura Mazda. Ahura Mazda achieved this act with the help of the six Holy Immortals.[14]

The liturgical hymns of Zoroaster, which may have been written by Zoroaster himself, are called *Gathas*. They give us a lot of insight into what Zoroaster himself may have believed, but it was a later and larger book of sacred scriptures called the *Avesta* that became the authorized source of information about Zoroastrianism.[15] The *Gathas* talk of a physical resurrection at the end of time, when the world will be flattened by a "fiery flood." This is called the time of "the making wonderful," a moment when a changeless realm replaces the perpetual conflict of cosmos and chaos.[16] There is also a messianic figure known as the *Sayoshyant*, which literally translates to "future benefactor." This individual plays a major role in all that is to come. He is the great hero, who brings all things to fruition.[17]

What we know is that like all the other cultures of the Middle East Zoroastrians had specific words that embodied the concepts of order and chaos. *Asha* was the word that designated order while *druj* meant "the false" or "the lie." Zoroastrianism was distinct among Middle Eastern religions in that it seemed to give a greater place to Ahura Mazda than any other pantheon gave to their own chief deities. Like all the other myths there is from the beginning a great cosmic battle. Angra Mainyu (also called Ahriman) represents the forces of the world that choose *druj* over *asha*. The war is fought between this god and the representative of Ahura Mazda, a god known as Spenta Mainyu, which can be translated "Holy Spirit." There are five other deities that assist Angra Mainyu in his tasks of destruction: Indra, Saurva, Nanghaithya, Taurvi, and Zairi. These deities serve as the main counterparts to the Holy Immortals.[18] One of the chief defenders of order is Mithra, the Iranian version of the Vedic Mitra. He is associated with the day or the sun, like the Egyptian Ra. In addition to all these gods it was believed that *Fravashis*, spirits of dead heroes or ancestors, could help one in this life.[19]

Zoroastrian myth differed somewhat from other religions when it came to the idea of the separation between the material and spiritual world. In fact, Zoroaster believed that the material world could be just as good as the spiritual world as long as it was infused with "moral purpose and directed by spiritual striving." This is a central idea in Zoroastrianism, and it comes close to proposing the modern idea of free will, since individuals are thought to have a choice between *asha* and *druj*.[20]

At some point life on the steppes of Asia passed into a "typical heroic age," a "turbulent" and "restless" age. Under this regime "military prowess" achieved "its highest value and the seizing of booty" its "highest aim."[21] "Zoroaster…was inspired by the ancient and potent combat myth to create a different and even more potent combat myth," and this combat myth has made its way to us in the form of apocalyptic faith.[22] How this happened is not hard to understand when we look at what Norman Cohn calls the "Syro-Palestinian Crucible," the place where early Hebrew myth was born, and then evolved over centuries into the early Jewish apocalyptic myth.

There were three major deities in the Syro-Palestinian pantheon in the fourteenth century BCE: El, Hadad (later Ba'al), and the goddess Anat. Eventually, Ba'al became the chief deity of this area. He is the one who is attributed with creating order out of chaos. His chief nemesis is Yam, the god of the sea. In mythology the sea is usually associated with chaos because of its unpredictability. Ba'al must subdue Yam in order to establish his order and to cement his own status as king of the gods. During this struggle Ba'al does not fare too well. He is killed by another god called Mot, the god of death, drought, and sterility. The goddess Anat, in a clear homage to Egyptian myth, has to find Ba'al's body and give it a proper burial. Having done this the ritual restores Ba'al to life. This does not end the story because Ba'al can still not overcome the power of Mot, so El has to intervene and tell Mot to step aside. This story, like all the others we have told so far, has many lessons in it. One of the central lessons is that "chaos is a perennial possibility, death the most certain of certainties," and "both are ineluctable parts of reality."[23]

By the time the Hebrew people came to rule Palestine (Israel) in the eleventh century BCE, Yahweh was already associated with the chief deity of the Syro-Palestinian pantheon, El. It was believed that El would be able to overcome and reestablish cosmos when need be, and that he possessed power the other gods did not. As was mentioned above, though, the Hebrews had not yet adopted a strictly monotheistic perspective. Like the other inhabitants of the Middle East they believed their god was simply stronger than others. The term *henotheism* is used to designate those who believe that many gods exist but that only one is deserving of worship. As in other Near Eastern societies ritual was very important and mistakes made at the temple could prove disastrous to cosmos. In early Hebrew tradition *mishpat* and *tsedeq* were two words that closely associated earthly rule with the divine order. This shows that even in early Hebrew tradition it was thought that earthly and heavenly order, and chaos, went hand-in-hand.[24]

It took the exile to Babylon to transform the *henotheistic* Hebrews to monotheists.[25] It was during this time that their defeat in battle and their exile began to be seen as punishment for not worshipping the one and only true god, Yahweh. Much of this view developed after the Hebrews returned from exile in the sixth century and began to rebuild their temple. Some priests, called Deuteronomists by modern scholars, claimed to have found some ancient documents relating to Israel's past and their relationship with Yahweh. The documents revealed a lost series of 614 commandments and prohibitions, and encouraged the Jewish remnant to adopt this way of life in order to reestablish the glory of ancient Israel. At this same time a smaller group of Jewish monotheists began to "look forward, impatiently, to a glorious consummation, when all things would be set to rights" for the Jewish people. For these Jewish believers there would be no more compromise. "Extermination, no less, is to be the fate of all who refuse to adhere to Yahweh alone and remain obstinately polytheistic." [26]

The first hint of monotheism found in the Old Testament is in the second half of Isaiah, which scholars believe was written by two different authors. Chapters 40 through 55 were clearly written by someone who was observing the events of the day. A great clash of empires was occurring as the Persians gobbled up nearly all of the Middle East into what has been called the *Achaemenid Empire*. This empire was the largest that had ever been known to that date and some have estimated that as many as fifty million people lived under the rule of the Persians at the beginning of the fifth century BCE. The second author of Isaiah, seeing all this, thought that "the end of Babylonian exile" was "inaugurating an age in which Yahweh's sovereignty" would "be made manifest, unchallenged and unchallengeable, once and for all." The second half of Isaiah, along with two other books, Zechariah and Joel, look forward to a time of future salvation. The "messiah," or *anointed one*, is not at this time seen as an otherworldly figure but merely as a great king, so "the notion of a transcendental savior in human form, so important in Zoroastrianism and so central to Christianity, is totally unknown in the Hebrew Bible."[27]

The Jewish apocalyptic tradition, which would become so important to Christianity, got its start very late, in the third and second centuries BCE. In the official Judaism of sixth-century Deuteronomists there was no room for "notions about chaos, cosmos, and the world to come." However, by the third and second centuries, as the Jewish state was again under threat, this tradition begins to develop, as evidenced by the appearance of the Book of Daniel, Jubilees, and I Enoch. All of these books were written from an apocalyptic perspective, which drew from the traditions of the cultures all around the Jewish people, and easily imported by the Hellenistic traffic that went from Macedonia all the way to Bac-tria (present-day Afghanistan). Canaanite and Zoroastrian influences can be seen. Works like the Egyptian *Demotic Chronicle* and the *Oracle of the Potter* spoke to the idea of being freed from political persecution, as did the Persian *Oracle of Hystaspes*. All of these writings purported to be ancient prophecies. Typical of these books is a final battle between cosmos and chaos where the faithful passively suffer until salvation is realized. Passively suffering was seen as necessary for salvation because it purified the believer for the coming world.[28]

Eventually these ideas would be passed on to small Jewish sects. We know of two that were possibly influenced by these ideas. The first was a sect at Qumran; the other was a group called the Essenes.[29] These groups relied heavily on I Enoch and Jubilees, both of which detail the last judgment and the world that would be established afterward. This event would be made apparent through the cessation of time itself, in a second phase called "the Renewal," but first there would be a messi-anic age of government.[30] This is an idea that would be familiar to most American evangelical Christians who adhere to a millenarian perspec-tive, and it is here, in Christianity, that the apocalyptic tradition really takes the western world by storm. This became particularly true after the temple at Jerusalem was destroyed in 70 CE. Prior to this the follow-ers of Jesus were seen as Jews with a few peculiar ideas about this man from Nazareth. If the gospels and other works are any indication Jesus and his followers were "deeply imbued" with a "dualist eschatology" that "was central to their worldview."[31]

The identification of Christianity with the apocalyptic tradition reached its peak in the first century CE. The Book of Revelation is the epitome of this eschatological fervor. Of course, none of this prophecy came true, at least not manifestly, so it had to be interpreted in a variety of different ways.[32] This is why the apocalyptic schemes of early Chris-tianity gave way to a belief in the gradual working out of the kingdom of God on earth through his Church. This was established belief by the fourth and fifth centuries CE. Earlier we mentioned Augustine and his book *The City of God* (410). In that book Augustine defended Christians against the charge of morally weakening the empire because they were abandoning the traditional Roman pantheon. Augustine also went on to argue how God would work his divine purpose through the Church on order to one day establish the *new Jerusalem* mentioned in chapter 21 of *Revelation*.

Beginning in the fourth century the Christian Church and the Roman state would merge into a single entity, which would last until secular governments and commercial interests began to reassert their power beginning in the eleventh century. It is not surprising that Christianity, and its apocalyptic narrative, so easily fused with the Roman state. Rome had its own narrative theodicy, the *Aeneid*, written by Vergil between the years 29 and 19 BCE. As mentioned earlier this explains why the nobility of Europe was constantly trying to trace its roots back to Adam, Aeneas, or some other ancient historical representative of God. By the fourth century CE the apocalypticism of Christianity had become sufficiently allegorical and distant in time that it became a perfect complement to the state. There is nothing more powerful than believing that God is on your side when engaging in social, economic, and political battle.

In the next couple of chapters we will explore the developing relationship between church and state, and how it infused society with a progressive view of the future. This progressive view of the future was rooted in the Church's vision that it would eventually work out the purposes of God on the earth. As we will see, though, that all began to come crashing down beginning in the late fifteenth century, as the Renaissance, the Reformation, the Scientific Revolution, the Enlightenment, and finally the secularization of life and politics, made it all but impossible for the Church to command anymore the spiritual and political obedience of Europeans. By the nineteenth century western society was largely freed from the morally repressive influence of traditional religion but it just could not shake those centuries of belief in progress, which was supposed to be accomplished through the Church. So, the Church's vision of progress merged with the Enlightenment and the Scientific Revolution, convincing many that what God could not do through his Church they would now accomplish through science, reason, and markets.

Chapter Eleven

Behold I Come Quickly

And, behold, I come quickly; and my reward is with me, to give every man according as his work shall be.

Revelation 22:12

The first three centuries of the Christian experience involved a struggle between those who represented what was to become the orthodox Christian faith and those who represented a myriad of other ideas about Jesus' divinity, his mission, and what he had accomplished through his death and resurrection.[1] The arguments of the first century or so of Christianity's history were heavily influenced by the general conviction that Jesus might return at anytime to establish the promised kingdom of God on earth. This *apocalyptic* strain of Christian thought was abandoned only after centuries of waiting for something to happen, and after leaders of the Church began to encourage believers to interpret Christian prophecy differently. We already mentioned Augustine's *City of God*, written around 410 CE, but even before that Christians were being encouraged to see the Church as Christ's representative, an institution that would eventually work all the purposes of God on earth. So, when Constantine made a nominal claim of Christian faith, because of a vision he had prior to the Battle of the Milvian Bridge (312 CE). It was only a matter of time before the extensive organizational structure of the Church would come to play a role in the new political order of Rome.[2]

Like the Zoroastrians before them, Christians eventually abandoned the idea of the imminent return of their spiritual leader. They replaced the immediacy of early Christian apocalyptic thought with the notion that the kingdom of God would come about gradually through the work of the Church and its power over the state.[3] However, this *gradualism* allowed the regressive *meme* of apocalypticism to survive in an intellectual form that theologians call *amillennialism*. This was the idea that the millennial kingdom of Christ was to be understood allegorically. The power of the Church was to be seen as the establishment of the kingdom of God on earth, and the "thousand year reign" was to be viewed not as a literal thousand years but as just a metaphor for "a very long time." This gradualist form of apocalypticism allowed the more immediate, and otherworldly, prophetic tradition to remain in stasis for centuries, but the early apocalyptic fervor of Christianity began to revive as the Church began to lose control of European society and the European political structure after 1000 CE.

***

Constantine began his new reign with the Edict of Milan (313 CE). This edict legalized the Christian faith throughout the Roman Empire. Prior to this Christianity had not been formally recognized because of the general animus of a polytheistic Roman society. The reason for the animus was that Christians refused to recognize any other gods, because they thought doing so would be idolatrous. This worried the Romans because they thought their religion very important in the maintenance of the empire. You will remember that this idea was touched on in the last few chapters.

Legalizing Christianity did not allow it to dominate the state immediately; that took many centuries. The Church faced many challenges, including an "apostate" emperor who attempted to return Rome to its ancient pagan roots. Julian the Apostate is called the last pagan emperor of Rome, 361-363 CE. It would take two centuries before the eastern and western halves of the empire would be for all practical purposes totally dominated by Christianity. Many have attributed the "dark ages" to the Church's dominance of the social and political structure after 500 CE, but this may not be completely fair. The empire had structural problems that no religion could have fixed. However, the Church did itself no historical favor by trying to destroy nearly all pagan intellectual culture, the same culture that we laud today in our history books and in our jurisprudence. Briefly understood the "dark ages" should be seen as a full-frontal assault by the Church on pagan thought and worship. This included much of the scientific and philosophical work that had been done by the Greeks. For centuries the Church, with the help of the state, ferreted out heresy, destroyed icons, established their orthodox positions, and destroyed nearly every vestige of pagan thought, which was only rescued because Arab traders and scholars kept all these works for centuries sealed up for us in Arabic. This would change, though, in the late medieval period as these works were re-translated back into Latin and Greek.

In the West the relationship between Church and state is difficult to follow because it was not necessarily an even relationship. At times it seemed that the state told the Church what to do and at other times the Church hounded those in power to get what it wanted. In the end the relationship between Church and state became one of mutual dependence, some might say *co-dependence*. While the state protected the Church's lands and primacy as a spiritual institution, the Church gave the secular government legitimacy by encouraging the people to obey the powers that be. The power of Church and state would swing back and forth for over ten centuries until a process began in the eleventh century that would erode the political, and sometimes the spiritual, power of the Church. This can be seen especially in the controversy over who should rightfully bestow Church offices, a controversy called the Investiture Contest. It was supposed to have been settled by the Concordat of Worms in 1122, but this agreement settled things only in principle, not in fact. So, the state and the Church continued to struggle against each other until the state finally won out by the seventeenth century, and the state did this with no small help from Martin Luther and his sixteenth-century Protestant Reformation.

Another force that played a role in what was happening in Europe during this time was the rise of Islam in the early seventh century. A Bedouin trader by the name of Mohammed claimed to have received divine messages from the angel Gabriel, a message that he said would be the last one prior to the end of the world. He had expected both Christians and Jews to respond positively to his message; when they did not Mohammed converted his polytheistic Bedouin brethren to his own brand of monotheism, which began the fantastic growth of Muslim-Arab expansionism in the seventh and eight centuries. Within a century Islam was making inroads into Western Europe and menacing the eastern Roman Empire centered at Constantinople. The Mediterranean Sea became an "Islamic lake," just as it had previously been a "Roman lake."[4]

As mentioned before, the intellectual curtain had descended over Western Europe partly because of the attitude Christians took toward pagan learning. Even in the east anti-pagan fervor could be witnessed in the violent action taken against images, even sacred images found in the churches. This movement against icons has given us the modern expression *iconoclasm*. Today the word denotes those who try to break down conventions or destroy perceived ideas of the sacred. Originally the term was used to describe the eighth-century movement against iconography. In the early medieval period iconoclasm was usually limited in its duration, and the general population was always drawn back to their icons, often because the icons were thought to possess some kind of talismanic power. The last major iconoclastic movement occurred in the eastern half of the Roman Empire in the early ninth century. After this there was a general and formal recognition of iconography as part of the Christian tradition in both the east and the west.[5]

In the West, as the urban centers broke down in the fifth century CE, people fled to the countryside, to villas and small towns, which would eventually become small fortified cities. This began the long decline of western civilization which led to *manorialism* and *feudalism*. These two systems combined to create a localized economy in which people were tied to the land and to the noble who owned it. It was also a time when the nobility practiced a martial prowess which only the Roman state once dared to exhibit. The noble of a certain section of land became legislator, judge, and father to his people. The people on that land looked to the noble for physical protection in return for their services. These systems of social, political, legal, and economic interaction were by necessity based on barter, since most coinage had gone out of local use with the demise of the Western portion of the Roman Empire.

These systems of social and economic organization would also break down, but not before they had made a heavy impression on the minds of Europeans. Feudalism was slowly degraded by renewed commercial activity centered in cities that were being reborn in the twelfth century, especially in Italy. The *cash-nexus* gave the feudal lord an incentive to break the socio-legal relationship he had with his serfs in exchange for ready coin. That money would be used not only to buy luxuries but to purchase the noble's freedom from military service. For, as each of the nascent states of Europe became more centralized and more powerful they became more dependent on paid mercenaries to do their fighting for them. This did not happen overnight. It took centuries, from approximately 1000 to 1650 CE.[6]

Probably nothing played a more important role in turning Europeans away from feudalism than the attempt to expel Islam from the Iberian Peninsula and southern France. With an external enemy European Christians were finally united into what became known as *Christendom*,[7] and after successfully driving the Muslims back to Northern Africa, and beyond, Western Europeans began to imagine a world quite different from the one they had known for centuries. The return of trade and luxury goods created a new materialism within society, although it was still constrained by the Church, especially among the poor. Powerful city officials began to expand their power and also began to war against each other for consolidation. Retaking the Mediterranean Sea, however, was instrumental in breaking Islamic power, and in setting Europe on the course of looking for a direct route to Asia. If they could do that they would eliminate the hated Muslim middleman, who was a necessary part of trade with Asia. Europeans also thought they might be able to open up another front in their general war against the Ottoman Empire.

Preceding all this were the "holy crusades" of Christendom, which began at the end of the eleventh century. These crusades were just a continuation of the Iberian campaigns of the eighth through fifteenth century, campaigns known collectively as the *Reconquista*. Over a period of centuries the Spanish and Portuguese (their modern ethnic designations) joined together to drive the Muslims out of Spain and Portugal, and back to Northern Africa. However, once this conquest was completed by the early fifteenth century, economic and political ambition, and the need for more land, spurred the Portuguese and Spanish to look further afield. So began the great European exploration of discovery that would eventually map the western coast of Africa, yield an eastern water route to Asian markets, and also inspire the famed voyage of Christopher Columbus. The discovery of the Americas was an unanticipated bonus for Europeans, and it would benefit the Portuguese and Spanish crowns for several centuries.[8] Because the Spanish and Portuguese played a major role in mapping out the world and the seas the Church gave its imprimatur to the notion that the earth was to be divided into two spheres of influence. One half belonged to the Spanish while the other was given to Portugal. This policy was established with the *Treaty of Tordesillas* (1494), which because of inaccurate information left the Spanish controlling the bulk of North and South America. This history is too complicated to relate here, but the events above do illustrate that at the beginning of the sixteenth century Europeans were already thinking about carving up the known world for their own purposes.

Against the backdrop of this history let us now place the narrative of apocalyptic faith, which has survived in various forms up until the present day. As mentioned above, apocalypticism lived on in the mission of the Church to gradually work the purposes of God here on earth, but it also lived on in the prophetic traditions of the medieval and early modern European people. As we will learn in the next few chapters Christian *eschatology* was not the only source of millenarian expectation.[9] Since ancient times the general populace had been animated by tales of sleeping kings or emperors. It was thought that these heroes of a bygone age would one day awaken to bring equity and justice back to the world, releasing the poor and downtrodden from their bonds and establishing the final perfect kingdom. The details of these stories changed over the years but they maintained common themes. Sometimes the hero was a lone figure, a messianic warrior-king, serving in the dual capacity of savior and politician. Sometimes it was thought that two separate individuals would fill each role. These details do not matter as much as why these ideas continued to survive even as the Church tried to stamp them out. The short answer is that the general population of Europe cleaved to these ideas because they had little else for which to hope.

Is it possible that we may here find an explanation for the modern day problem of "the culture of fear"? I think so. When enough people are driven to the point of mere survival they lose all hope in the way things are and search for a new way of doing things, often radical ways of doing things. It should come as no surprise that the fourteenth-century peasant was easily drawn to those who promised to lift their burdens, and to punish the elites of society for their material wantonness and disregard for the poor. The last several years have shown this proclivity of the marginalized to rally against the elites of society. *Tea Parties* and *Occupy Movements* exhibit the ease with which people connect their own problems to a corrupt and dysfunctional system. Some blame it on corrupt and extortionate government. Some see capitalists as the chief malefactors. Yet others see a general social decay as the culprit. Of course, there is no reason it cannot be a mixture of all three, but that is a point we will take up in the latter part of this book. For now, let us continue to explore how the apocalyptic mindset has developed over the last few centuries and has become an integral part of the modern *zeitgeist*.

***

Most of what follows in the rest of this chapter is based on Norman Cohn's book *The Pursuit of the Millennium: Revolutionary Millenarians and Mystical Anarchists of the Middle Ages* (1957). The history I am about to relate must be placed in the context of what you have read up to this point. If you do not keep that history in mind you might get the impression that life before the modern world was dominated solely by religious and spiritual concerns. It was not. Until the modern era most people lived in abject poverty, working from day to day in the production of food and other necessities, barely feeding themselves and their families. As Professor Cohn has intimated throughout his book it was this hardscrabble existence that made millenarian ideas so potent to people living on the edge of material starvation. This speaks to the general topic of this book, because there is clearly an inverse relationship between the material conditions that people find themselves in and the level of *apocalyptic thinking* and *cultural fear* that exists among the general populace. This is especially true where material conditions are constantly in flux. However, to say that material deprivation is at the heart of the culture of fear is to tell only part of the story. Even more important may be what social scientists and psychologists call "relative deprivation," which means we are always comparing our lot in life to that of the person next to us. When we do not measure up we become anxious. When we do measure up we feel content.[10]

Millenarianism, according to Cohn, is a particular strain of apocalyptic Christian thought, and it possesses five main characteristics. First, it is *collective*, meaning it will be enjoyed by all believers. It is *terrestrial*, which means it will not be enjoyed in some distant location but here on earth. It is *imminent*, because it could occur at any time in the near future. It is *total*, since no area of the earth will escape its transforming power. Lastly, it will be *miraculous*. It will only be achieved through the supernatural intervention of God. These five characteristics constitute what has been termed "Salvationism," and it is the source not only of medieval schemes of utopianism but also of modern political philosophies from *Communism* to *Liberation Theology*.[11] Over the next few pages we will discover how these ideas have come to permeate Western society, even as religion has receded in importance. Let us begin, yet again, long ago.

***

Medieval Europe witnessed the rise of many different millenarian sects. The Franciscan spiritualists are one example. These ascetic agents claimed that the world was on the cusp of inaugurating a great "age of the Spirit." This would be a time in which the world would come together in "prayer, mystical contemplation, and voluntary poverty." These early movements would place an emphasis on rejecting material culture, but this would change by the late early modern era. There were others with similar spiritual programs: Joachim of Fiore and the Brethren of the Free Spirit are just two. All of them share a common characteristic: *they were all supported by the "rootless poor of western Europe between the eleventh and sixteenth centuries."*[12]

In order to better understand how European religious and social history got to this point in the eleventh century we must backtrack a little, reiterating some earlier points about Jewish and Christian history. Probably the most important point to make is that prior to the Jewish people only the Persians had developed an "unshakeable conviction that they were themselves the Chosen People of the one God," a view that would be adopted by Christians in the first few centuries of the current era.[13] This is an extremely important point because it will play a large role in the early modern conflict between millenarian Christians and the powers that be. It will also inform the views of those who eventually abandoned Christian orthodoxy in exchange for a blood-thirsty *Salvationism* that could justify the killing of anyone designated an *infidel* or *apostate*.

As mentioned in a previous chapter, some members of the Jewish community began to adopt apocalyptic views in the third and second centuries BCE. Several "Prophetical Books" encouraged the Jewish people to imagine a day when Palestine would become "nothing less than Eden, a Paradise regained." One of those prophetical books was the Book of Daniel, written sometime around 165 BCE. This book served as propaganda against all the invaders of Palestine, especially the Hellenistic cultural influences brought by the Ptolemaic kingdom of Egypt. In an interesting repetition of history, this type of literature, over and over again, appealed more to the "common people" than it did to the upper classes. This was because in Palestine the upper classes tended to be advantaged by the adoption of Greek culture while the lower orders of society saw no benefit to it whatsoever. The upper classes had no reason to view the invader solely as an oppressor, and the civilizing influence of the Greeks and Romans is still evidenced today in the ruins they left behind—not to mention the continued cultural influence they have had on modern western society.[14]

The annexation of Palestine by the Romans in 63 BCE did nothing to change the general attitude of the Jewish people toward the invader. The Romans were just the latest in a series of invaders who needed to be resisted, and if possible removed. That is why the *Book of Daniel*, and the *Apocalypses of Baruch* and *Ezra*, appealed to the general population at this time. In these books a singular man was coming to rescue Jerusalem from oppression. He was sent from god, a warrior-king with miraculous

powers. Miraculous or not, the "messiah," according to most Jewish interpretations, would be only a man. Evidence for this is found as late as
131 CE when Simon bar-Cochba led the last Jewish revolt against the
Romans. Only a man, he was still "greeted as Messiah."[15] It should be
pointed out here that the Christian idea of a solely spiritual kingdom,
established through the suffering and death of the messiah, was simply
not known to the Jewish people. In fact, there is a lot of evidence to suggest that this idea developed much later among early Christians.[16]

The millenarian strain of Christian belief is evidenced as late as 156
CE when a Phrygian by the name of Montanus claimed to be the incarnation of the Holy Spirit, and predicted that the second coming of
Christ was imminent. He called all Christians to Phrygia to pray and
wait for the coming day. Even after Christ failed to make his appearance
the *Montanists*, as they became known, continued to hold to a belief
in Christ's imminent return. They were not the only ones. Several, well
known, Fathers of the Early Church like Papias (mid-second century
CE) and Iranaeus (d. 202 CE) made much of Christ's imminent return,
which may explain why they happily went to their martyrdom, according to legend. However, by the third century some were already questioning whether the established Church should subscribe to this notion
of an imminent return. The *bloody vengeance scenario* put forth by many
Christian writers,[17] such as Lactantius (c. 240 - c. 320) and Commodia-
nus (c. mid-third century CE), may have disturbed a Church hierarchy
that was becoming more integrated into what was left of a declining
Roman Empire. Church leaders, like Origen and St. Augustine, discouraged these millenarian views, and attempted to convince Christians that
the true battle took place within the soul.

Augustine wrote in his book *The City of God* (c. 410 CE) that Christians should view the *Book of Revelation* as a "spiritual allegory" which
was "fully realized in the Church." However, the millenarian strain of
Christianity would not die. This is seen in the fact that once Christians
made common cause with the state, during the time of Constantine and

after, there is a renewal of millenarian faith, but it is now directed at the emperor who is seen as the last ruler before the coming kingdom of God.

This idea of the "Emperor of the Last Days" would become popular in medieval Europe, based on what were called "Christian Sibyllines," an extension of the accepted prophetic canon in the New Testament. They were very popular *outside the organized Church*. The oldest of these writings known to us is the *Tiburtina*. It dates to sometime in the middle of the fourth century, possibly as the Roman Empire is being divided into East and West. The emphasis in the Sibyllines is always the two warrior-kings who will appear during the end of days. In the Johannine tradition it is only one warrior-king, Jesus Christ. Often a mighty emperor in these Sibyllines will have gone to sleep only to wake at some future time to battle against the Antichrist. This is a common literary device used from ancient times, and it is no surprise that the French and German dynasties throughout the Middle Ages and the early modern period used these folk tales to legitimate their own "claims to primacy."[18]

It did not take long for pretenders to take advantage of the peoples' gullibility. Throughout the medieval period many rose to prominence, claiming to be Christ, an incarnation of the Holy Spirit, or the last emperor. These individuals usually developed a following among the poor and oppressed, people who were watching their lives upended by major changes in feudal society. By the eleventh and twelfth centuries feudal traditions, hundreds of years in the making, were being quickly eroded by the rise of new commercial interests, the movement toward a *cash-nexus*, and the rebirth of the city. Reform movements within the Church also exacerbated the people's hunger for spiritual solace, since by the sixth century the Church was already on its way to becoming a thoroughly corrupt institution. The Church was challenged early and often by monastic movements like the Franciscans and Dominicans, all of which encouraged the Church to abandon its worldly claims and to focus on spiritual things. Starving for spiritual leadership the common people were especially susceptible to the message of those unassociated with the Church—now viewed by many as corrupt and beyond redemption. These voices in the wilderness claimed to speak for God, and their lives were at first a testament to that message since they were usually ascetics or impoverished shepherds. It began with individuals like *Adelbert*, an eighth-century French cleric who claimed to be a living saint. His following, like most, was short lived. In the twelfth century two individuals stand out for mention. The first is a Breton known sometimes simply as *Eon*. He claimed to be the son of God. Afterward, *Tanchelm*, a twelfth-century monk of Antwerp, led the local people in a revolt against the Church and its corruption. The latter eventually began to reign like a messianic king in Antwerp before he was finally "dethroned."[19]

It is in these examples that we can see what factors contributed to the appeal of revolutionary millenarianism. Overpopulation, rapid economic change, and social dislocation, all contributed to an overwhelming sense of helplessness and uncertainty. By the eleventh and twelfth centuries two distinct proletariats were being born: the rural and the urban. These people, who often moved from one group to another, occupied the margins of society, in a "state of chronic insecurity," and the support structure of the extended family, although still existing in the upper classes, all but disappeared among the urban proletariat. The frustration associated with this way of life had to have some outlet, especially since the Church had been working to eliminate the internecine warfare of European Christians through the establishment of the *Truce of God*.[20] This was an attempt to limit the effects of feudal warfare, especially on the civilian population. However, the most effective way to draw off the steam of the sociopolitical mixing pot of early Europe was to give the people an external enemy. Herein lies the beauty of the Crusades, the first of which was announced by Pope Urban IV in 1096. The Crusades allowed the "messianism of the poor" to be directed toward the so-called *Saracen*, who possessed to the consternation of all Christendom the *Holy Land* (Palestine). There were many crusades, half a dozen or so formally declared over a period of several hundred years. The poor streamed to individuals like *Peter the Hermit* and *Raymond of Toulouse* in order to participate in the freeing of the Holy Land. However, the carnage of the *pauperes* (the poor) did not begin upon entering Syro-Palestinian territory; it usually began with a massacre of local Jews, a practice that became almost a prerequisite for any popular crusade.[21]

It was during this time that all infidels, especially the Jew and the Muslim, were made into demonic figures. When Islam was in its ascendancy up to the tenth century it was feared by Christians that the Antichrist would turn out to be a Saracen. Much of the animosity toward the Jew was simply because they would not assimilate to European Christian culture. This made them suspect in the eyes of the dominant Christian population, which imagined all sorts of secret and anti-Christian behavior. It did not help that the Jewish community also served as money-lenders, primarily because of the Church's prohibition against lending at interest. This ban on usury (any interest-bearing loan) would eventually be ignored by Italian and German bankers, but the stigma it brought to the Jew would not abate—even in modern times.[22]

The monastic movements of the Franciscans and Dominicans, the Conciliar Movement, and the widespread movement of evangelicalism, showed that the Church could change; however, the changes were not fast enough to suit those who started the Reformation of the early sixteenth century. They were also not fast enough for the poor and downtrodden. The poor saw themselves as the natural "custodians of the eschatological mission." That is why most of the revolutionary millenarian movements, and political anarchism, of the time involved the poor, and were usually led by some self-appointed demagogue. *Frank of Neuilly* led one such movement in the late-twelfth century. This was followed by the *Children's Crusade of 1212*. All of these movements ended in sadness for those who blindly followed these impostors of long dead counts or sleeping emperors, men like *Pseudo-Baldwin* or *Bertrand of Ray*. These individuals became so numerous that they acquired their own nomenclature. They began to be called *pastoureaux* because most of them initially dressed as shepherds. These many examples teach us a central lesson of history: *beware the humble man preaching power.*

The increasing importance of trade and urban manufacturing after the eleventh century encouraged the feudal lords of Europe to abandon the sociopolitical system surrounding the manor. These lords increasingly began to prize ready cash and the luxury goods that could be bought with that cash. This radically changed the relationship between peasant and feudal lord because the social obligations of both wealthy and poor, inherent in feudalism, dissolved as serfs fled the *manse* for the city, and as feudal lords converted their lands to rental incomes. As a result of these changes the poor, who were often animated by millenarian dreams, began to direct their animus more toward the rich and powerful and less toward corrupt clerics and demonic Jews. By the mid to late fourteenth century this redirection of energy began to take the form of pure political action aimed at the specific purpose of redistributing wealth, or at least getting a little more for the poor. In this movement of the poor for a greater share of the "commonwealth" we can see the influence of eschatological tradition, a tradition that was being transformed into "a vehicle for the new radicalism." Much of this fervor, though, was dampened in France and England because of the growth of strong, centralized government. It was only in politically volatile Germany that we continue to see radical religious and political action motivated by millenarian dreams.[23]

At this point one may be asking, "Where did all this come from? After all, weren't most of these people illiterate? How were they reading these Christian Sibyllines?" Yes, it is true that the common people were largely illiterate, but by the sixteenth century this was becoming less true. However, it was not primarily through the written word that people were informed about these ideas. Preaching would have been the main source of information about these ideas, and there were plenty of people preaching various millenarian messages in the medieval period.

It is the same today. If you want to understand how apocalyptic ideas are communicated to the general population you cannot just study modern religion. You must also study modern film and literature, the chief means by which people are fed apocalypticism in all its varying forms. However, in the late medieval period preaching would have been the chief means of communicating these ideas, which is the method men like Joachim of Fiore used.

In the twelfth century Joachim of Fiore (1145-1202), a Calabrian abbot and hermit, put forth the idea that history was split into three different ages: the *Age of the Father*, the *Age of the Son*, and the *Age of the Spirit*. This view of history allowed for the development of a new millenarian idea that was both anti-ecclesiastical and ultimately secular. Joachim believed that his eschatological scheme would transpire between the year 1200 and 1260. However, once this window of time had passed Joachim's ideas were incorporated into the popular sibylline narrative. The "chastiser of the Church in the Last Days" was merged with Joachim's eschatological scheme and people began to believe that the German emperor would chastise the corrupt Church. So, in the thirteenth century many looked to the Emperor, Frederick II (1194-1250), to chastise the Church, but he died in 1250. After that a legend developed that he had gone to sleep in preparation for the day when he would awake to judge and chastise the Church.[24] Another legend associated with this one, was that *Prester John*, an oriental monarch of dubious existence, had given Frederick three magical items: an asbestos cloak, a ring that made the wearer invisible, and an elixir that would keep whoever drank it young.

It should be remembered that while all these ideas were gaining popularity in the twelfth and thirteenth centuries the Church and the state were still at loggerheads over the issue of who could appoint clergymen and invest them with their offices. This became known as the *Investiture Contest* (1075-1122) and culminated in the war between the Church and the German states, a conflict that lasted beyond the official settlement of the controversy, the *Concordat of Worms* (1122). The only thing accomplished by this war was that the German principalities and the Church were so severely weakened by the end of the thirteenth century that the French and Spanish, in turn, came to dominate them both. Due to French dominance in the fourteenth century the Church was relocated, for nearly seventy years (1309-1377), to Avignon, France. During this same time the German principalities continued to engage in nearly perpetual hostilities amongst themselves, or against others.

Amidst all the political chaos of the German states, Frederick lived on in the imagination of the German people as the "messiah of the poor," who would one day return to set everything right. These ideas were laid out in several books the first of which was called *Gamaleon* (1409 or 1439). Others like the *Reformation of Sigismund* (1439) and the *Book of a Hundred Chapters*, which was written at the beginning of the sixteenth century, continued to meld apocalyptic and sibylline ideas of a salvific future emperor. At this point the task of the emperor and his followers—mostly the poor—was to engage in an all-out war against the infidel, to massacre all who would not accept the millenarian message. These millenarian movements were usually anti-capitalist and chauvinistic, since the German people were now seen as the chosen of God whose path had been corrupted by "capitalist, inferior, non-Germanic peoples and the Church of Rome." There was a general belief that primitive German culture must be restored and that the fifth and greatest empire was to be realized through the German state, and that Mainz would be the glorious new capitol, a *Third Rome* or *New Jerusalem*. It was in this millenarian-doused history, argues Cohn, that the seed of twentieth-century German nationalism was sown. This environment gave birth to a type of millenarianism that morphed into a revolutionary model, distinguished by its belief that God had called righteous men to wet their swords with the blood of infidels and blasphemers.[25]

Also during this time of great social, economic, political, and religious upheaval, there was yet another movement that proved popular among the poor. It began in the eleventh century, often going hand-in-hand with the rise of millenarian fervor and other types of mystical hysteria. It began in Italy, among the monastic communities of Camaldoli and Fonte Avellana. However, it soon burned itself out in Italy and moved over the mountains into Germany. If millenarian faith excited one's hope for a better world that could arrive at any moment, *flagellation* was thought to bring one closer to God through the ecstatic infliction of self-mutilation. There were many events that lent themselves to the popularity of this movement. The incessant warfare in Italy and Germany, and the arrival of plague via the trade routes from the East, convinced Christians of their need for heartfelt and public penance. What better way to show one's penance than to suffer as the Lord had at the hands of the Romans? The flagellant movement was seen as a way for the community to enter into the passion of Christ by beating themselves until they bled. At one point, a flagellant group known as "the secret flagellants of Thuringia," led by one Konrad Schmid, baptized newborn babies in their own blood. This was accomplished by beating the child until he or she bled. These Cross Bearers, Flagellant Brethren, or Brethren of the Cross, had largely run their course by the time of the Protestant Reformation. However, it was then that a whole new revolutionary interpretation of apocalyptic literature came into being.[26]

Things only got more unorthodox as Gnostic-like groups developed around what became known as the "heresy of the Free Spirit." This tradition ultimately became associated with quasi-mystical anarchism and antinomianism because these groups and individuals were convinced they had grown so spiritually adept that common notions of sin did not apply to them. They were so spiritually pure that no physical act, however impure, could sully their souls. Mystical texts like *Le Mirouer des simples ames* (*The Mirror of Simple Souls*) argued that excessive sensuality was itself proof that one had passed beyond this life into "spiritual emancipation." Like Joachim of Fiore these folks broke history down into three ages, ending with the *Age of the Spirit*. However, where they differed was in their belief that each individual could experience an incarnation of that Spirit, and that at some point in the future this would be a universal experience. Within this framework heaven and hell became to them merely two different states of the soul. The final destination of the soul within the Free Spirit doctrine was to move beyond standard Christian understanding, to become a pantheist who sees himself as part of the mystical fabric of the universe. In the end they would become one with God, so in tune with the divine that there would be no real distinction between the self and God. This idea probably does not sound too unfamiliar to the modern reader, but combine these views with a millenarian eschatology and you get what Cohn argues were "amoral supermen" who could justify any amount of violence to bring about their own version of the ultimate spiritual order, as they understood it.[27]

Another idea popular among spiritualists and millenarians in the late medieval and early modern period was the notion that mankind used to live in an "egalitarian state of nature." This idea had been put forth in classical Greek and Roman literature, and adopted by the Christian Church. Ovid's *Metamorphoses*, Virgil's *Aeneid*, the philosophical treatises of the Greek Stoics, and even Clement, a father of the early Church, all agreed; there was a time when man lived in an "absolute" state of egalitarianism, which, of course, had been marred by man himself. That nearly everyone accepted this idea meant that it was easy for the Church to maintain that the "more perfect way" for a society to live was communally and in poverty. Here we see the roots of an egalitarian millennialism that would develop in the early modern period, an idea that would lend itself to modern secular utopianism. This was a central idea that animated the Romantic Movement at the turn of the eighteenth century, and the later development of communist and socialist reforms in the nineteenth century.[28]

The egalitarian ethos was exhibited in action several times during the fourteenth century. The whole idea of egalitarianism implies a society without distinctions of status and wealth. John Ball and the *English*

Peasant Revolt of 1381 exhibit just how prevalent this idea had grown in the common man's imagination by the fourteenth century. This was particularly true once the paternalism of the feudal system had been destroyed. In an early fourteenth century dialectic called the *Dialogue of Dives and Pauper* there is a clear indication that people were generally convinced that under "Goddes lawe all thynge is common." This was in contrast to the Church's official stance, which allowed for distinctions in status and wealth as long as the upper classes paid attention to the basic needs of the poor. That the powerful and wealthy were not doing an adequate job is proven by three major uprisings in the fourteenth century: the 1323 and 1328 rising of Maritime Flanders, the *Jacquerie* of 1358, and the aforementioned English Peasant Revolt.

The Bohemian Taborites provide more evidence of what happens when the strains of socio-economic dislocation are mixed with the millenarian expectations of the common people. By the middle of the fifteenth century the Taborites were calling for their lords, nobles, and knights to be hunted down like "outlaws" in the forests. John Capek, a graduate of Prague's university, said it was the "inescapable duty of the Elect to kill in the name of the Lord." The Taborite army itself was defeated in 1434 but the spirit of their movement did not die with them. One of the most celebrated, or "infamous," individuals to become the heir of revolutionary millenarianism was Thomas Müntzer. He had originally broken away from Catholic orthodoxy when he followed Martin Luther. However, as happens when religious divisions begin, Müntzer soon abandoned Luther and turned toward a more millenarian and violent strain of reform. Müntzer's actions are now seen as part of a larger revolt at the time. This movement by the lower classes has been given the historical designation *Bundschuh*, which is the German equivalent of the French Revolution's *sans-cullote*, the difference being that the first referred to a type of shoe while the latter referred to pants—or a lack thereof.

Müntzer's "League of the Elect" proclaimed that "the ungodly have

no right to live" and even after Müntzer's death in May 1525 the revolutionary millenarian movement continued to live on in a group of
believers who called themselves Anabaptists. Jan Bockelson, an early
modern European version of David Koresh,[29] and better known to history as John of Leyden, led the town of Münster (not to be confused
with Thomas above) against the forces of Lutheran and Catholic princes.
These forces were seen by Leyden and his followers as the attendants
of the Antichrist. In 1534 Leyden and his followers took over the town
of Münster and established their own version of egalitarian primitiv-
ism with a heavy overtone of millenarian expectation. They claimed
that Münster would be the New Jerusalem and that the end of time was
about to occur. Anyone not in the city of Münster at that time would be
killed. The town was eventually besieged while Leyden made himself
into a messianic warrior-king. The depredations to which he subjected
the city were not only sensual but often inhumane. His appeal soon wore
off and he had to flee the city. John of Leyden was captured and executed
in 1537.[30]

What this history shows us is that the apocalyptic tradition survived
the Church's attempt to curtail what some have called the "imannentiz-
ing of the eschaton."[31] Socio-economic and political changes that were
revolutionizing Europe throughout the late medieval and early modern
period helped to sustain and bolster an interest in apocalyptic themes,
especially among the poor. The millenarian dream was stripped of all
moral inhibition in the late medieval period, and that allowed men to
believe that it was justified to slaughter all who stood in the way of establishing a God-centered, egalitarian world. Cohn argues that revolutionary and millenarian zeal is perpetuated by social and economic upheaval and for this reason "revolutionary millenarianism and mystical
anarchism are with us still," albeit stripped of its "religious idiom."[32]

We will extend Cohn's argument when we examine the history of
the United States in chapter thirteen. From its origins as a British colony
to its present-day pre-eminence as a military, economic, and political

power, we will learn that what has been called *American Exceptionalism* is ultimately rooted in a secularized millenarianism built on the foundation of political liberty and self-determination, seen as gifts bestowed by God upon the faithful. We will also examine why this is ultimately problematic when it comes to addressing the issue of what we have called *the culture of fear.*

The transition to the secular model begins in the sixteenth and seventeenth centuries with the work of luminaries like Copernicus and Galileo. It continues throughout the seventeenth century with Newton and others. By the eighteenth century we can speak of a full-fledged secular *Enlightenment* pushed forward by the development of the modern, secular nation-state. The separation of church and state is a relatively new idea, and even in its early infancy the United States was not a completely secular state. They were still animated by the notion that they had been chosen by God—a leftover of their Puritan heritage which had been reinforced by two national "Great Awakenings." However, by the end of the Revolutionary War "civic millennialism," which was a largely secular interpretation of Christian prophecy, had come to dominate American social thinking. This was true even in the South where the distinctive strain of race-tinged premillennialism, mixed with the notion that the South would rise again, only came into being after the Civil War. It was this milieu, this mixing of religious and secular political ideas, that helps to explain the modern conundrum of "the culture of fear," but before we get to this we must examine a little deeper how utopianism and science merged in the eighteenth century.

Chapter Twelve

The Utopianism of Science

Scientific progress makes moral progress a necessity; for if man's power is increased, the checks that restrain him from abusing it must be strengthened.

Madame de Stael

In the last few chapters we have engaged in something of a *tour de force* from the ancient world to the beginning of the early modern period, roughly 1600 CE. Now we must fill in another historical gap extending from approximately 1600 to 1800 CE. This will get us to the point where we can analyze the role of the United States in world history, and assess the influence that Christian apocalyptic thinking has had on that role. We will also explore how each of us—even without the benefit of direct and conscious religious experience—has been exposed to all of these ideas through literature and film. I should apologize ahead of time to those who know history, since the following is just a brief overview and I have simplified things for the sake of brevity. Still, I believe I have captured the *spirit of the age.*

As you read this chapter keep the following general history in mind. The Renaissance was a "rebirth" of classical learning, art, and architecture. This movement was not anti-religious or anti-Christian, and the humanist movement it morphed into later was embraced by the community of Christian scholars who dominated the Church-based university system of Europe. It was only when scientists began to question the works of Aristotle—which had become virtually Church doctrine—that they got into trouble. Some scientists began to insist that the universe operated, for the most part, on its own, and with very little intervention by God. This perturbed a Church sensitive to the development of any competing cosmological explanation, especially any cosmology that took God out of the equation.

The Scientific Revolution, involving names we have all heard: Copernicus, Galileo, and Newton, continued to diminish the role of God in the world until, eventually, the *Deism* of the Enlightenment largely replaced the intimate and jealous God of Christianity. Philosophers, scientists, politicians, statesmen, and capitalists would abandon the God of *pathos* for a *clockmaker*. It was upon Enlightenment principles that a few dozen men built a new nation at the end of the eighteenth century, but they had to do so within the constraints of a society that still held dearly not only to the God of fire but to the promised return of Eden here on earth. However, before we can move forward to consider the apocalyptic history of United States we must travel once again backwards in time. For, every social, intellectual, and political advance is preceded by another, a different age with differing principles, even if they may overlap in many ways. There is always an individual or two that occupies that area between the known and the unknown. In geographical development we call him the *frontiersmen*. In intellectual pursuits we call them *paradigm shifters*.[1]

The same was true of the Renaissance. The intellectuals who preceded the Renaissance were known as *Scholastics*. These were Church-educated individuals committed to a paradigm consisting of *a priori* assumptions, usually rooted in Christian theology, and connected by logical conclusions that resulted from organizing all Christian thought into a holistic system. Until the beginning of the sixteenth century the Roman Church dominated the intellectual and social life of Europeans, which is why Scholasticism held such sway prior to the Protestant Reformation, the Scientific Revolution, and the Enlightenment.

Within the Scholastic tradition there were several different competing paradigms, but "Thomism" was the dominant school of thought within the Scholastic tradition after the fourteenth century. This tradition started with Thomas Aquinas (1225-1274) who in the thirteenth century attempted to organize all Christian thought in his *Summa Theologica*, written between 1265 and 1274. This book was meant to be a primer for all those interested in questions like "How can we know that God exists?" or "What is the purpose of man?" To all these questions Aquinas gave what he thought were well-reasoned answers. He also tried to reconcile biblical thinking with the pagan philosophy of Aristotle (384-322 BCE). The latter was attempted in his work *Summa contra Gentiles*, written around 1264. The latter can be viewed as a sort of *grand unified theory*, an attempt to integrate theology with all the other sciences (*scientia* = knowledge). Aquinas's work was initially condemned by Etienne Tempier, a bishop of Paris, but by the fourteenth century Aquinas was made a saint and in the mid-sixteenth century he was declared a Doctor of the Church (*Doctor Angelici*). Even today the Thomistic intellectual spirit inspires Catholic thought and teaching. Pope Pius X (1835-1914) declared in his *Doctoris Angelici*, on June 29, 1914, that no Catholic could understand the teachings of the Church outside the framework of Thomistic teachings.

It is not difficult to understand what was happening here in the centuries leading up to the secular and religious events that would result in the diminishment of the Church's social and intellectual influence. As mentioned several times already, by the end of the eleventh century the Church was involved in a full-blown battle over who would control the appointment and investment of certain Church offices. It was at this same time that Pope Urban IV called the first crusade. A little over a century later, at the Fourth Lateran Council (1215), the Church continued to narrow its definition of orthodoxy and began to persecute those who would not conform. It was shortly after this council that the Dominican-led *Inquisition* began to systematically hunt down and torture Jews and heretics. However, the Church could not stop the tide of secularism, especially since it was largely goaded by commercial and materialist considerations. By the end of the fourteenth century, as the

Papacy returned from Avignon to Rome, they found themselves a political shadow of their former self, and then came the Renaissance.

The Renaissance, which lasted from approximately the mid-fifteenth century to the mid-sixteenth century, saw a "rebirth" of interest in ancient and classical learning, art, and architecture. This movement was still within the Thomist intellectual tradition of the Church, but eventually "Christian humanism" and "secular humanism" would be seen as two distinct pursuits. Allen G. Debus gives us a brief history of this movement in his book *Man and Nature in the Renaissance* (1978). Debus shows that there was a clear desire on the part of Christian scholars to glorify God through their discoveries. At the same time Europe was going through a process of cultural integration, even as the lines of nation-states were beginning to be drawn because of hardening ethnic identity. John Hale in his book *The Civilization of Europe in the Renaissance* (1994) points out that Europe was developing a larger sense of sociocultural identity during the Renaissance, largely centered on the growing influence of centralized power in the royal courts of Europe. It did not hurt that Europeans also had a common enemy in the Muslim Ottoman Empire, which had as recently as 1453 captured the eastern Christian empire of Byzantium. Yes, these individuals were the wayward Orthodox cousins of the Roman Catholics, but they were still Christians, members of what was becoming known as *Christendom*. It was also around this time that the great artistic improvements of Rome began under the patronage of wealthy families like the Borgias and the Medici, a patronage still enjoyed today by those who visit the Eternal City.

The Church, though, was not willing to give up completely. Even with the secularizing spirit of the Renaissance and the religious challenge of Protestants, the Church still found itself able to command kings and emperors, as well as millions of the faithful. It was only by chance that two of the most Catholic kingdoms of Europe, Portugal and Spain, took the lead in the oceanic discoveries of the fifteenth and sixteenth centuries. These two countries came to dominate African, Asian, and American trade in the sixteenth century and the first half of the seventeenth century. They did so with the blessing of the Catholic Church, which used these discoveries as an opportunity to add new souls to the Church. The Church would also leverage their influence with the Spanish and Portuguese crowns to continue exerting some force over the intellectual developments of Europe. The most celebrated case in which the Church directly challenged the growth of science was probably that involving Galileo and his promotion of Copernicus's solar-centric world.[2]

Galileo Galilei (1564-1642) initially published his *Dialogue Concerning the Two Chief World Systems* (1632) with the approval of the Church. However, upon closer examination some began to complain about the potential heresy of the work. The book placed the solar-centric world of Nicholas Copernicus (1473-1543) against the earth-centric view of Ptolemy (90-160 CE). The famous trial of Galileo in 1633 is often viewed as a blatant attack on the nascent Scientific Revolution. The Church maintained, as did their approved second-century astronomer Ptolemy, that it was the sun and all the other planets that revolved around the earth. This theological and astronomical principle could be found in Joshua's command for the sun to stop in its course across the sky so that he could defeat the Amorites. (Joshua 10:12-13)

If empirical astronomy was questioning something clearly laid out in scripture then it was the obligation of faithful Catholics to choose the scriptures over what could be known through observation. An anecdote about the Jesuits is illustrative here. It is said that Jesuit astronomers refused to look through Galileo's telescope in order to see the mountains on the earth's moon or to see moons of Jupiter. What had already been written was good enough for them. They needed no physical proof for or against it. This attitude of the Church is what forced Galileo to recant in 1633, after which he was placed under house arrest until his death.

The Church initially embraced the work being done by humanists and early scientists, but by the early seventeenth century—probably exacerbated by the success of the Protestant Reformation—the Church began to grow suspicious of science, which was slowly breaking away from the confines of Thomism. This was all part of the process historians call the Scientific Revolution. The Church's view was that science was fine as long as it continued to reinforce scripture's notion that nature revealed the work of God. Theology was thought to be the "Queen of the Sciences." All other knowledge (*scientia*) was meant to serve the purposes of theology. However, when some scientists began to suggest that God was not necessary to explain the natural world, things got tense. The age-old assumption was that God could be revealed in his creation. The Apostle Paul spoke of it in his letter to the Romans (1:19-20). The idea is also found in Psalm 19:1, where it says, "The heavens declare the glory of God; and the firmament sheweth his handywork."

The Church could not stop the progress of science. Science continued to move forward into it was full-blown intellectual revolution. That revolution began with Isaac Newton's *Philosophiae Naturalis Principia Mathematica* (1687). Newton (1642-1727) was born the same year that Galileo died. His greatest claim to fame was his development of Calculus (contemporary with Leibniz's own independent discovery) and his mathematization of physics and astronomy. This was part of a process that had begun during the Renaissance, a process to which Nicholas Copernicus, Tycho Brahe (1546-1601), Johannes Kepler (1571-1630), and Galileo had contributed. Newton had, as he said, "stood on the shoulder of giants" in order to make his contributions to science. Of course, this was only in the area of physics and astronomy. There were other areas of knowledge that also grew by leaps and bounds during this time.

In biology Andreas Vesalius (1514-1564) began the modern movement toward our understanding of human anatomy while William Harvey (1578-1657) discovered the process by which blood flowed through the body. Both of these new discoveries upset the accepted works of Galen (129-200 CE). In Chemistry Robert Boyle (1627-1691) discovered the inverse relationship between the volume and pressure of gases, a concept with widespread scientific and technological import. Boyle represents an interesting example of one of those individuals who straddles two separate worlds. While Boyle was a contributor to the modern age of science he was still fascinated by *alchemy*, the notion that one could transmute a base metal into a precious metal through a process not wholly physical. Rene Descartes (1596-1650) also represents another transitional figure. His contributions to philosophy—like his famous *cogito ergo sum*—are equally matched by his contributions to mathematics. Descartes' analytical geometry made Newton and Leibniz's discovery of the Calculus possible. Descartes also claimed to be a devout Catholic, but nothing in his philosophical or mathematical work justifies such an assertion. He was most likely a Deist, like many of his fellow intellectuals at the time.

These men of science straddled the world between superstition and knowledge. Boyle was not the only one intrigued by alchemistry and theology. It is said that Newton actually wrote more about theology than he ever did about physics and astronomy. Newton was intrigued by Christian eschatology, frequently trying to figure out when the prophecies of the Bible would be fulfilled. If anything distinguishes these men from the philosophers and scientists of the eighteenth and nineteenth century it is their view of God. The subsequent era, which we call the Enlightenment, although having its roots in the Renaissance and the Scientific Revolution, is distinctive in its commitment to what some have called the "clockwork God," a demiurge unconcerned with the daily lives of those who are the product of his creation. The Masons, associated with the building trades, would call God the "Grand Architect." Is it any wonder that the early followers of Yahweh, who were themselves shepherds, referred to their lord in heaven as a shepherd? (Psalm 23:1)

As with the Renaissance and Scientific Revolution there was overlap in the transition from the early modern to the modern world. The "Age of Enlightenment" was less a concerted effort than it was a confluence of forces, often associated with the work of individuals like Baruch Spinoza (1632-1677), John Locke (1632-1704), and Voltaire (1694-1778). Each of these men, along with many others, contributed to the *spirit of the age* (*zeitgeist*). It was an intellectual spirit that saw God—if he existed at all—as uninvolved with his creation, and the world as a self-operating mechanism that could be reduced to basic principles and mathematical formulas. Probably nothing represented this spirit better than the work of Denis Diderot (1713-1784). His *Encyclopédie* (published between 1752 and 1772) was a compendium of everything that was then known or becoming known. In other words, there was a general belief that mankind would eventually conquer what could be known, and that things which could not be known, things like metaphysics, were not much worth knowing anyway.

Modern atheism was largely unknown in early modern Europe. As Lucien Febvre argues in his book *The Problem of Unbelief in the Sixteenth Century* (1937), the idea that people in the sixteenth century could believe in nothing is an anachronism. Atheism in the sixteenth century was defined not necessarily as disbelief but rather as immorality. One might say that an atheist was one whose belief did not rise to the level of keeping one on the straight and narrow. It is only in the modern era that we get the idea of modern unbelief, as presented in famous literary treatments like Dostoyevsky's Grand Inquisitor, who concludes in the end that if God does not exist then "everything is permissible." This is still a common misconception of those who fear the modern atheist. At the beginning of the Enlightenment atheism would be a word applied to Deists like Spinoza and later Thomas Jefferson, even though these individuals did believe in a supreme, conscious being of some kind.

The most important contribution which the Enlightenment philosophers and scientists contributed to society was the idea that man could shape his own destiny through reason and science. Carl Becker explores this idea in his book *The Heavenly City of the Eighteenth-Century Philosophers* (1932). The main thesis of Becker's book is that the Enlightenment philosophers of the eighteenth century were actually products of a medieval education, and that they replaced the religious idea of the *City of God* with their own mathematical and reason-worshipping *City of Man*. Of course, this sowed the seeds of overweening optimism in science and in mankind's own ability to control his destiny. As John Gray has written,

> The decline of Christianity and the rise of revolutionary utopianism go together. When Christianity was rejected, its eschatological hopes did not disappear. They were repressed, only to return as projects of universal emancipation.[3]

We will return to this idea in the next chapter as we explore the topic of American Exceptionalism.

It is difficult to ferret out how much of this scientific utopianism was a result of scientific dreaming or merely the popularization of scientific ideas by amateur scientists. In Rene Dubos's *The Dreams of Reason: Science and Utopias* (1961) the author addresses the same subject as Becker with a little different slant. Dubos writes that as science moved *from learning to doing* there was what he called a "narrow-minded intellectual arrogance" that seemed to take hold of the scientific establishment but most scientists continued to understand the limits of their knowledge.[4] Lewis Mumford addresses the same question in his book *The Myth of the Machine* (1970) where he argues that the technological advances that science has made possible in the modern world has given mankind the conviction that progress is unlimited. So, modern man is convinced that what is possible should also be desirable regardless of the consequences. We touched on this topic earlier when we discussed what Neil Postman termed "technopoly."

Scientists have not always been the best communicators. Therefore, it is no surprise that individuals like Sir Francis Bacon (1561-1626) would have greater influence on the western *zeitgeist* than say a Lavoisier or Fermat. Two works published by Bacon in the early seventeenth century set the stage for the way the western world would come to view science and technology. *Novum Organum* (1620) was a treatise on inductive logic and established the general principle that all scientific endeavors should involve observation (*empiricism*). With this work Bacon was challenging the Scholastic method, wedded too intimately to syllogisms based on *a priori* assumptions. Bacon's next publication *New Atlantis* (1627) was meant to illustrate through fiction what kind of society could be built with a proper appreciation for right religion, science, and technology. Bacon's novel is a continuation of utopian writing going back as far as Plato's *Republic* (c. 380 BCE) and directly influenced by Thomas More's *Utopia* (1516). This whole notion of utopia would later be ridiculed by Voltaire in his novel *Candide* (1759), where the overly sanguine Dr. Pangloss claims that "all is for the best in the best of all possible worlds."

It would be incorrect to say that all Enlightenment figures were easily bowled over by the magnificent possibilities of science. As mentioned just above, Voltaire (1694-1778) took pains to burst the balloon of those who sought to impose on society a secular, science-based utopianism. Voltaire was not the only one to question this type of utopianism. Jean-Jacques Rousseau (1712-1778) would also point out why this type of utopianism was not possible in his book *Of the Social Contract, Or Principles of Political Right* (1762). Although, he would make his point by arguing that an equally dubious primitive and egalitarian utopianism once existed in the distant past. Rousseau argued that an elysian-like society had once existed prior to the development of the chain-ridden, hierarchical system of modern society, and that modern forms of government should take note of this because it was a fact that argued for the "general will" of the people in government, i.e., democracy. Voltaire and Rousseau were not the only ones to question the merits of a secular utopia. Many religious leaders during the first half of the eighteenth century were also critical of this secular vision.

Several leaders within the Anglican and other Protestant churches rose up to challenge the coldness of the Enlightenment's God, a God that could not satisfy the passionate needs of the human soul, a God that had no personal concern for each individual, even if that concern was in the form of threatening his creation with hellfire. In England and the British colonies of America the First Great Awakening of the 1730s and 1740s can be seen as a reaction to the Enlightenment and reason. Jonathan Edwards (1703-1758), George Whitefield (1714-1770), and the brothers John (1703-1791) and Charles (1707-1788) Wesley, were all involved in calling the general population back to the fold of traditional faith. The latter three were also instrumental in the creation of Methodism, which became one of the most popular denominations in the United States, next to the Baptists. These evangelical preachers challenged the existing hierarchy since they were not traditional religionists who supported Anglican, Presbyterian, Episcopal, or Congregational organizations. These were the denominations of the establishment. This *awakening* was a revival movement with all the associated anti-intellectualism and inveighing against institutional corruption. The historian Nathan Hatch has even suggested that this evangelical movement may have later solidified support for the American Revolution because the American British colonies could be seen through the eyes of religionists as part of a group that was resisting corrupt leaders in the form of King George III and Parliament.[5]

The Methodist and Baptist denominations began to dominate the religious experience of Americans, especially in western areas of the United States, where expansion was quick. This began in the late eighteenth century and has continued until the present day, with several lulls along the way. We will deal with this in more detail in the next chapter, but suffice to say here that the American Revolution both animated religious sentiment and was animated by it. Each contributed to a political ecosystem where liberty, both political and religious, came to be the single most important issue for Americans. The United States rediscovered, albeit in mostly secular form, that vision of a "city on a hill," a light of liberty to the rest of the world. They believed their cause not only just but part of a grand, divine scheme. These traditional Christians, though, were not the only ones to challenge the dominant materialist themes of the Enlightenment.

At the end of the eighteenth century the Romantic reaction to what Wordsworth referred to as the Enlightenment's proclivity to "murder" in order "to dissect" was becoming more pronounced. This was a whole-sale reaction to what became known as *reductionism*. The rest of Words-worth's poem is a paean to Romantic sentiment. We should not dissect, jar, or catalogue the world; we must simply let nature sweep over us, we should take it in whole, and alive. As Wordsworth writes at the end of his famous poem "The Tables Turned,"

> Enough of Science and of Art;
> Close up those barren leaves;
> Come forth, and bring with you a heart
> That watches and receives.[6]

This was the reaction to the cold, vivisected worldview of the scientist and the mathematician. Romantics rejected the notion that humanity, or nature in general, could be reduced to mere numbers. They thought there was more to nature, that there was an *elan vital*, a "great chain of being," and that we dismissed it at our own peril. There would always be, the Romantic argued, an ineffable quality to life, a quality that simply could not be captured and studied by science.

Many rejected the *overemphasis* of reason but not reason itself, and not just because they were orthodox Christians. In fact, many of them were considered well outside the mainstream of orthodoxy. William Blake (1757-1827) is a good example of a non-sectarian, who opposed all organized religion but who adhered to an almost Gnostic version of Christianity. He opposed what he thought was an excessive emphasis on rationalism in the eighteenth and nineteenth centuries. His art and poetry challenged the rational, Newtonian, and Enlightenment view of the world, as captured in the following verses of his most famous poem:

> Tyger! Tyger! burning bright
> In the forests of the night,

What immortal hand or eye
Could frame thy fearful symmetry?[7]

Implied here is the notion that even creation exceeds the Immortal's own ability to understand. This pantheistic view of nature is quite in contrast to the God of Job, who challenges anyone to question his status as creator of the universe.[8]

A contemporary of Blake's, the German writer Johann Wolfgang von Goethe (1749-1832), saw the world in much the same way. Goethe's two most celebrated works, *Faust* (c. 1806-1808) and *The Sorrows of Young Werther* (1774), are both commentaries on mankind's inability to free itself from human passion and ego, problems that often lead to either the loss of the soul or suicide. Goethe has a quote that gives us insight into the Romantic mind. He writes, "He who possesses art and science has religion; he who does not possess them, needs religion." This shows that the Romantics did not reject science. They rejected the idea that scientific and technological endeavors could be engaged in willy-nilly, without any thought about the consequences for society or the soul.

Another English writer, Mary Shelley (1797-1851), commented through fiction on the inability of men to appreciate the awesome power that science had laid at mankind's feet. Her *Frankenstein, or, The Modern Prometheus* is not so much a tale of horror, as it is in some modern movie versions. It is a cautionary tale about placing too much power in the hands of those without the wisdom to deal with it. The novel is not really about the monster. It is about Viktor (Dr. Frankenstein) who through science makes himself into a "modern Prometheus," an individual who in Greek mythology stole fire (*fire = technology*) from the gods and gave it to man. Through a series of other events related to this theft Pandora's Box is opened, releasing all sorts of misery on mankind. For his crime Prometheus was chained to a rock, and an eagle would come each day and eat at his liver. It would then grow back so the process could be repeated the following day. For Viktor's transgression, he loses everything he holds dear and dies while hunting down his own creation.

The Romantics were not the first to warn against knowledge and technology being placed in the wrong hands. The Greeks had warned of the destructive potential of technology when they told the story of Daedalus and his son, Icarus. The latter learned the hard way what happens when you put technology in the hands of individuals who do not possess the wisdom to use it. In this story Daedalus makes two sets of wings, a pair for himself and another for his son. The wings are made of feathers and wax. Before they set off from Crete, where they are being held captive, Daedalus tells Icarus not to fly too high or the sun will melt the wax and make his wings ineffective. Overcome by the glory of flight Icarus forgets his father's warning, flying ever closer to the sun. The wax melts, the feathers fall out, and Icarus plunges into the sea and drowns. The lesson: *tragedy awaits those who blithely adopt every technological development that comes their way.*

The Romantic reaction to Enlightenment hubris was not enough to stop the juggernaut of science and technology. The religious reaction was also not enough to slow things down. While traditional Christians might have rejected the cosmological conclusions of eighteenth-century science they could not help but embrace the technology that grew out of that intellectual milieu. This technology was instrumental, especially in the United States and Britain, in creating unprecedented concentrations of wealth, a wealth that seemed for a time open to many. Christians, especially in the northern United States, also embraced science because they still believed it proved the glory of God. The Deists would come to be seen as allies when compared to the modern, "godless" Darwinist. However, before that happened, the United States had to be forged from a political and social revolution decades in the making. That revolution would be the product of Enlightenment optimism mixed with a jaundiced view of mankind's moral nature, and that is the subject of the next chapter.

Chapter Thirteen

The Apple of His Eye

Keep me as the apple of the eye, hide me under the shadow of thy wings....

Psalm 17:8

By the end of the eighteenth century western society had gained a considerable amount of self-confidence, a confidence that even permeated the religious world. In the last chapter we talked about those who critiqued the Enlightenment, those who stood against an overzealous faith in reason and science, but the truth is that most people stood firmly on the side of scientific, social, and political progress.

The eighteenth-century Congregationalist minister Samuel Hopkins believed that technology would play a chief role in releasing mankind from his material burdens, giving him the leisure he needed to commune more often and more deeply with the divine. In a 1793 work entitled *A Treatise on the Millennium*, Hopkins suggested that technology would be instrumental in the gradual institution of the kingdom of God, which would only be realized when everyone on earth was a true Christian. Hopkins did not believe that the kingdom of God would be realized quickly or through supernatural intervention, which is why he and most Revolutionary-era Americans were firmly in the *post-millennial* camp.

Hopkins also rejected the *pre-millennial* notion that "carnal Israel"[1] would have to be restored to its status as a nation before Christian prophecy could be fulfilled. This was nonsense, as far as he was concerned. The kingdom of God, according to Hopkins, and most early nineteenth century Christians, would only be implemented through a completely spiritual process, which would require universal Christian conversion.[2]

It is not difficult to see how this view could easily support what has been called "civic" or "civil" millennialism, a belief that the state could be organized to serve the purposes of God here on earth, as long as it was dominated by believing Christians.[3] It should also come as no surprise that Hopkins was an early opponent of African slavery. The "Spiritualist" view of the coming millennial kingdom of God was consistent with the notion of universal brotherhood. In 1776 Hopkins wrote *A Dialogue concerning the Slavery of the Africans, showing it to be the Duty and Interest of the American States to emancipate all their African Slaves.* The title says it all.

This view, which had been shared for decades among northern and southern clergy, would grow into the American Anti-Slavery Movement, a movement that would contribute in no small part to the social, religious, and political division of the country, and to the start of the American Civil War.

The takeaway here is that at the end of the eighteenth century and the beginning of the nineteenth century Americans were generally forward-looking and rejected the standard *millenarian* version of Christian prophecy, a millenarianism that emphasized God's action over man's inaction. This was not true of all since many American millenarian groups did form in the 1830s and 1840s, chief among them the Millerites (Seventh-day Adventists) and the Latter Day Saints (Mormons). However, these groups were still only forming at the fringes of society. For example, in New York State's "burned-over district," an area that had experienced extensive religious agitation in the early days of the Second Great Awakening from 1790 to 1870, several millenarian groups came into being. Those mentioned just above both fit within Michael Barkun and Norman Cohn's theories about millenarian group formation. These groups thrived in environments where there was increasing social dislocation, and where there was what Michael Barkun called "decremental deprivation." This type of deprivation occurs when people are unable to *keep up with the Jones's*, when expectations become more difficult to realize, either because the expectations are unrealistic or the environment does not allow those expectations to be realized.[4]

So, religious agitation was not the only reason millenarianism began to appeal to segments of society in the second quarter of the nineteenth century. The United States was in a constant state of flux exhibited by the social, political, and economic changes that were occurring throughout the first half of the nineteenth century. To understand how dramatically American society was changing one merely has to examine the move westward, the huge influx of immigrants in the 1830s and 1840s, the growth of industry, and the growing fear among southerners that their way of life was being threatened by forces beyond their control. There were simply a lot of people who as a result of American social and economic dynamism felt left behind.[5]

During the Second Great Awakening there was a huge increase in church membership among all denominations, but especially among the Methodists and Baptists. These two popular denominations would eventually split into northern and southern confessions by the 1840s, primarily because of their differences over the question of slavery. Even then, though, there was general agreement among these splintering denominations about how the kingdom of God would be established: it would be gradual, it would *not* involve the re-establishment of old Israel, and the state would play a major role in its consummation.[6]

This is one of the reasons American religious history becomes complicated just before the Civil War, because northern and southern clergy generally held the same eschatological views before the war, but they differed in the way they thought the kingdom of God would be implemented, especially what role African slavery would play in the coming kingdom. It might be difficult for the modern Christian to accept but most southern clergy had no problem imagining that the kingdom God would be led by the United States and that African slavery would continue to exist. By the 1850s, as many were arguing that slavery was a "positive good," southern clergymen like William Gannaway Brownlow were arguing that slavery was an institution that would continue to exist even after God's kingdom had been realized on earth. The reason for this is that southern clergymen by the 1850s conceived of the kingdom of God in far more parochial and earthy terms. The northern clergy believed the kingdom of God would be implemented through universal Christian conversion while southerners believed the kingdom of God would be established by political Christian elites who would rule over the "infidel."[7] For southerners there was clearly less cognitive dissonance in this view.

So, how did things get this way in the United States by the second quarter of the nineteenth century? We have read previously about how the Catholic Church had kept millenarianism at bay through its own interpretation of prophecy, an *amillennial* (allegorical) interpretation that made the Church the prime mover in the gradual realization of the kingdom of God on earth. The Protestant Reformation had freed millions of people from the social and religious control of the Catholic Church, but for the most part Protestant Christians did not abandon the post-millennial view, they merely exchanged the Church for the state as the primary agent of change. The "Christian state," whether in the form of a universal community of believers or a government led by the political elite, would now be the means by which the kingdom of God would be established on the earth.

To understand where this idea came from we must go back to mid-seventeenth-century England when these ideas were exported along with the emigration of the Puritans to what would be called New England. It was during this time that particular interest in the restoration of the Jewish people to their homeland began to agitate the prophetically minded. According to many prophecy watchers, the restoration of the Jewish people to Palestine signified that the end would soon come. There were even those who thought they could expedite the coming of the kingdom of God through the conversion of souls, and still others who thought they might be able to establish the kingdom of God through a Christian takeover of government. So, the restoration of Israel was not always interpreted literally. It was more often interpreted to mean that an existing government, like England's, was a new "spiritual" Israel. So, thought some, by establishing a theocratic government in England it would be possible to spiritually restore Israel to power and immediately inaugurate the kingdom of God. Writers like Joseph Mede, Thomas Brightman, and John Colton trumpeted this idea. What is significant here is that people continued to accept the common notion that a Christian-led government would be at the forefront of the literal fulfillment of Christian prophecy—not a new idea, as we have seen.

This type of millennial fervor reached its apex in England during the 1640s.[8] This is when a cadre of zealous Puritan revolutionaries attempted to set up a theocracy during one of England's civil wars. These individuals were called the Fifth Monarchy Men because they thought they were establishing the everlasting fifth kingdom, which was spoken of in Daniel 7:26-27:

> But the court shall be seated,
> And they shall take away his dominion,
> To consume and destroy it forever.
> Then the kingdom and dominion,
> And the greatness of the kingdoms under the whole heaven,
> Shall be given to the people, the saints of the Most High.
> His kingdom is an everlasting kingdom,
> And all dominions shall serve and obey Him.

There are similarities here to the accounts given in the Christian Sibyllines, which were mentioned in a previous chapter. Pay particular attention to the line about how the "greatness of the kingdoms...shall be given to the people, the saints of the Most High." On that one line stood much of what has been called *post-millennialism*.

The Fifth Monarchy Men built on this idea of post-millennialism. They were a small, radical group within the larger English Puritan movement. They were all persecuted, and like all ideologically-oriented groups there were some who were always less flexible than others. In general, though, all Puritans roundly criticized the Anglican Church for not going far enough in stripping itself of Catholic influences. They wanted to get rid of things like music and iconography, and they opposed the centralized control of the Church, especially any control by the state, which had been established in England with the *Act of Supremacy* (1559). Like many radical Christian movements they wanted England to return to a more *primitive* Christianity.[9] The Fifth Monarchy Men—and Puritans in general—saw themselves as the saints of God, the New Israel, or as the *chosen* nation of God whose task was to make the world fit for Christ's return. Many believed that before the second coming of Christ could take place, and before the kingdom could be established, that the whole world had to have at least one chance to hear the gospel. How else could God hold them accountable?

There were other radical groups that existed at the time: the Diggers, Levellers, and Ranters, but the Fifth Monarchists were the most extreme example of the fusion of millennialism and politics.[10] Oliver Cromwell, the Lord Protector of England, disavowed the extreme theocratic agenda of the Fifth Monarchy Men and quickly earned their enmity, but the group was too small to effectively oppose Cromwell. After Cromwell died in 1658, and the English restored Charles II to the throne in 1660, the Fifth Monarchy Men disappeared into obscurity within two decades. However, their ideas lived on in various degrees within other millennially-oriented groups. The most familiar was the British Israel movement. This movement consisted of people who thought the British people were descended from the ten lost tribes of Israel. These ten tribes, according to legend, had been scattered to the four winds during the Assyrian invasion of Palestine in 720 BCE. We still do not know where these tribes ended up, and it is still the subject of much speculation.

Prior to the English Civil War (1642-1651) some Puritans sailed for

America with the intention of establishing a godly community, "a city set on a hill." They still believed that England could be redeemed as a nation, they only needed an example. The colonial Puritans were determined to show their wayward brethren back in England what kind of government could be built by a community of the faithful. Edward Johnson (1599-1672) had come to America in 1630 on the *Arbella*, along with John Winthrop. So, Johnson's *The Wonder-Working Providence of Sion's Saviour* (1654) displays the level of animosity which this group had toward the English crown.[11] The opening paragraph of his work lays it all out plainly:

> When England began to decline in Religion, like lukewarme Laodicea,[12] and instead of purging out Popery, a farther compliance was sought not onely in vaine Idolatrous Ceremonies, but also in prophaning the Sabbath, and by Proclamation throughout their Parish churches, exasperating lewd and prophane persons to celebrate a Sabbath like the Heathen to Venus, Baccus and Ceres; in so much that the multitude of irreligious lascivious and popish affected persons spred the whole land like Grashoppers, in this very time Christ the glorious King of his Churches, raises an Army out of our English Nation, for freeing his people from their long servitude under usurping Prelacy; and because every corner of England was filled with the fury of malignant adversaries, Christ creates a New England to muster up the first of his Forces in; Whose low condition, little number, and remotenesse of place made these adversaries triumph, despising this day of small things, but in this hight of their pride the Lord Christ brought sudden, and unexpected destruction upon them.[13] Thus have you a touch of the time when this worke began.

This Puritan animosity lasted for a generation or two, but Puritan faith and reform-mindedness waned with time. Puritan society changed dramatically after the first few generations as more attention was directed toward material concerns. When they arrived Puritans believed they had been divinely chosen to establish a colony for God. That belief never really diminished, even as adherence to certain doctrines became less important. They did, however, change their view about what role they would play on the world stage. They had begun with the wilderness motif—a type of Israel's wandering through the desert. That was the overriding metaphor for their spiritual experience in the New World, about which the historian Sacvan Bercovitch has written extensively.

The wilderness motif proved extremely important to the identity that Americans would adopt for themselves. This motif, and the accompanying tradition of the *jeremiad*, kept fresh in the minds of Americans their unique position as the chosen of God. A jeremiad was a call to repentance, an exhortation to return to godly obedience. Both the Old and New Worlds had jeremiads, but they differed in that America's always had a happy ending. Affliction from God was not punishment but reproof.[14] The American jeremiad was always meant as chastisement to bring the children of God back to obedience. It was seen as the application of discipline for their own good.[15] In time, though, the American Puritans went from pilgrims wandering through a wilderness to the chosen people of God occupying a new Canaan.

Samuel Danforth (1626-1674), a seventeenth-century preacher and poet, epitomizes the use of the jeremiad. Danforth's *A Brief Recognition of New England's Errand into the Wilderness* (1670) uses the wilderness as a rhetorical device. With it he calls New Englanders back to God, back to being responsible members of society. This tradition of calling the people back to the basic principles of the faith became a part of American culture. It continued even as Puritan theocracy faded in influence. It showed that even with a lack of agreement on political principles society possessed an "ideological consensus—in moral, religious, economic, social, and intellectual matters."[16] Danforth's jeremiad was probably a response to the growing worldliness of New England society. The institution of the Halfway Covenant in 1662, a political accommodation for those who could not prove a Christian conversion experience, was probably at the root of Danforth's concern. Puritans, Danforth and others thought, were starting to lose their moral way. They were starting to forget their original mission.

Danforth was right. New Englanders were beginning to think of themselves differently. They were no longer just outcasts, sent to wander in the wilderness; they were becoming a beacon to the rest of the world, a beacon of liberty and virtue. As Bercovitch writes, "The Puritan jeremiad set out the sacred history of the New World; the eighteenth-century jeremiad established the typology of America's mission."[17] So, when the colonies gained their independence from England they had already begun to think of themselves as New Israelites, and of America as a new Canaan.[18] During the first half of the nineteenth century the religious tone of millennialism was replaced by a *civil millennialism*, what the American journalist John L. O'Sullivan in 1845 designated as "Manifest Destiny."

Beginning in the early nineteenth century Americans began to believe that they would be *the* force behind the moral and political redemption of all nations. This was particularly true after 1815, once they had beaten England a second time in war. Human progress replaced the sudden establishment of a millennial kingdom. In the nineteenth century the American jeremiad became part of the secular culture with readings of the Declaration of Independence and a political oration replacing the traditional lamentations of the preacher. Voting and political campaigns became the sacraments of a new civil religion.[19] It was this fusion of the American jeremiad and the political tradition that made the idea of "Manifest Destiny" possible.

As has been said before, the First Great Awakening of the 1740s had caused an "explosion" in millennial thought, and Jonathan Edwards exemplified this thinking. The *parousia* (the second coming of Christ) and the end of the world were events that Christians looked forward to rather than feared. For, evil men would be brought under control and righteousness would prevail. After an initial time of judgment, a peaceable kingdom of the faithful would be established, and they would reign for a thousand years. Again, the thousand years here may have just been a allegory for a very long time. Eternal punishment would come only with the last judgment, when the whole world, past and present, would be weighed in the balance. As for the millennium, Edwards placed cataclysm, providential government, and the personal return of Jesus Christ in the background of Christian eschatology. For Edwards history was progress, and "the earthly kingdom was foreseen this side of judgment and cataclysm."[20] These things, according to Edwards, would occur after the millennial age had come to a close. So, the First Great Awakening "spread the millennial tradition of New England Puritanism into the rest of the colonies,"[21] and by the 1760s and 1770s the early settlers of New England had become bigger than life. Their immigration to America began to be viewed, *anachronistically*, as a struggle for civil and religious liberty.[22]

The American Revolution also brought a change in millennial thinking. New England Puritans had considered themselves the chosen remnant of God sent into the wilderness of the New World.[23] The American Revolution served as a chrysalis in which the chosen *people* of God metamorphosed into the chosen *nation* of God. In many minds the infant United States became the New Israel. Revolutionary-era Bible commentators began to write that the formation of the United States was the fulfillment of the prophecy found in Revelation 16:17-21:

> [17] And the seventh angel poured out his vial into the air; and there came a great voice out of the temple of heaven, from the throne, saying, It is done. [18] And there were voices, and thunders, and lightnings; and there was *a great earthquake*, such as was not since men were upon the earth, *so mighty an earthquake, and so great.* [19] And the great city was divided into three parts, and the cities of the nations fell: and great Babylon came in remembrance before God, to give unto her the cup of the wine of the fierceness of his wrath. [20] And every island fled away, and the mountains were not found. [21] And there fell upon men a great hail out of heaven, every stone about the weight of a talent: and men blasphemed God because of the plague of the hail; for the plague thereof was exceeding great. (emphasis mine)

Many interpreted "a great earthquake" as an allegorical type that meant the disruption of human government. Both the American and French Revolutions were seen as proof that this prophecy had come to pass,[24] even if radical French opposition to established religion horrified many Americans.

As far as late eighteenth-century American Christians were concerned they stood on the brink of judgment. In fact, "judged by the number of sermons and books addressing prophetic themes, the first generation of United States citizens may have lived in the shadow of Christ's second coming more intensely than any other generation since."[25] America's millennial role had already been revealed to those who were looking for it, and as Ruth Bloch has written, "In the late 1780s the nationalistic hopes of supporters of the Constitution [Federalists] were expressed in decidedly millennial terms."[26] Religion historian Alan Heimert adds, "Throughout the post-Revolutionary years the evangelical mind had continued to interpret the progress of millenarian history in the light of the events that have taken place in America."[27] Yes, the *parousia* did not occur, but that did not matter since the United States had now become the vehicle through which the millennial kingdom would be established.

Nathan Hatch and Ruth Bloch have both written extensively about the transformation of the North American British colonies from theological millennialism to "civic millennialism." Both have shown that Americans during the Revolution believed they stood at a prophetic watershed. Bloch argues that "millennialism…can illuminate how…Americans understood the ultimate meaning of the revolutionary crisis and the birth of the American Nation." This was because "religion deeply informed political ideology." This explains why the most millennially-oriented groups tended to support the Revolution more fervently than others.[28] Nathan Hatch writes that the clergy thought the "antichrist had altered his tactics and sought to crush the church through civil oppression." This meant the distinction between establishing the kingdom of God and achieving specific political goals became obscured and fused.[29] Liberty itself became the cause of God's people because it was seen as the surest way of protecting the Church from political oppression. This fusion of millennial goals and political goals required the secularization of millennial ideas, and these ideas had to become less attached to their religious moorings if they were to become a political force. They had to become a secularized form of Christian millennialism known as *civic millennialism*.[30]

Christian eschatology provides meaning and purpose to those who must see themselves as the supreme act of creation, especially in a universe that from all observation is indifferent to their existence. The same thing happens as Christian eschatology is transformed into the chief means by which a national identity is formed. As Ernest Tuveson writes, "apocalyptic theory, whatever its type, tends to chain men to the wheels of the juggernaut of history."[31] That was the contribution of Christian eschatology as it was transformed into a secular faith in America's national greatness: *it allowed Americans to believe they were still part of the great universal drama without necessarily subscribing to any particular creed other than that which emanated from the Declaration of Independence and the United States Constitution.* It is here that we find the roots of what has been called American Exceptionalism, and it is with the strengthening and waning of this faith that much of United States history is explained.

From the War of 1812 (1812-1815) to the Mexican-American War (1846-1848) to the Civil War (1860-1865) the American nation marched forward as the chosen nation of God. Over the period of a century they had conquered the premier military power of the era—Britain, and they had quelled the internal rebellions of Native Americans. The "domestic imperialism" embodied in the phrase "manifest destiny" came to a close in 1893 when Frederick Jackson Turner declared in his famous historical essay that the "frontier" was closed.[32] It was now time for Americans to turn their gaze outward, although they had already briefly done so when Commodore Matthew Perry threatened Edo (present-day Tokyo) in 1853. Perry's show of military might yielded the *Convention of Kanagawa* (1854), which opened up the door to American trade in Japan. It also inaugurated the modernizing program of the Meiji period, which would yield interesting results in the twentieth century. American foreign policy in the late nineteenth and early twentieth century had more to do with trade than it did political considerations, which shows that some things never change.

In many ways Turner's essay is a recapitulation of the wilderness motif. It was meant to show how the frontier had changed the nation, how it had made the nation distinct in character. That argument of distinctiveness fit right into the prevalent belief of most Americans, and it would help to unite them in 1898 when the U.S.S. Maine went down in Havana Harbor. It would unite them again when they entered the "war to end all wars" in 1917. That same sense of unity, even after it had been challenged by a decade of economic depression, returned to strengthen them against Nazi Germany and the other Axis Powers. This "last good war" would leave the United States the preeminent economic, military, and political power on the planet, but it would not ensure the future faith of Americans in themselves. Women and minorities had tasted the power of the economic system during the war. They had bled beside their white fellow soldiers. They had experienced the freeing effects that war often has on society. There was no going back, and the next several decades would see a major shift in how people viewed race, gender, and even age. If these major shifts in social relations were not enough, the two atomic bombs detonated over Japan initiated the age of "atomic diplomacy,"[33] a policy that effectively started the Cold War and gave birth to the idea of Mutually Assured Destruction (MAD).

What came of America's faith in science, technology, and progress? Surprisingly enough it did not completely disappear after World War II. However bruised and battered the faith of the American people has gotten at times they have remained relatively optimistic throughout history. Even throughout the narcissistic 1970s and 1980s most still continued to believe that the United States was the chosen nation of God, and that it stood as the only effective defense against *godless Communism*. For many, the Cold War was not just a geopolitical struggle. It was a struggle of good versus evil.

Yes, there were many who turned to the consolation of fundamentalist religion, especially as the national revival movement initiated by Billy Graham and others made its mark in the 1950s, but even these folks believed that the battle would not last forever. They were sure God would soon bring history to an end and inaugurate his eternal kingdom, even if the United States proved it was not up to the task. This is why the religious community in the United States has never had a problem with an American foreign policy that is ultimately apocalyptic and utopian in its aims. Either way, they believe God will work through the nations of the world to achieve his ultimate purpose. As we will see in the next chapter this is still very much the case, and it makes for a dangerous and unsustainable foreign policy.

PART FOUR

WHAT GOD AND SCIENCE
HATH WROUGHT

Chapter Fourteen

The American Theocratic Empire

All governments are ordained by God, but none compare to government by God, theocracy.

William R. Bowen, *American Government: In Christian Perspective*

The idea of national Exceptionalism, which we explored in the last chapter, is alive and well in American politics. Even those on the left side of the aisle, who claim they want to reduce the U.S. military footprint, push the idea that without American leadership the world would simply not be able to get along. Some might see this as mere political games-manship on the part of the left, but there is a more practical reason for the left's continued support of military spending, and that is the amount of money the Pentagon and private contractors spend in each electoral district of the United States. That is why recent articles about the fast approaching deadline for automatic spending cuts to the federal budget has emphasized how private contractors are wringing their hands over their almost guaranteed profits.[1] It is not difficult to understand why since there are tens of billions of dollars at stake in the cuts proposed for 2013. Even without these immediate economic and political concerns, though, there is still a general belief among both the left and right that the United States is exceptional and must play a fundamental role on the world political stage. This is nowhere better exhibited then in the fervor with which evangelicals support Israel, and with which they look forward to the literal end of history, often associated with the establish-ment of an American theocracy, or at least quasi-theocracy. The agenda of the religious Right often seems a contradiction. For example, they support family values yet promote a libertarian economic agenda that disrupts family and community life in every way, or they want to establish a semi-theocratic government yet pine for the day when fire will reign down upon it all. As is true of all religions or ideologies people tend to exhaust logic and common sense when they try to put into practice their aspirations.

Why should evangelical support for secular Israel be of concern to us? Because, American Exceptionalism directly influences foreign policy choices that might not be good for the nation in the long run, and American Exceptionalism is still largely driven by religious sentiment. Of course, evangelical support for Israel is not the primary consideration when the White House devises its foreign policy strategy for the Middle East. The nation's need for oil and a decades-old policy of denominating all sales of Saudi oil in U.S. dollars—so-called *petrodollars*—is the dominant consideration in policy making.[2] Combine the neo-con policy of exporting U.S. democracy and capitalism abroad with evangelical support for Israel, and the policy of petrodollars, and you have a recipe for disaster.

Kevin Phillips has laid out in his book *American Theocracy* (2006) the many problems inherent in American-style theocracy and imperialism. He compared the United States under the presidency of George W. Bush to late-sixteenth century Spain under Phillip II, who ruled as a "dull and prayerful Habsburg dynast." During Philip's reign Spain continued to import huge amounts of silver and gold from the New World, a corollary of modern-day Wall Street's financialization of the U.S. and world economy. Another analogy is the sixteenth-century Genoan bankers who financed the wars of the Spanish crown against rebellious Protestants just as Asian banks are now financing the U.S. "war on terror."[3] All of these things led to huge increases in prices (inflation) without any real growth in the European economy.[4]

The parallels between this early modern history and today are eerie, and instructive for the U.S. and world economy. It also does not change much under Democrat administrations. For example, Bill Clinton was heavily criticized by the far left for his movement to the right on issues of welfare policy and his refusal to recognize the "peace dividend," which was supposed to come from budget cuts to the Pentagon, cuts made possible by the end of the Cold War. Obama has fared little better at the hands of the far left because of his slow action on gay marriage, his reversal on closing Guantanamo Bay, and his surge strategy in Afghanistan. It is my view that a better distribution of national income, and a severe reduction in the U.S. role as "world policeman," would dramatically change the social and political dynamic of American culture, but more on that later.

Of course, the position we find ourselves in today, as a quasi-theocratic empire, did not happen overnight. As we have read, Americans long believed they were to play a special role in the grand scheme of history. However, the way in which the United States came into its imperial role was haphazard at best. Pushed by commercial interests, and resisted by ultranationalists and xenophobes, the United States only achieved its standing as a world power after World War II, although the foundation for power was laid during the First World War. The U.S. became a dominant world power because of its relative isolation from the destructive capacity of modern war, its access to abundant natural resources, and because it and the U.S.S.R. were the only two intact governmental and economic systems after World War II.

For thirty years after World War II the United States enjoyed the fruits of this dominance, but as U.S. oil reserves reached what Marion King Hubbert called "peak" production capacity there was a shock to the system,[5] primarily because it was accompanied by OPEC restrictions, which drove up prices by artificially drawing down supply.[6] The reason the OPEC embargo of 1973 is such an axial event is because it was a direct response to the United State's decision to resupply Israel with weapons during the *Yom Kippur War* (October 1973). Here we have a confluence of U.S. foreign policy and American eschatological agitation, so it should come as no surprise that Bantam re-released the same year Hal Lindsey's *The Late, Great Planet Earth*. This book had originally been published in 1970 by the Christian publishing house Zondervan, but it was the "secular" Bantam that made it possible for the book to sell 28 million copies by the early 1990s. There was also a movie released in 1979, and narrated by none other than Orson Welles. This allowed Lindsey's premillennial eschatology to be disseminated to millions of people outside the evangelical Christian community.

In brief premillennial Christians believe there will be a rapture (a taking up into heaven) of true-believing Christians at some undesignated point in the future. The New Testament book of I Thessalonians is believed by many Christians to refer to this event when it says that Jesus will return as "a thief in the night." (I Thessalonians 5:2) Once this event occurs, the clock will start ticking. For seven years the people who are "left behind" will suffer, although at first it will seem as though the one-world government that has been established is going to bring about perpetual peace and prosperity. At some point during this seven-year period Satan will have free reign over the earth and will install his emissary, "the antichrist." This individual will eventually take the reins of the one-world government and make everyone worship him, persecuting those who resist. Following the "seven years of tribulation" Christ will return to do battle with the forces of evil at a place called Meggido, the place name from which we get our word *Armageddon*. After this battle Christ will set up his kingdom and rule for a thousand years, sometimes seen as merely a long time and not necessarily a literal thousand years. At some point after this Satan will be released on the world again, at which point he will finally be defeated, and a new heaven and a new earth will be created to replace the old.[7]

Since the 1970s the situation has only grown more hysterical. American evangelical Christians continue to read within the events of the Middle East,[8] or the election of any insufficiently Christian U.S.

president, signs of prophetic fulfillment. This becomes more and more problematic as domestic politics and the need for international oil intersect. Foreign policy begins to grow into an attempt to satisfy three prevailing goals: retaining access to oil through U.S. global supremacy, maintaining the role of the dollar in the trade of oil (*petro-dollars*), and an attempt to satisfy, even if facilely, the Christian Right's desire to strike at whichever power they now see as the "new Babylon"—presently Iran. All of these goals were evident in the 2003 invasion of Iraq, although the dubious argument that Saddam Hussein had or was acquiring Weapons of Mass Destruction (WMDs) was the main reason given for the invasion. So, American foreign policy is now meant to satisfy five major constituents: 1) politicians concerned about peak oil, 2) oil companies looking for new areas of exploration, 3) the U.S. financial community concerned about the foreign exchange implications of *petro-dollars*, 4) climatologists concerned about the environmental damage caused by fossil fuels, and 5) millennial Christians who pine for "the end" of it all.[9]

If these Christians merely represented a fringe movement with no implications for American politics or foreign policy we could just catalogue the movement as an interesting subculture and move on. However, they have grown to a level of influence in local and national politics which makes it impossible to ignore them. We can see their influence in the attempt to eliminate evolution from the classroom, or to give equal time to the pseudo-religious alternative known as "intelligent design"— thinly-veiled *creationism*. They are making all types of legal inroads when it comes to abortion, trying to narrow the rights of women when it comes to the question of reproductive choice. Some have even begun to imagine the creation of a new, biblically-based United States government. These latter individuals are sometimes called "Reconstructionists" because they believe they are returning the nation to its Christian roots. They tend to oppose modern culture, support a hawkish foreign policy, and call for the literal establishment of a Christian theocracy through the democratic process, or by *other means*. That these individuals do not have a problem circumventing the democratic process is what makes their agenda so disturbing, especially since they are well-organized, well-financed, and above all, zealous.[10]

This explains why these types of Christians so easily make common cause with those known as neo-conservatives, even when many of these noted neo-conservatives reject traditional religion, or even belief in God. In his book *Black Mass: Apocalyptic Religion and the Death of Utopia* (2007) John Gray has explored in-depth this relationship between religious utopianism and the secular political agenda. He starts off by pointing out that neo-conservatives believe that the universalization of democracy and the free market system are inevitable. This belief has become particularly pronounced since the demise of the U.S.S.R. and the effective elimination of Communism as a practical political and economic philosophy. In the end, writes Gray, the neo-conservative view is a secularized version of Christian apocalypticism. They have taken the fervor of religious utopianism, stripped it of its religious façade, and have made it into a project for "universal emancipation." The problem is that unlike their Enlightenment predecessors they have chosen to ignore the fundamental flaws of human nature—much as the French did during their bloody revolution.[11] Of course, as we have seen in previous chapters this is not new. The United States has a long tradition of this type of political utopianism. The difference is that Americans now have the power to impose the American ideal on the rest of the world and are nonplussed by the use of violence to achieve that end.

Before we go on, let us make a distinction here between the civic millennialism of the early nineteenth century and the twenty-first century political utopianism of today. The former operated in a post-millennial framework, where the gradual improvement of the human race would lead to a better world. Americans animated by civic millennialism were not above using violence to achieve their ends, as their treatment of Native Americans proves. However, the goal of American civic millennialism was primarily secular rather than moral. Land and markets always mattered more than God. Yes, there were Christians who sought to impose on the rest of the country their views about the evils of alcohol—among other things, but this was generally done peacefully and through moral suasion. In other words, nineteenth-century Americans were animated by the eschatological hope of postmillennial Christianity but they sought a rather pedestrian fulfillment of prophecy in the form of the yeoman farmer. This has changed today. There is now a large segment of the population animated by the promise of science and the elimination of human frailties—including our moral frailties. These individuals are fellow travelers with religious believers when it comes to the arena of secular foreign policy, and they have no patience to work slowly through cultural, social, and economic accommodation. It is either their way or the highway. The religious advocate of foreign intervention demands, in particular, the immediate upending of civilization to establish the kingdom of God on earth, or to hasten the end of history. Neo-conservatives are ready to oblige because they share the same revolutionary spirit as the apocalyptic believer, especially when it comes to their vision of future human history. In their view it is okay to export democracy and markets at the point of a gun. Religious or secular, those who still argue for the limits of human action and for moral improvement are shunted aside as Luddites or Romantic sentimentalists. There is no room for criticism; you are either for "progress" or against it.[12]

The neo-conservative view may have always existed in a nascent form in the United States but it was not until the country had achieved the status of a fully urban society that the general population began to imagine building the machine that would relieve us of all our burdens. Two hundred years ago when most people lived on farms and their nearest neighbor was several miles away these utopian beliefs mattered little. As we learned in a previous chapter cosmos and the millennial kingdom have always been associated with the city. We should not be surprised that the twentieth century saw such movements as Nazism, and Soviet and Chinese Totalitarianism, all associated with a major city where the central bureaucracy was housed. It was inevitable that some in the twentieth century would start to believe that they could not only make over the world but that they could make over man himself. After all, these movements can be traced back in many ways to the Enlightenment and the Counter-Enlightenment, or to the Romantic Reaction of the late eighteenth and early nineteenth century. Even modern-day Islamic fundamentalism can be traced back to a mix of Western Enlightenment thought and Islamic eschatology as embodied in the writings of the radical Islamist Sayyid Qutb (1906-1966).[13]

The neo-conservative vision is a *theodicy*, a story of how the gods work out the fate of mankind. Thatcherism—one could include Reaganism—is a form of neo-liberalism which came to dominate the political right in the last quarter of the twentieth century. What it ended up doing is giving governments, both left and right, too much optimism about the future, making it impossible for them to prepare for the problems associated with nationalism and violence. This has been seen time and again everywhere the West has chosen to intervene in other countries. One of the problems is that neo-liberals do not share the classic liberal's skepticism when it comes to human nature, so they are prone to turn free-market faith into utopianism. It was right-leaning intellectuals like F. A. Hayek who convinced many that the irrationality of a planned economy should be replaced by a rational, self-correcting, and laissez-faire economy, ignoring the fact that the free market is not necessarily rational or self-correcting.[14] The evidence for this is all around us today, five years after the worst financial meltdown in eighty years.

Still the utopian faith of the neo-conservative abides, in all its "crackpot realism" and "chiliastic fantasy." In the United States it is a continuation of that persistent belief in the American *mission*, which was alone challenged by the early Federalists. However, the Federalists could not dislodge what would become termed the nation's "manifest destiny." John Gray writes, that "the United States is the last militant Enlightenment regime and the only advanced country that is still unshakably

Christian." For this reason the nation is particularly susceptible to the neo-conservative foreign policy view, which is rooted in the left's historical opposition to Soviet totalitarianism. Neo-conservatism, like Soviet totalitarianism before it, has now morphed into a criticism of anyone who would question the American way of life, or whether it should be exported to other countries. The Project for the New American Century (PNAC), formed in 1997, is an organization which makes clear that neo-conservatives have no intention of letting the United States lose its military and political sway around the world, and that those who criticize such a project become in the eyes of neo-conservatives "counter-revolutionaries."[15] Again, he who is not with me is against me, they argue.

Democracy cannot be forced on a country, an important lesson learned in Iraq and continuing to be learned in Afghanistan. Those who would intervene in the affairs of others by force justify it on the basis of the liberal argument that all governments which do not ensure the basic rights of their citizens are illegitimate. Unfortunately, this requires long-term commitments, and violence is always counter-productive when trying to build a political system. "No constitution can impose freedom where it is not wanted or preserve it where it is no longer valued." In the case of the "war on terror," neo-conservatives ignore both the limited scope of the problem and the limitations of military action in addressing the problem. Terrorism is primarily a political act; so, it should be treated as a crime against which all the nations of the world work. Beyond criminalizing terrorism, creating political outlets for social and economic frustration have been shown to be effective in the past against feeding the terrorist mindset. The IRA in Ireland was eventually given political legitimacy through Sinn Féin, and it is this type of practical political solution that stands in stark contrast to the US policy of "pre-emptive war," which only encourages "rogue" states to seek nuclear technology in order to prevent future U.S. "pre-emptive" attacks or invasions.[16]

Modern secularists fail to see how much Christianity has contributed to their world view and how important the myths of religion are to human beings. Secularism is not treated as an intellectual viewpoint so much as it is a political stance, and political secularism unmoors us from the moral limitations inherent in religious myths, making secular utopianism possible. If we are to avoid the minefield inherent in utopian thinking we must reject all utopian schemes and simply address problems as they arise. "Realism" demands a humility with which utopian dreamers are not acquainted. Not every problem has a solution, and no problem, social or political, is ever simple. Realists understand that international relations are at their core moral questions, to which a harmonious resolution may never come. That is why balance rather than equity should dominate political decisions. The human need to be part of a narrative explains why we are drawn to religious myth and secular utopianism. However, both are dangerous since they ultimately convince us of a future harmony that can never be. In the end, "religions are not claims to knowledge but ways of living with what cannot be known."[17] This is the lesson we must learn if we are to disentangle ourselves from utopian schemes and all the problems they entail.

What results when a nation is convinced it has right on its side, and it possesses the might to make it happen? An answer to this question can be found in the work of two authors: Chalmers Johnson and Andrew Bacevich. The late Chalmers Johnson wrote a trilogy of books about the *American empire*. The first of the books, *Blowback: The Costs and Consequences of American Empire* (2000), was a prescient warning about the unintended consequences of what the CIA calls "mission creep." This is when an organization sets itself a task and continues to widen the scope of the task because of ill-defined or unrealistic goals. However, the bigger problem with American empire is that the American people are largely ignorant of their empire's existence and cannot therefore put historical events into context. So, when events like the first bombing of the World Trade Center in 1993, the bombing of the US Embassies in Kenya in 1998, or the bombing of the USS Cole in 2000, occur one cannot put them all together in a cohesive narrative. One is left wondering why these people hate America so much, because most of us are ignorant of the extent to which the U.S. military is involved with other governments around the world, an involvement that often takes the form of befriending or propping up dictators and autocrats who are hated by their own people. So, the United States begins to gain enemies by proxy.

In his subsequent books, *The Sorrows of Empire: Militarism, Secrecy, and the End of the Republic* (2004) and *Nemesis: The Last Days of the American Republic* (2007), Johnson argues for redefining the defense goals of the United States. Johnson criticizes the continued use of Cold War organizations to fight the new shadowy enemies of the post-9/11 world, and warns that by not changing our *militarized* foreign policy stance we will eventually begin curbing domestic freedoms in the name of security. Patriot Acts, warrantless wiretaps, and the indefinite detention of American citizens suspected of terrorism are only a few ways in which the American security state has already begun to violate the Constitution. Like John Gray and others, Johnson argues for a smaller footprint in the fight against world terrorism. That means a dramatic reduction in the nearly 800 military bases that the United States maintains around the world in dozens of countries. Before his death Johnson issued a final warning in a short book titled *Dismantling the Empire: America's Last Best Hope* (2010). In it he recommended three things: the dissolution of the CIA and its clandestine activities, the closing of many of our overseas bases, and a dramatic reduction in defense spending. All of these things, he believed, would be the first steps in restoring American democracy.

Johnson was not a lone voice in the wilderness, and Andrew Bacevich in his book *The Limits of Power: The End of American Exceptionalism* (2008) lends a certain military gravitas to Johnson's view of American power abroad. Presently a professor of international relations at Boston University, Bacevich graduated from West Point in 1969 and then did two tours of duty in Vietnam. Bacevich retired two decades later at

the rank of colonel. Like Johnson, Bacevich contends that the empire
of bases needs to be dismantled. In the 1990s, after the Cold War had
ended, politicians decided to expand the Pentagon rather than shrink
it. When the United States was attacked on September 11, 2001 politicians, the Pentagon, and others began to use the attacks as a reason not
only to keep the expanded military-industrial complex but to extend it
even further. The "long war" against world terrorism was declared by
the Bush administration, and this narrative of good versus evil justified
the desire of many to maintain a bloated military and intelligence community. One is reminded of the words of Shakespeare in *Coriolanus*:
"Do not cry havoc, where you should but hunt with modest warrant."

The real reason for this was more subtle and not directly related to
national security. The real reason was to maintain the growth of *globalization*, which is just a catch-all word for the unrestrained activity of
multi-national corporations and capital. So, the United States has taken
a unilateral lead in keeping the world safe for commerce, especially oil.
However, the United States is reaching its economic limits. It can no
longer practically sustain its empire of bases, which prompts Bacevich
to opine that,

> Rather than insisting that the world accommodate the United
> States, Americans need to reassert control over their own destiny,
> ending their condition of dependency and abandoning their impe-
> rial delusions.[18]

Americans are defined by their unquenchable desire for more, so
they have adopted a foreign policy based on the notion that they can
continue to consume massive amounts of the world's resources without any social, political, or economic ramifications. This policy ignores
the obvious gap between available natural resources and the demand
for goods. If the United States continues to follow this policy then hard
choices will be forced on the American people at some point in the near
future. Making the choice now to dramatically reduce the empire of bases would mitigate the more onerous decisions the country will be forced

to make later.[19] Yes, these decisions are largely economic but they also have a military component because the military has been spread far too thin in its many theaters of operation. The solution, according to Bacevich, is a consumption model less dependent on the rest of the world and a foreign policy that is more in line with the reasonable capacity of the United States military.[20] However, Bacevich is less than sanguine about the possibility of this happening. He says that it is more likely that overconsumption, unbalanced budgets, and debt will eventually be the only way to humble the American people, to teach them the *limits of power.*

Kevin Phillips identifies five criteria by which we can judge the level of national decline in the United States: 1) growing cultural and economic decay, 2) growing religious fervor, 3) the favoring of faith over intellect, 4) belief in a cosmic battle, and 5) imperial over-reach. The U.S. is experiencing all five of these to some degree, just as Rome, Spain, the Dutch, and the British experienced them previously. *Christian Reconstruction* movements support various agendas like using the Bible as a basis for law, giving all education responsibility over to religious institutions, and subordinating women. "Faith-based initiatives" are just one way in which Republicans are trying to pull church and state together, while the Christian Reconstructionists work in stealth, clearly sensitive to the animus of the general population to their whole political agenda.[21]

Chris Hedges calls this movement "Christo-fascism." It is a movement made up of thirty million evangelical Christians who constitute a "culture of despair." These folks have not only abandoned the "reality-based world," which they feel has failed them, but they look with orgiastic glee to the approaching end of the planet and the suffering of those they see as evil: gays, single mothers, and even the poor. Yes, the poor! Why the poor? Because, many evangelical Christians have come to believe that the poor in America, those needing public assistance, have some type of moral failing, or that they lack faith. For, surely God takes care of his own.[22] It is interesting to note that although Christians reject Darwin's theory of biological selection they have no problem accepting what has been called Social Darwinism.[23] It is also interesting how these folks ignore the basic injunction to minister to the poor, and to work for social justice, an injunction that permeates both the Old and New Testaments, according to Pastor Jim Wallis.[24]

What may help these Reconstructionists achieve some of what they want to do is that the United States has put itself on an unsustainable path of debt accumulation, what the New York Times labeled in 2005 the "borrower-industrial complex." This industry is now well over 20% of the United States' GDP, and in 2004 forty percent of all corporate profits were created in the financial sector of the economy. The problem with this is that it is a system that accrues wealth at the top rather than spreading it around, so we have seen the opposite of the trend which occurred from the 1920s through the 1970s when unionized, blue collar jobs lifted tens of millions of people into the middle class. The working man has become prey to what Phillips calls the "Judas economy," where in order to make ends meet the average worker must go deeper and deeper into debt. The closed factories, blighted neighborhoods, broken families, and the useless skills of those unable to escape the crumbling urban landscape, are all that is left in certain sections of American society, a society that once held the general promise that each generation would be better off than the last. Instead we have become a "rentier society" in which those at the top of the income scale have become so adept at avoiding taxation that it has widened the gap between the economic haves and have-nots, and has made it nearly impossible to sustain either the imperial aspirations of the nation or its social safety net. Both are now in danger of being destroyed by huge amounts of public and private debt.[25]

Lest you think that Phillips is just being a Cassandra read the following words,

> ...the fallout from a 10 to 20 percent national housing-price slump could make the analogy [of indenture] somewhat more credible. Bankruptcies or shattered credit might well put millions of card-holders in thrall to dozens of issuers and mortgage lenders. And

if household America slowed its consumption, thereby ceasing to play locomotive to the world, the domestic and global effects could be incendiary.[26]

Now, remember, Phillips wrote this paragraph in 2006, two years prior to any sign that the world financial system was on the verge of melting down! If he could see it, why could not others? Could the answer be that we are blinded to the real problems and real solutions by the illusion of general moral decay and by our desire, still, to be the chosen of God, those who are destined to bring liberty and light to the rest of the world?

In the next chapter we will consider whether religion is still of any value to a modern society. The answer is not quite as simple as that given by the New Atheists and it is somewhat less ambitious than the mystic's answer of not trying to conceive of God at all. The answer ultimately lies in knowledge. We must learn to know not only the world around us but ourselves. Greater knowledge of the universe humbles us while knowledge of ourselves gives us the confidence to move forward. We may not be destined to progress forever as a species, but a commonsense commitment to reason and science may keep us from returning to the trees.

Chapter Fifteen

Tiger, Tiger, Burning Bright

Science and religion—being antithetical ways of thinking about the same reality—will never come to terms.

Sam Harris, *The Moral Landscape*

A debate rages today between some intellectuals and a very well-organized, well-funded movement of anti-intellectualism, a movement rooted in the fundamentalist evangelical community. This anti-intellectual movement has manifested itself over the last thirty years in its opposition to equal rights for women and gays, its desire to curb a woman's right to make her own reproductive decisions, its demand for the unrestricted return of prayer and God to the public square (primarily in the form of Christianity), and its virulent denunciation of Darwin's theory of biological evolution. It is this last point that has raised the ire of individuals like Richard Dawkins, who has since the 1986 publication of his book *The Blind Watchmaker*, taken to task "creation science" proponents. These are folks who have attempted to outright curtail the teaching of evolution or to get their own "scientific" view equal time in the biology classroom.

This is not a new debate and you have probably heard of the famous Scopes Trial of 1925—sometimes called the Scopes "Monkey" Trial. This was the case that forced evangelical fundamentalists into a rearguard action when it came to science instruction in American public schools. For fifty years scientists and science instructors appeared to have the upper hand when it came to what would be taught in the classroom, but this all changed as organizations like the Moral Majority and the Christian Coalition began to dominate certain segments of politics in the 1980s.[1] Where they focused much of their effort was in getting Christians elected to local school boards. This allowed them to control not only what would be taught in science classes but also what would be taught in U.S. history—often seen as lacking an emphasis on the Christian origins of the American republic.[2]

This debate is complicated by the long history of animosity between traditional religion and the growing scientific knowledge of the western world. As we have learned more about the world and ourselves it has become difficult to swallow without question the literal, Bible-based accounts of many religionists, e.g., the story of the earth's creation just 6,000 years ago. The literal-minded believer claims that the account in Genesis has historical value, the same historical value we derive from Julius Caesar's account of the Gallic Wars or Plato's record of the life and teachings of Socrates. Modern geologists, physicists, and biologists, view the earth, the universe, and mankind as extremely old, beyond any span of time that we can practically appreciate when compared to our own 75-odd years of life on this planet. On the side of the scientists stands the evidence of the earth itself, the evidence of the cosmos, and a long trail of evidence that man can now trace back to his own origins using the fossil record, molecular clocks, and radiological dating.[3] The creationist has a brief (around three pages), late iron-age account of how God brought the universe and the earth into being. From a historical perspective the only thing that the Genesis account of creation can tell us is that sometime around the sixth or seventh century BCE some Jewish believers wrote this story down and included it among their religion's sacred documents. We cannot even be sure they ever meant it to be taken literally. It might have just been an allegorical argument for the supremacy of the Jewish god.

Part of the problem here may be that most people assume that if one part of a biblical account has historical validity it must be through and through a historical account. Of course, this does not have to be true, since we know that stories can easily be woven from both fact and fantasy, and that over time a tale always gets bigger with the telling.[4] In the end, the debate between the anti-intellectual evangelical community and modern secular intellectuals is rooted in a basic issue of epistemology, which is the study of *what can be known*. However, since most fundamentalist Christians simply ignore any physical evidence that does not accord with their beliefs, and they demand that non-scientific, iron-age accounts of creation be given the same epistemological weight as geology, physics, and biology, it is nearly impossible to engage in any productive dialogue. That does not mean, though, that everyone has given up trying to reconcile the two, but can it be done?

There are three assumptions made by most evangelical Christians that relate directly to this general debate. The first is that religion and God are the same. The second is that we cannot have morality without religion. The third is that religious belief and national heritage are so inextricably bound together that it is nearly impossible to disengage one from the other, especially without offending a whole host of individuals. For example, those put off by overzealous patriotism might have their religious faith questioned along with their loyalty to the nation. This happens among the many Christian communities that Chris Hedges examines in his book *American Fascists: The Christian Right and the War on America* (2007). Can atheists, these American evangelicals wonder out loud, ever be true patriots without faith in God? Since religion, faith in God, and patriotism are all one in their eyes, evangelical Christians cannot conceive of a world in which they are separate. All of the views above are ultimately rooted in a literal interpretation of Christian scriptures.

This is not to ignore that some Christians have made an attempt to accommodate modern thinking. For example, there are some modern

Christians who say that the account of Genesis should not be taken literally, that the calendrical calculations of the mid-seventeenth-century bishop James Ussher should be dismissed.[5] These modern Christians argue that there is no intrinsic tension between faith in God and science, which is why many claim to believe in God but still subscribe to the prevailing view that evolution is a natural, unguided process of biological selection.[6] These people have clearly concluded that they can side with God and science against the literal-minded religionist.

The author Karen Armstrong is a proponent of this view and presents a compelling argument for it in her book *The Case For God* (2009). Armstrong says that many religious leaders and thinkers over the centuries have found the solution to this conflict in their conception of the *unknowable God*, and that it is only the literal-minded religionist and the "new atheists" who stand in the way of a proper understanding of how God should be contemplated. The problem, as Armstrong sees it, is that people do not understand the essential purpose of religion; they are unaware that the way in which we get to know the world and the way in which we get to know God require two different epistemological perspectives. The way in which we get to know the world is through *logos*—what we call *reason*; the way in which we come to know God is through *mythos*, timeless tales about the human condition and our ineffable relationship with the universe or God.[7]

Armstrong believes that if *mythos* were restored to its proper place that religion and science would have little reason for conflict, a conflict she blames on fundamentalist Christians, because they demand that their faith be consistent with *logos*. As in the song "My God" by Jethro Tull:

> People—what have you done—
> Locked him in His golden cage.
> Made him bend to your religion—
> Him resurrected from the grave.
> He is the god of nothing—
> If that's all that you can see.

The requirement that faith be a "reasonable" intellectual position to take has meant that the literal-minded religionist must challenge any view that is both contrary to religion and based on *logos*. This often goes to the point of undermining the very notion of *logos* itself, which is ironic when one listens to the evangelical community bemoan cultural and moral relativism.

Armstrong is convinced that if we could all somehow come to see religion aright that it would end the conflict between God and science. Seeing religion aright, which means seeing it through the language of *mythos*, would mean rediscovering the *unknowable God*. It would also mean admitting to ourselves that religion is just a tool used to help us in the contemplation of God. Viewed in this light the present conflict between religion and science is actually between science and those who have adopted a perverted (*logos*-based) view of religion. So, it is not a conflict between God and science. However, although Armstrong has done a marvelous job of tracing the history of mystical and Gnostic faith she ignores a fundamental flaw in her proposal to enlighten people and decouple religion from *logos*. The reality of practical religious belief militates against the program she suggests.

Richard Dawkins sums up the problem with Armstrong's proposal in a 2009 article published in the Wall Street Journal, a response to Armstrong's book *The Case For God*. He writes,

> Now, there is a certain class of sophisticated modern theologian who will say something like this: "Good heavens, of course we are not so naive or simplistic as to care whether God exists. Existence is such a 19th-century preoccupation! It doesn't matter whether God exists in a scientific sense. What matters is whether he exists for you or for me. If God is real for you, who cares whether science has made him redundant? Such arrogance! Such elitism."
>
> Well, if that's what floats your canoe, you'll be paddling it up a very lonely creek. The mainstream belief of the world's peoples is very clear. They believe in God, and that means they believe he exists in objective reality, just as surely as the Rock of Gibraltar exists. If sophisticated theologians or postmodern relativists think they are rescuing God from the redundancy scrap-heap by downplay-

ing the importance of existence, they should think again. Tell the congregation of a church or mosque that existence is too vulgar an attribute to fasten onto their God, and they will brand you an atheist. They'll be right.[8]

The problem with Armstrong's suggestion becomes apparent when you look at the results of a 2009 Harris poll conducted on what the American people believe. For example, over 70% of respondents believe in God, miracles, Heaven, the divinity of Jesus, angels, eternal life, and the resurrection of Jesus while only 45% believe in Darwin's theory of natural selection.[9] How do you think the people in these surveys would respond to the idea that religion has little to say about God, that it only provides us with the environment (rituals) and the language (mythos) necessary to contemplate him, or that it is irrelevant whether he exists at all? Might people get worried about other issues like the reality of eternal life and whether angels are watching over them, or whether bad people will eventually be punished in Hell? The problem still remains. However negatively people view established religion, and they have viewed it quite negatively throughout history, they still cannot quite escape from the notion that religion gives us insight into who and what God is, how he operates, and how we can make him our ally. As critical as people may be about organized religion they are still fundamentally convinced that religion somehow equates to belief in or knowledge of God.[10]

So, most people believe that when we are talking about religion and God we are essentially talking about the same thing. The only people who appear to be able to see the difference between the two are those who have committed themselves completely to *logos* or those who have come to a semi-Gnostic view of God and revealed religion. This relates to the debate we have been talking about because it feeds into the second issue we mentioned above: the equivalence of religion with morality. Most seem compelled, as if instinctually, to believe that if we were to get rid of religion and/or God that we would somehow be set morally adrift, that there is no intellectual means by which we can fix our moral compass.[11] This is one of the central themes of Dostoyevsky's *The Broth-*

ers Karamazov (1880), where the young, cosmopolitan, and university educated, Ivan Karamazov argues that without belief in God and the immortality of the soul "everything" would be "lawful." Ivan has even written an article on the subject. He contends in the article that God and immortality must cease to exist if social reform is to be implemented, since as long as people are looking to the next life for relief from their earthly burdens then no program of social reform can go forward to improve life now. Later in the novel, Miüsov, the elder Karamazov's first wife, claims that Ivan's ideas are "stupid" and that his atheistic stance could even justify cannibalism. Ivan cannot disagree with her, although one is not quite convinced he does agree, especially when he goes nearly insane after his illegitimate brother, Smerdyakov, kills their father in order to steal some money, and then his older brother Dimitri is wrongly blamed and tried for the murder. Dostoyevsky does an excellent job of leaving us to draw our own moral conclusions, as all great literature does. However, one is not quite convinced by the novel itself that God, immortality, or atheism, have anything germane to contribute to how we form our moral views. Could it be that we all simply possess a generally universal "moral sentiment" that manifests itself in different ways?

Formal research into this question may have first begun with William James's *The Varieties of Religious Experience: A Study In Human Nature* (1902), although David Hume and other modern thinkers had previously theorized about man's moral life. James's book was based on a series of lectures he gave at the University of Edinburgh in 1901 and 1902. James was a researcher in the area then called "functional psychology," which was founded on the *Pragmatism* of Charles Sanders Peirce. James viewed religion from a purely "existential point of view," by which he meant *empirical*. Religion, according to James, could only be studied as a physical phenomenon; metaphysics had to be left to others. So, as far as he was concerned it mattered not whether religion was true or not, only that it was *useful* to someone. James first observed that most religious belief is communicated via culture. Little conscious thought goes into the ideas before we adopt them from our family or society. The second thing he observed was that we believe one line of religious thought to be superior to another when it delights us or provides us with some practical benefit. James also observed that religious experience is subjective, which is why the word *religion* does not clarify things; it obscures them. *Religion* is a catchall word that is meant to describe that moment when moral sentiment and reason *seem* to come together.[12]

James argues that the purpose of some religions is to impart to its adherents what he calls "healthy-mindedness." Those who possess this perspective tend to be more positive, more optimistic, and they believe good will always triumph over evil—if only in the end. Those James called "mind-curers" encourage healthy-mindedness through a process of psychologically letting go—a spiritual advisor might, for instance, encourage you to "let go and let God."[13] This is in keeping with the injunction of Jesus to be as a grain of wheat, which must first be buried in the ground and die before it can bring forth its fruit. (John 12:24) The same sentiment is put forth by the Buddha when he encourages his followers to free themselves from ego so they can experience oneness with the universe, *nirvana*. There is also another strain of religious thought which James calls the "morbid-minded way." These folks view the "healthy-minded" as "blind and shallow," unable to grasp the deeper truth of religion because they do not choose to suffer rather than live fully.

The *healthy-minded* view the *morbid-minded* as "unmanly and diseased," but it is clear that these views are rooted more in culture than religion. James points to Leo Tolstoy, who thought modern bourgeois life was itself the source of modern neurosis.[14] Tolstoy alludes to this in several of his novels. In *Anna Karenina* (1878) Kostya Levin struggles with his own feelings about the people he employs on his land. He watches them and works beside them but cannot achieve the same bucolic serenity that they seem to get from their simple work. Kostya is tortured by what he knows—which is too much, just like the main character of another Tolstoy work, *The Death of Ivan Ilyich*, a novella published in 1886. In this story we watch as a man crumbles physically under his own success. In what appears to be a mere case of hypochondria, brought on by nerves, Ivan ultimately succumbs to death from unknown causes.

When it comes to the subject of conscious religious conversion, teenagers and those with a certain temperament tend to be more susceptible, [15] and once converted a certain type of life is preferred to that of ordinary living. The life of the *saint* is venerated. Very often saintliness is associated with a rejection of the material world. Celibacy and poverty are seen as the surest means by which to achieve true spirituality. This, of course, is a problem in the modern capitalist world where, as James points out, "We have grown literally afraid to be poor." This contempt for poverty makes it nearly impossible for anyone in search of non-material rewards to turn their backs on "money-making." We even begin to lose the ability to see how any type of deprivation, no matter how modest, can sometimes open up a whole new world to the spiritually hungry. The religious believer is looking for a world not dominated by the *bribed soul*, the soul motivated solely by material gain and paralyzed with fear at "material ugliness and hardship." However, the problem for the spiritual seeker is that the western world is dominated by "aggressive members of society always tending to become bullies, robbers, and swindlers." Yes, says James, we need these aggressive types to push forward the kind of society we now have, but excessive aggression on the part of all leads to the breakdown of society. [16] Christopher Lasch echoes James's sentiments here when he talks about the "war of all against all."

In the end, James says that how people *feel* about religion has a greater influence on how people *think* about religion. Philosophical and theological arguments are usually a by-product of those feelings, a justification after the fact. So, religion will continue to exist as long as it is *useful*. The sixty-four thousand dollar question is whether religion can ever be made redundant as long as men possess the nagging sense that life encompasses more than we are ever consciously able to take in at any one time.[17] Michael Shermer, a science historian, has tackled these questions, and others, in his book *The Believing Brain* (2011). Shermer concludes that we are "natural-born immortalists" and that evolution has equipped us with two finely honed abilities: the ability to see patterns—even where there are none, and the natural tendency to ascribe agency to anything that moves. These abilities were quite useful in the distant past since mankind lived most of the time outside the confines of civilization. It was wise to assume that there was pattern and agency in a bush that moved even when the wind was not blowing. Why do we favor patterns and agency? Well, there are two errors that can be made in the situation above: Type I and Type II. The former is a *false positive*; we think it is real when it is not. The latter is a *false negative*; we believe the event is unreal when it is real. The latter would be a far more dangerous mistake to make if lions and other carnivores are known to roam around where you live. That is why we tend to favor Type I errors. We tend to assume that all patterns are real and run away at the first sign of something moving in a bush. So, Shermer writes, we "believe weird things because of our evolved need to believe nonweird things."[18]

How does all this relate to religious belief? Well, our tendency to *patternize* and *agentize* is the basis for all human beliefs, and once those beliefs are adopted it is very difficult to dislodge them because we always favor confirmation over contradiction, and the smarter we are the better we are at rationalizing what we already believe. We rationalize away anything that does not fit into our dominant paradigm.[19] Most Christians have a problem with the idea that the world is ruled by "chance, randomness, and contingency." They believe everything must have significance.[20] That Christians believe this is not unusual. Read Luke 12:7, where Jesus is purported to have said that God "numbers the hairs on your head." One can see how this could offer a great sense of well-being to those looking for control over their lives. Even if they cannot control everything themselves they can leave it to a benevolent power to take up the slack.[21]

The bad news, depending on your view, is that belief in God and religion is hard wired into the brain. So is the appeal of storytelling. As Shermer writes, "It feels good…to believe in God." The reason it feels good is because the discovery of patterns, even ones that do not exist, releases dopamine into the brain. Dopamine is similar to morphine in its effects on the brain. It gives you a sense of euphoria and well-being. What this means is: *not believing* is very hard work. There are no strong analytical systems in the brain used for error detection, especially errors that have to be detected at a statistical level. Instead our brains have evolved to deal with anecdotes, and we tend to focus on and remember short-term trends and small number runs, something called *folk numeracy*. So, we are stuck with brains wired to believe, but there is hope: *science*. If we are to settle our disputes, we must turn to science, and its tried and true methodologies, and we must continue to collect "higher quality data" and develop more comprehensive theories.[22]

Okay, so we all have a tendency to equate God with religion and morality, and many of us, especially within the evangelical community, have bound faith in God so tightly to patriotism that atheism is seen as merely one side of the coin of social and national disloyalty. To top this situation off we are learning that we do not have a lot of control when it comes to what we believe. We are all natural believers because evolution has equipped us with the ability to connect things, even things that are not necessarily connected. Our only hope of turning things around is to look outside ourselves to a shared paradigm about how the world operates, and the only way to do this is through science. However, can science give us answers about God and morality? Sam Harris, a member of that group we call the "new atheists," thinks so.

In his book *The Moral Landscape: How Science Can Determine Human Values* (2010), Harris stridently denies that morality is the sole domain of the religious community. He criticizes the secular liberal community for abdicating any responsibility for establishing an objective foundation upon which to build a moral system. He says that the moral relativism of the secular liberal community is rooted in the cultural relativism of anthropologists and others who see moral relativism as "intellectual reparations for the crimes of Western colonialism, ethnocentrism, and racism."[23] He also says that the development of any ethical system does not require the moral absolutism of the religionist. A reasoned ethic can bring about consensus on moral principles, and how they can be implemented, but we must accept one simple premise: *that all ethical systems are ultimately rooted in the question of "human well-being."*[24] This is at the heart of every ethical system. This is not to say that all moral questions should be easy for the non-religionist. Morality will never be a matter of plugging variables into a mathematical formula. It does mean, though, that an ethical system with an eye to human well-being will always yield betters results than an absolute morality divorced from any consideration of human suffering. We must reject moral relativism because it paralyzes us in the face of human suffering; we must reject moral absolutism because it makes of human suffering a burnt offering to fantasies. When we separate human suffering from moral concerns we open the floodgate to great harm, because people easily lose sight of what leads to human well-being and happiness.[25]

What we are learning from science is that our brains are hard-wired to make moral decisions based on two general principles: *tit for tat* (reciprocity) and *defection*. The latter is the idea that changing sides in a social situation will benefit you more than loyalty. This idea is played out each week on the popular television show *Survivor*.[26] Most of this moral decision-making appears to occur in what is called the medial prefrontal cortex (MPFC) of the brain. This is the area that processes "emotion, reward, and judgments of self-relevance." That is why we cannot ignore the emotional component of a decision, and why "anxiety and fear… serve as anchors to social and moral norms."[27] For example, you know that doing X would benefit you in some way but you also know it will hurt someone you care about, or expose you to social ridicule. Will you do it? Maybe, but you will have a tough time making the decision and will possibly be filled with fear and anxiety before, during, and after the act. To avoid that situation you must develop a way of justifying your decisions, making what you do right in your own eyes.[28] Most people acquire their beliefs about the world through their emotional and social lives, and often feel as though they know far more than they actually do. They are also convinced that they are the master when it comes to free will. Of course, all this research calls into question many ideas put forth by religious believers. For example, the extent to which certain pathologies are genetically, socially, or emotionally determined. Harris concludes, "With respect to our current scientific understanding of the mind, the major religions remain wedded to doctrines that are growing less plausible by the day."[29]

Harris clearly has an ax to grind, but he is right. Science confirms his views more and more each day. Daniel Kahneman, Paul Slovic, David Eagleman, Michael Shermer, Steven Pinker, Jonathan Haidt, and many others continue to dig deeper into the processes of the brain. What we are now beginning to understand is that Freud and others were right, a lot more lurks under the surface than we imagine, a fact we learned about in part one of this book when we discussed the biology and psychology of fear. Jonathan Haidt uses a good analogy to help us understand the general way in which our brains work. He compares it to a man riding an elephant. The man is our conscious mind while the elephant is everything else. In this situation the man may be able to guide the elephant where *he* wants to go but the elephant ultimately has a mind of his own, which we sometimes learn to our chagrin.[30] For the most part, though, we believe ourselves to be in control, that we possess what we commonly call "free will."[31] Whether this is true or not, science will probably learn in the coming years. The evidence up to this point suggests that our "fate" is determined by a complicated mix of biological factors, environmental influence, and individual will—and the last factor is not as dominant as we like to think.

The good news, for Harris and society in general, is that most of those who say they believe in God are not Christian fundamentalists. Most of those who claim to believe in God have a rather nebulous view of the Christian religion and its moral demands.[32] The evidence for this can be seen in the demand for *New Age* answers to human problems. Books like *The Celestine Prophecy* (1997) and *The Secret* (2006) propose alternative approaches to understanding ourselves and the universe. It is very likely that the consumers of these books, who also believe in God, can be engaged in a dialogue, and should be, since religion does ultimately train one to see the world more holistically—which is not a bad thing, as long as the pitfall of religious literalism is avoided. That is why the philosopher Daniel Dennett has suggested that creating a more secularized and inclusive moral dialogue would first require that people understand religion better. He believes this would serve as a prophylactic against literal-mindedness when it comes to religion. However, the goal here is not to destroy faith but to guard against the simplistic mindset of the fundamentalist, for whom morality is merely a series of rules and for whom religion is just a list of beliefs that can be checked off. The goal of any religious studies program should be to develop an appreciation for the larger lessons that religion has to teach while making it difficult for people to fall prey to beliefs that are intrinsically antagonistic to the physical world. The chief lesson of religion is that in the grand scheme of things we mean very little, although many have turned this lesson on its head, using religion to bolster our innate narcissistic tendencies.[33]

A historical and literary appreciation of religion may be our best bet in protecting children, and others, from the worst effects of fundamentalist religion. It may also allow us to develop a healthy respect for the central lesson of religion: *our own limitations.* Is it possible for us to combine the broad lessons of religion with the knowledge that comes from reason and science? I don't think this is as tall an order as do some. The reason is that we already have plenty of literature that helps us to better understand religion and ourselves, although, as Dennett suggests, we may have to create new material and courses that are accessible to the young. For example, most young people might have difficulty traversing the prose of William James's *The Varieties of Religious Experience: A Study of Human Nature* (1902), but this book could easily be included in the reading list of a college course on religious history and thought. We could also have a whole course for young people that focuses on James's singular insight: *that religion is good when it is useful.* Children tend to be very literal in their view of things, the first to point out inconsistencies, so I think it would be fascinating to hear a group of children discuss whether you should believe something, whether it is true or not, if it improves the quality of your life.

If we wanted to teach about religion in general then Joseph Campbell's fascinating book *The Hero With a Thousand Faces* (1949) might be a good starting point. This is not an easy book, but it is a fun book because it is full of stories like the tale of Prince Five-Weapons and Sticky-hair, a forest ogre. Prince Five-Weapons is actually a story of the Buddha in a previous incarnation, one who through knowledge had conquered his fear of death. Since we are all naturally inclined to tell and listen to stories this book might be easier than some of the more cut and dried works of Richard Dawkins or the late Christopher Hitchens. Campbell's work is also less belligerent toward religion, since he believed that religion had something to teach us. As we discussed in a previous chapter, Campbell argued that all religions are dominated by what he called a *monomyth*, the myth of the hero. Most of the stories of religion can be reduced to a three-stage process of separation, initiation, and return.[34] How much of this is accomplished through the hero's own ability and how much is accomplished through the help of others changes with each story. However, the goal is always the same: the attempt to break free from one way of looking at the world to another, usually a view that allows you to master multiple worlds at the same time. Campbell writes,

> Dream is the personalized myth, myth the depersonalized dream; both myth and dream are symbolic in the same general way of the

dynamics of the psyche.[35]

This is why Campbell and his mentor, Carl Jung, believed that dreams give us insight into the psychic problems of the modern age, and that religion, properly understood, could help us through those problems.[36] What does it mean to properly understand religion? For Campbell it meant understanding a general process of human psychological development, a process that involved a "down-going" and an "up-coming" which would eventually lead to *katharsis*, the purging of sin and death. Of course, the path of the hero is for the few while most of us will prefer the "less adventurous way of the comparatively unconscious civic and tribal routines."[37] One can see how the fundamentalist Christian would fit into this latter category, and we know Campbell would have agreed since he writes that when "the poetry of myth is interpreted as biography, history, or science, it is killed."[38] In another place he writes,

> Mythology is defeated when the mind rests solemnly with its favorite or traditional images, defending them as though they themselves were the message that they communicate.[39]

In other words, those who approach mythology *literally* only perceive absurdity, unless they commit fully to it, but then that destroys the usefulness of religious teaching, which is meant not to delude but to free from delusion.[40]

In Campbell's view mythology, and therefore religion, should teach us how absurd our lives are in the grand scheme of things. Mythology is for this reason a "Divine Comedy," not tragic poetry or indignant moralizing.[41] In the modern age one might read Douglas Adams's *Hitchhiker's Guide to the Galaxy* as an antidote to the belief that our scientific and technological progress makes the universe more cognizant of us. It doesn't. "Humor," writes Campbell, "is the touchstone of the truly mythological" and it is "distinct from the more literal-minded and sentimental theological mood."[42]

The problem of the modern world is that where religion once provided the individual with meaning through the group, today the individual is all on his own, which may explain why man still looks for answers in traditional religion.[43] However, Campbell warns against the "tribal, national, or sectarian" view of God, which only leads us to fight for his alleged causes. Those who travel the road of the hero come to view the universe in a different light, they begin to understand the essential oneness of existence, a unity that makes *all men* brothers. They come to understand that any metaphysical conceptions we might have are best seen as the manifestation of our unconscious lives. The hero finally comes to terms with the knowledge that life is lived on a symbolic battlefield where we are all forced, to some degree or another, to live through the death or sacrifice of another.[44] This is the lesson of religion, but it can also be the lesson of science, if we keep ourselves open to *the world as it is*.

Chapter Sixteen

Our Brave New World

Until they become conscious they will never rebel, and until after they have rebelled they cannot become conscious.

George Orwell, *1984*

In his book *Civilization and Its Discontents* (1930) Sigmund Freud addressed the fundamental tension that exists between the desires of individuals and the demands of the societies in which they live. Freud was not the first to point this out. Jean-Jacques Rousseau had intimated much the same thing in his book *Of the Social Contract, or Principles of Political Right* (1762), in which the author harkened back to a mythical time in which all men lived in *Edenic* equality. The American writer Henry David Thoreau was animated by the same spirit when he wrote his *Walden; or, Life in the Woods* (1854). A desire to escape the increasing demands of the urban experience is addressed in all these works, and the cry has only grown shriller in the twentieth and twenty-first centuries, which we have observed in previous chapters.

Freud argued in *Civilization and Its Discontents* that the source of many psychological maladies are a product of the repression by various social structures on the individual's will. After dispensing with religion as only a band-aid for man's inability to face the world as it is, Freud explains how the chief aim of civilization has been the assertion of dominance over the natural world. The problem is that mankind generally seeks pleasure or freedom from pain, both of which civilization can supply but at the price man's fundamental desire: *freedom*. Much of that price is exacted in the form of restrictions on sexuality and aggression. Restrictions on sexuality are dealt with in George Orwell and Aldous Huxley's often-cited dystopian novels, and both address it in an interesting fashion.

In Orwell's *1984* "The Party" restricts sexual pleasure to marriage in an attempt to harness man's sexual energy so it can be used for the state's purposes. They also want to make sure that none of the relationships among party members interfere with devotion to "The Party." In *Brave New World* the ruling class encourages everyone to engage in a hedonistic sexuality. Those who desire a monogamous relationship are viewed with suspicion, because as everyone learns while a child, "Everybody belongs to everyone else." What is interesting is that both achieve the same purpose: *the breakdown of the commonly experienced emotional bond between men and women.* In a 1949 letter to Orwell, Huxley argued that the ruling elite will always find it easier to provide material abundance as a soporific to the masses. The "boot-on-the-face" policy that Orwell writes about in his novel, according to Huxley, simply requires too much work for the ruling elite.[1] I tend to agree with Huxley, and the popularity today of *Prozac, Paxil, Ambien,* etc., has an eerie similarity to the drug *soma* in *Brave New World.*[2]

The problem individuals encounter with any program of social repression is that they eventually internalize those restrictions into what Freud called the *super-ego,* an internal agent that attempts to curtail our two chief desires: *sexual satisfaction and freedom.* The German philosopher Friedrich Nietzsche had earlier espoused a similar idea that he called *will to power.* Developed in various writings like *Beyond Good and Evil* (1886), Nietzsche suggested that it was natural for men who stand characteristically head-and-shoulders above the herd of humanity to aspire to power, to express their will in and over the lives of others. It is for this reason that Nietzsche denounced Christianity as a *morality of the herd,* a decadent philosophy meant to keep in-check the natural leaders of society.

Freud saw it a bit differently. In his view the internalization of authority—which could be here a synonym for morality—was a problem for every individual in society, not just those with a will to power. The internalization of authority into the super-ego meant the individual would be racked with guilt when he inevitably violated the restrictions of society, and by extension the super-ego. The reason for this is that the super-ego monitors our relationship to society, which we early on come to see as a protector. Once we have that sense of protection we become fearful of losing it through actions that might displease society. *Ostracism* becomes death, often merely social death but occasionally real death. So, our super-ego is assiduous in repressing our true desires until they begin to manifest themselves as neurosis.

Freud was correct in pointing out that human beings try to direct the world to satisfy their own ego, and that the result is always an acute narcissism: *the inability to distinguish between the self and the world around us.* This is a problem that has only become more pronounced in modern society, as Christopher Lasch pointed out in his best-selling book *The Culture of Narcissism: American Life in An Age of Diminishing Expectations* (1979). According to Lasch, modern America had become a society of self-involved individuals who had lost nearly all faith in the notion of expertise, although, ironically, still demanding it. Americans had also lost nearly all sense of self-reliance and had given themselves over to a program of *extreme* individualism which fostered a "war of all against all." However, unlike the narcissist of Freud's day and age, the modern narcissist is animated not by guilt but by anxiety.[3]

Lasch points out that by the 1970s it was generally agreed that liberalism had become politically and intellectually bankrupt. Liberalism was no longer the pursuit of maximized freedom; it had become a movement of personal fulfillment through the identification of one's self as a victim. What animated the liberal cause was not fixing the system but simply identifying those who were victimized by it, and then helping them to limp along in life as best as possible. As Lasch writes, we ended up demanding "too much of life" and "too little of ourselves."[4] What was happening in the 1960s and 1970s was that the radicalism of the nineteenth century was becoming in the twentieth century an attempt to "drown" our own "sense of personal failure in collective action." What made it worse was that modern radicalism was exemplified in mindlessness and a blind adherence to political doctrines. The attempt to build a better world was abandoned for the promise of "psychic self-improvement," evidence that people in the main had abandoned faith in political action. The "awareness craze" of the 1970s was an attempt to internalize our desire for a viable social order. The idea was that each of us could achieve some kind of individual spiritual utopianism, and "the devil take the world!"

The conundrum, though, was that neither inner peace nor a viable social order was now possible since most, if not all, found the former completely elusive and had abandoned the latter for *facile grandiosity*. Lasch is here diagnosing the problem long before the "Big 80s" and the cultural phenomena of "Dynasty," "Dallas," or "Lifestyles of the Rich and Famous." What was happening in the 1970s, and what continued for decades after, was that people were being trained to idealize the rich and famous. People were being encouraged to loathe the "herd," or in other words: *themselves*. This had the effect of only increasing the social anxiety that already existed, making people feel even more victimized by a society that promised so much but delivered so little. The retreat into the self was an admission that we now lived in a society where surviving, not thriving, would be the order of the day.

The last thirty years has been an attempt to camouflage the common man's loss of self-reliance through the notion of punctuated self-aggrandizement. Everyone is told to expect the possibility that they will get "fifteen minutes of fame," and we remain ever in hope that it will one day happen. However, since this is not a likely outcome for most, society has encouraged us to see another way in which we can make our lives matter in the grand scheme of things. This is done by making us all experts at one thing above all: *consumption.* Think of the common parlance of business, which makes the word *consumer* a hallowed designation. The consumer has become a sanctified practitioner of the only religion that Americans really practice: *commerce.* Politicians and business leaders try to convince us that consumers do not just know best but they know all. The *market,* which is just *a collection of consumers,* has become omniscient, and we reject their almost divine, homespun wisdom at our own peril.[5] We exult in the common man while maintaining a society that is largely antagonistic to his basic needs and wants.[6]

Still, though, we cannot rid ourselves of the anxiety of life without pills and endless therapy sessions. We still hope the professionals, the scientists and technologists, will someday figure it all out. We continue to ignore the chief problem of the human condition, even as we stare it straight in the face. We refuse to deal with the fact that we are frail and finite creatures, that our infinite desires will always be physically limited in their satisfaction. Our hunger will never be sated; our thirst will never be slaked.

I have thought a lot about this idea of limits and all roads lead back to one thing: *the issue of morality.* Of course, we might substitute the word *ethics* for *morality,* because the former implies a greater level of intellectual thought while the latter implies a code of conduct revealed to mankind through traditional religion. I think the distinction is instrumentally irrelevant in the modern world since there is pretty conclusive evidence that moral sentiment is universal.[7] However, the distinction between morality and ethics is important when a society finds it necessary to discuss what kind of behavior is acceptable and unacceptable in that society. Sam Harris has done an excellent job of starting this conversation with his recent book *The Moral Landscape: How Science Can Determine Human Values* (2010). I cannot say that Harris has satisfied every concern I have about this subject but I generally agree with his view that those who discuss morality must always do so in light of whether an action causes or alleviates human suffering. This shows the core problem with a morality based on what is called "fundamentalist" Christianity.

The fundamentalist is ultimately a literalist in every meaning of the term. To lie is wrong, no matter what the situation. To abort a fetus is wrong, no matter what the situation. To kill the infidel is always right, no matter what the situation. The inflexibility of the fundamentalist mind extends even to that which can be empirically known, which is why these folks reject hundreds of years of geology, chemistry, physics, and biology, preferring a science based on the first few chapters of Genesis. It is because of this mindset that the New Atheists have it mostly right: *fundamentalists must be for the most part marginalized.* They cannot be practically engaged in a dialogue concerning the social ethic that should inform our political and economic lives.

If you want to see how the literal-minded religionist views politics just read Thomas Frank's *What's the Matter With Kansas? How Conservatives Won the Heart of America* (2004). The first thing you will learn is that the literal-minded religionist sees a conspiracy of liberalism in everything that is done by the "obnoxious eastern elite" of society. These "backlash theorists," as Frank calls them, believe there is a national conspiracy of the "wealthy, powerful, and well-connected," and that the "liberal media" and "atheistic scientists" are their mouthpiece. These elites, it is believed by Kansans, "pull the strings and make the puppets dance." Convinced they are *morally superior*, Kansans attribute their economic woes to an orchestrated persecution by a shadowy, liberal conspiracy. Kansan economic woes have nothing to do with the *Freedom to Farm Act* (1996), which provides huge subsidies to ADM, Cargill, and ConAgra, and which prices many small farmers out of the market. Because Kansans cannot see the connection between laws that protect large-scale agribusiness and their own economic plight they turn to Republican candidates who preach "family values:" opposition to abortion, gay marriage, atheism, and evolution. Kansans are convinced their economic problems are really just a symptom of the moral problems plaguing the country, not that the capitalist system is being gamed against them.[8]

Professionals and experts are also seen by Kansans as a tyrannous bunch, and conservative politicians like to play up this antagonism, caricaturing the educated and the agnostic as interlopers seeking to oppress Middle America. It is not actual physical oppression with which conservative Kansans are concerned but rather the criticism of things like religion, creationism, or traditional morality. They see criticism of these things as a form of persecution. No one likes to be made fun of, and conservative politicians claim they are coming to the aid of these much-maligned simple folk, offering them an "authentic" alternative to the patronizing, east or west coast, elites. This is one of the reasons that, above all, anyone running for office in Kansas must be a Christian. Atheists need not apply. Conservative Kansans are convinced that there is no economic class war, that there is only a conflict between the hardworking and the parasitic—usually identified as an elite liberal or a welfare recipient.[9] However, the whole political process in Kansas, as in many other areas of the country, is a bait and switch operation.

Conservative politicians get into office running on social issues but once in office they begin to pass legislation favorable to entrenched business interests. Kansans, fearing that their way of life is changing too fast or wanting to reverse modern trends, vote for representatives that only make things worse, because the real issue in Kansas politics, as in the rest of the nation, is *the breakdown of democratic capitalism*, which can be loosely defined as capitalism loosely regulated by the democratic process. So, Kansans, and many other Americans, clamor for more deregulation, the shrinking of the welfare state, the destruction of unions, and the selling off of nearly all state-owned assets. They do this because they are convinced that the roots of their problems are not economic but social and moral.[10] The irony is that Kansans are right about the problems being a moral and social, but it has nothing to do with fornication, abortion, or gay marriage. It is about the great economic disparity that exists in a country given almost completely over to the notion that anything can be bought.[11] Not until we stop looking at everything through the filter of an actuarial chart or a balance sheet will we be able to address the real issues plaguing American society.[12]

The problem with our "brave new world" is that it has become so disproportionately geared toward material well-being that little else is thought about on a daily basis. We have become a hedonistic society, in which those unable to consume are seen as somehow morally corrupt, even when the structures of society militate against their consumption unless they go heavily into debt. This is not the only economic contradiction in our society. The commitment of many to what are called "family values" is militated against by what Daniel Bell called "the cultural contradictions of capitalism." Starting in the early twentieth century many of the "bourgeois" expectations of the middling and the lower classes were challenged by the growing tension between social mores and the libertine aspects of a market economy. The market, especially in the form of modern advertising, encourages individuals to pursue anything that is "new," to explore their sexuality, and to liberate themselves from the restrictions of society. In order for this to be achieved many things had to change in society during the twentieth century. It not only required the general breakdown of social consciousness; it required the acceptance of nearly perpetual debt, which in an earlier age had been viewed as economic servitude, or worse: *an act of immorality*. From a moral perspective, what science could not achieve, was easily achieved by modern technology and advertising, things which led directly to what we call the "counter-culture," whether in its libertine enjoyment of the economic self or in its rejection of the material world.

Daniel Bell concludes,

> American capitalism, as I have tried to show, has lost its traditional legitimacy, which was based on a moral system of reward rooted in the Protestant sanctification of work. It has substituted a hedonism which promises material ease and luxury, yet shies away from all the historic implications of a "voluptuary system," with all its social

permissiveness and libertinism.[13]

This is not the only contradiction of the modern economic age. Michael B. Crawford has pointed out in his book *Shop Class as Soulcraft: An Inquiry Into the Value of Work* (2009) that work has ceased to be something we own, that corporations have become so efficient at expropriating labor that few of us still experience the joy of working with our minds and our hands. Even Aristotle and Adam Smith realized that this would be a problem in a society where people were reduced to the drudgery of physical, mindless labor.[14] What we have done is substituted consumption for all other activities. It does not matter whether you find your job satisfying, no matter how drudge-like it might be, and no matter how inadequately it provides for your needs. We have a drug for that, say the pharmaceutical companies; we have a line of credit, say the banks. This is the biggest contradiction with which most of us must live because our jobs dominate a large portion of our lives, and the latest trend by corporations is to convince us that if we cannot enjoy having our labor expropriated then there must be something wrong with us. We just need an attitude adjustment, not economic equity or the ability to feel engaged by the work we do. So, we are forced to spend our time in seminars that teach us about "core values" and how to operate in the "new economy," and then we are told that if we cannot keep up with all the changes that are happening in the business world then the fault lies solely in our inability to overcome and adapt to the situation—even though it is gamed against us from the start.[15]

This situation is reminiscent of the seventeenth century, when liberal capitalism was in its infancy in England, and still fighting against the mercantilist spirit of an earlier age. Christopher Hill lays out this story wonderfully in his book *Liberty Against the Law: Some Seventeenth-Century Controversies* (1996). The book is organized around the English "enclosure movement" of the seventeenth century. This is when land owners began to enclose their lands and turn them to pasture rather than agriculture. This had several effects on the general population.

One was that it made food prices more volatile since grain now had to be imported to feed the population. It also meant the destruction of what was called "the commons," a shared agricultural plot, which has its corollary in the modern *community garden*—although it was far more important, since it may have been the local workers only source of fresh fruits and vegetables.[16] The irony is that the enclosure movement caused such devastating dislocation that many began to roam the land, turning to brigandage in order to survive. This was before the English Industrial Revolution was able to soak up all the excess labor created by the enclosure movement. Some have estimated that during this time England had a chronic problem with unemployment, often exceeding 25% in the seventeenth century. It is no wonder that the government had to turn to forced emigration to solve many of these problems. This was first tried in the New World, but famously got redirected to Australia in the late eighteenth and early nineteenth centuries.[17] Britain's history shows what happens when people criminalize poverty rather than addressing its root cause: the lack of an adequate distribution of national income, which is the foundation of any democratic capitalist system that seeks to maintain a large middle class.

I would like to end this chapter by suggesting that merely distributing income properly is not the only thing we must do to improve our society. Yes, it may be one of the most important parts of the equation that we must consider when addressing our larger social problems. However, any solution to the problems that ail our society: poverty, violence, hunger, homelessness, physical and psychological abuse, rape, etc., must also take into consideration human psychology. If we ignore Freud's insight into the individual's desire to satisfy the ego we will be unable to fully address those needs at a social or political level. In other words, we must commit ourselves to creating a society that allows the greatest amount of flexibility for the individual without allowing him or her to excessively exploit others only to satisfy their ego. The turn-of-the-century writer Thorstein Veblen understood that economic activity and ego often go hand-in-hand.

Most mainstream economists today disparage the notion that Thorstein Veblen put forth in his book *The Theory of the Leisure Class* (1899), but the idea that people are driven by ego in their economic pursuits is obvious to anyone who has worked in an organization. Veblen's concern was with those who flaunted their excess wealth in the form of *conspicuous consumption*, but his general view that economic behavior is driven by ego seems valid along the spectrum of economic activity. If you have ever worked as a manager you have observed firsthand the jockeying for position that goes on among those you supervise. Why would this occur even when there is clearly no economic benefit derived, or even sought, from having a little more power over others? This clearly shows that we are first and foremost social animals, not rational economic players, a truth that is reinforced by reading Thackeray's *Vanity Fair* (1848) or any of Charles Dickens's numerous works.

The "conspicuous consumption" of the Gilded Age can be seen as just another manifestation of the Native American *potlatch*, a tradition in which the chief of a tribe would nearly ruin himself materially in order to obtain something even more fundamentally valuable: *the esteem of his tribe.* In the modern age, where consumption generally continues to be viewed as the highest achievement, we are in awe of those with the *power* to consume, and that is why a fundamentally more just distribution of national income is important in our society, because *money is power*. Without an adequate income the average individual cannot meet his or her basic needs, but even more important he or she ceases to have any power over their life, and this begins to manifest itself in other problems, which debt only exacerbates. So, a more just distribution of income may be the starting point, but we must also address other fundamental issues related to the human condition: mainly, the needs of the ego.

Epilogue

A politics emptied of substantive moral engagement makes for an impoverished civic life. It is also an open invitation to narrow, intolerant moralisms. Fundamentalists rush in where liberals fear to tread.

Michael Sandel, *Justice: What's the Right Thing to Do?*

When I was a child, I spake as a child, I understood as a child, I thought as a child: but when I became a man, I put away childish things.

1 Corinthians 13:11

We have discussed a lot in the last few hundred pages; however, my hope is that you have arrived at this point of the book with the understanding that we are all, whether we like it or not, part of some moral narrative. That narrative begins the moment we are born. It is determined by genetics, by the type of family we are born into, by the sociocultural milieu in which we find ourselves, and to possibly a lesser extent by the dominant political economy of our society. No man, to use the old cliché, is an island. It is because we are surrounded by other beings that we must engage in some contemplation of the moral universe. For, a moral universe is one that is more predictable, one that ensures greater survival through an understanding of how that moral schema works and how we should operate in it. One of the problems with this is that from a cosmological standpoint each of us has all the moral value of a speck of dust when placed beside the practically infinite universe of modern science, but that view is no help in our day-to-day struggle to figure out how to survive, or maybe even thrive, in this demanding world of ours.

We have explored in the third part of this book how the early development of cosmological thought was meant to impose some type of order on the primal chaos that was thought to surround us all. The irony is that we have been so successful at imposing that order through *civilization* that we are taken aback and confused when chaos comes rushing back into our lives. After all, did not the Enlightenment philosophers tell us that the whole universe was an ordered place where God's natural laws, both physical and moral, were always at work? Is not the world some kind of beautiful, self-correcting mechanism that will work properly if we simply leave it alone? Do we really need to worry about the malefactor or those in need? Will not nature take care of them, giving them their just deserts?

Well, the moral world is not as simple as the one conceived of by some Enlightenment thinkers, or their admiring nineteenth-century religionists. First of all, the morally progressive world appears to be limited only to man's experience. It is a natural product of our cognitive evolution. That moral landscape has been and continues to be reshaped to meet the demands of the world we inhabit everyday: *civilization.*

The last several centuries man has attempted to escape from the moral narrative into which he has been thrown, to gain through science an advantage over nature, and through economics and politics the dominance of others.[1] There is the rub, as Hamlet might say, because we can never escape the moral narrative. The only one who achieves a momentary moral advantage over others is the sociopath, and as Aristotle said, a man who has no need of society is either a beast or a god. There are still some who think they can live in *civilized* society as a beast or a god, but they do not understand the impossibility of it. For, we eventually kill both.

Why are we moral rather than immoral? Well, that would be a subject for another book and I can suggest several to start you on your way. You might begin by reading the works of Steven Pinker, Jonathan Haidt, or Ian Macintyre. Pick up some of Plato's works or Aristotle's writings. You also might find some insight into the topic by reading of Robert M. Pirsig's *Zen and the Art of Motorcycle Maintenance: An Inquiry Into*

Values (1974). In this book a motorcycle journey across country, meant to solidify the bond between father and son, becomes a journey inward, into what really matters in life and how we can know it. Be warned, you may find the answer unsatisfying.

Another book to put on your reading list is Michael Sandel's *Justice: What's the Right Thing to Do?* Again, you will not have all the answers at the end of the book, but you will also be convinced that no one else does either. Therein lies a central lesson in any discussion about morality: *it is a difficult endeavor and should not be taken up lightly.* The formulaic answers that traditional religion offers simply do not work anymore—if they ever did. However, since we cannot avoid the moral universe of which we are naturally a part, we must discuss it, know it, agree on it, and proceed to build the type of world we want to live in based on those shared moral principles.

It is here that we arrive at the nub of the problem associated with *the culture of fear* and its close cousin, apocalypticism. Apocalypticism represents the desire to establish a utopian world of justice, a type of justice that is simply not possible. The word *utopia* tellingly means "nowhere." *The culture of fear*, on the other hand, exemplifies the belief that we are too distant from experiencing justice in our own lives, that the deck is stacked against us. Whether this latter belief is real or only perceived is still the subject of much debate, but millions of people appear to be convinced that the *injustice* is real enough that things should be changed. Would it not be prudent for us to at least have a dialogue about it rather than relying on modern bromides about "liberty" and "free markets"? Shouldn't we ask whether these bromides are merely a way of distancing ourselves from social and economic changes that we do not like, or whether they are an attempt to assuage our guilt at past and present injustice? Some are already having the dialogue but it is one-sided. The religious believer, and those politicians who cow tow almost solely to that constituency, argue that the many problems which plague our society can only be remedied by a return to Judeo-Christian values.[2]

However, to accept this solution requires that we swallow by faith the simplistic moral universe upon which they frame their own lives. This is not a solution; it is merely sticking one's head in the sand.

So, how can we build a more harmonious social and economic system when millions of people dread each day's sunrise? How can we have a proper functioning political system when so many people are looking forward to the destruction of this world and the coming of the next one? In the words of the popular 1980s band Midnight Oil, "How can we dance when our earth is turning? How can we sleep when our beds are burning?"

Well, if we hope to build a better, although always imperfect, society we must not only set aside our utopian visions we must dispense with its doppelgänger: dystopianism, or what we now call *the culture of fear*. We can only do this if we are unafraid to talk about morality in the public square, not the simplistic morality of a bronze-age people three thousand years ago but a more robust and modern morality, a morality built on the foundation of modern reason, common sense, and science. We still have a choice, and we should not allow the culture of fear or apocalypticism to rob us of the opportunity to choose a better future for ourselves and our posterity.

Notes

Preface

1 Author Richard Horne has already written a light take on the end of the world in a book called *A Is for Armageddon: A Catalogue of Disasters That May Culminate in the End of the World As We Know It* (New York: Harper Paperbacks, 2010).

2 The defrocked tele-minister Jim Bakker is now hawking "time of trouble" survival gear and food. Watching this program is a real education in the use of fear to sell both religion and over-priced dry goods.

3 Jonathan Edwards, "Sinners in the Hands of An Angry God," a sermon preached in Enfield, CT, on July 8, 1741.

4 An example of this is the Roman Catholic Church's stance on the use of condoms in Africa. Even in the face of a widespread AIDS epidemic the Church continues to discourage the use of condoms. On its face this is not only morally skewed because it encourages the spread of a deadly disease but because it encourages human reproduction at a time when we should be encouraging people to have less children, not more. Accessed on June 12, 2012, http://www.pbs.org/newshour/bb/health/jan-june11/vatican_05-30.html.

Chapter One - Be Afraid, Be Very Afraid

1 Daniel Gardner, *The Science of Fear: Why We Fear the Things We Shouldn't—and Put Ourselves in Greater Danger* (New York: Dutton, 2008), 289-304.

2 http://www.reuters.com/article/2011/10/19/us-usa-antidepressants-idUSTRE79I7FI20111019, accessed on October 28, 2011.

3 http://www.washingtonpost.com/blogs/checkpoint-washington/post/foreign-hackers-broke-into-illinois-water-plant-control-system-industry-expert-says/2011/11/18/gIQAgmTZYN_blog.html, accessed on 1/13/2012; http://www.msnbc.msn.com/id/45409799/ns/technology_and_science-security/t/illinois-water-plant-not-hacked-foreigners-us/, accessed on 1/13/2012.

4 Michael Crichton, *State of Fear* (New York: Harper Collins, 2004), 445-60.

5 H. L. Mencken, *In Defense of Women* (New York: A. A. Knopf, 1922) [Originally published in 1918].

6 Frank Furedi, *Culture of Fear: Risk-Taking and the Morality of Low Expecta-*

tions (New York: Continuum, 2002), xii.

7 There is no way to know these statistics with any certainty. Nick Rosen in his book *Off the Grid: Inside the Movement for More Space, Less Government, and True Independence in Modern America* (2011) suggests the number may be anywhere from 300,000 to 500,000, depending on how you do the count. For example, there are some people who only live off the grid part-time, and there are those who minimize grid time while living still living in large urban areas, 13.

8 Dan Gardner, *The Science of Fear: Why We Fear the Things We Shouldn't—and Put Ourselves in Greater Danger* (Boston MA: Dutton, 2011).

9 See Paul Slovic, *The Perception of Risk* (Sterling, VA: Earthscan Publications, 2000) and Daniel Kahneman *Thinking, Fast and Slow* (New York: Farrar, Straus and Giroux, 2011).

10 Frank Furedi, *Culture of Fear: Risk-Taking and the Morality of Low Expectations* (New York: Continuum, 2002), xiii-xv.

11 This narrative became particularly dominant in the United States as the frontier closed, and more and more people were subject to an urban, industrialized lifestyle. This became a dominant theme in American history writing with the publication of Frederick Jackson Turner's paper on "the close of the frontier," a paper he gave at the 1893 annual conference of the American Historical Association, held in Chicago, Illinois. Oswald Spengler's early twentieth century tome on the "decline of the West" was also very popular, especially since it was published after the horrors of World War I. There have always been groups in society that believe we are in perpetual decline, that civilizations like human beings are born, live, and then die.

12 Barry Glassner, *The Culture of Fear: Why Americans Are Afraid of the Wrong Things* (New York: Basic Books, 1999), 5.

13 Ibid., 8.

14 Ibid., 6.

15 The movie "Bowling for Columbine" (2002) makes the disturbing assertion that gun violence in America is not just a result of the ease with which Americans can buy guns, but that Americans are much more trigger-happy when it comes to solving their problems. Evidence for this is that Canada has more guns per capita than the U.S. but has far less gun violence. Michael Moore suggests this may have something to do with the general influence of the military-industrial complex and the hawkish nature of U.S. foreign policy. United States citizens are raised to believe that violence is more socially acceptable. Could this also explain why 76% of all serial killings occur in the United States? This statistic is taken from Peter Vronsky's *Serial Killers: The Method and Madness of Monsters* (New York: Berley Books, 2004), 32.

16 Barry Glassner, *The Culture of Fear: Why Americans Are Afraid of the Wrong Things* (New York: Basic Books, 1999), 3-9.

17 Ibid., 5, 133, 9, xxvi, xxii-xxiii, 207-210.

18 http://www.washingtonpost.com/opinions/this-summer-of-the-shark-its-all-about-saving-them/2011/08/03/gIQAVQfnwI_story.html, accessed on

January 17, 2012.

19 Barry Glassner, *The Culture of Fear: Why Americans Are Afraid of the Wrong Things* (New York: Basic Books, 1999), 23-49.

20 Steven D. Levitt and Stephen J. Dubner, *Freakonomics: A Rogue Economist Explores the Hidden Side of Everything* (New York: William Morrow, 2005), 105-32. An article in *The Economist*, http://www.economist.com/node/5246700?story_id=5246700, argues that Levitt's initial research was flawed.

21 http://www.fbi.gov/about-us/cjis/ucr/crime-in-the-u.s/2010/crime-in-the-u.s.-2010/tables/10tbl01.xls.

22 Barry Glassner, *The Culture of Fear: Why Americans Are Afraid of the Wrong Things* (New York: Basic Books, 1999), 131-150.

23 Ibid., 210.

24 Frank Furedi, *Culture of Fear: Risk-Taking and the Morality of Low Expectations* (New York: Continuum, 2002), 9-11.

25 Ibid., vii-xvii.

26 Ibid., 63.

27 Ibid., 66-68, 162.

28 Ibid., 56.

29 Ibid., 90-103.

30 Ibid., 25-26.

31 Ibid., 185-92.

32 Dan Gardner, *The Science of Fear: Why We Fear the Things We Shouldn't— and Put Ourselves in Greater Danger* (Boston MA· Dutton, 2011), 125-154.

33 Steven Pinker, *The Better Angels of Our Nature: Why Violence Has Declined* (New York: Viking, 2011).

Chapter Two - A Century of Fear

1 David Halberstam, *The Best and the Brightest* (New York: Fawcett Crest, 1972), 296-301.

2 Joanna Bourke, *Fear, A Cultural History* (Emeryville, CA: Shoemaker and Hoard, 2005), 25-50.

3 Ibid., 51-71.

4 Ibid., 81-108.

5 Ibid., 109-158.

6 Ibid., 149.

7 Ibid., 198-221.

8 Ibid., 222-254.

9 Ibid., 2005), 167-188.

10 Ibid., 255-285, 295-321, 322-351, 357-391.

Chapter Three - The Biology of Fear

1 Kenneth L. Woodward, "Religion and the Brain," *Newsweek*, 7 May 2001.

2 This example was given to highlight the workings of the limbic system, not to assess the relative safety or danger of living in the city. For all the talk of rampant crime in the United States we cannot ignore the statistics, we live in one of the safest places in the world. However, always use your own good judgment.

3 Actually this is an exaggeration since science could not exist without sensory input from the world around us. When it is said that science encourages us take pause, when it comes to what we can sense, this is only to say that our senses may be faulty enough not to trust them every single time. That is why science requires multiple observations to confirm that something actually happened.

4 Richard Dawkins, *The Ancestor's Tale: A Pilgrmage to the Dawn of Evolution* (New York: Houghton Mifflin Harcourt, 2004), 36.

5 Desmond Morris, *The Naked Ape: A Zoologists Study of the Human Animal* (New York: Dell, 1967), 22, 24, 33, 41.

6 This is a common mistake made by those who do not understand natural selection through environmental adaptation. Evolution can only be explained *post hoc*, because the complexity of biological development does not allow us to predict with certainty how a single adaptation will affect the organism. The minute an adaptation becomes fixed it may prove deleterious for survival, which may argue for the notion that those organism that tend to be prove more flexible tend to survive.

7 Craig Stanford, *Upright: The Evolutionary Key to Becoming Human* (New York: Houghton Mifflin Harcourt, 2003), xvi, xvii, 39, 59-60, 121, 140-141.

8 Ibid., 103.

9 This timeline for this has changed significantly since 1967. Paleontologists and evolutionary biologists now believe that the last common ancestors of the species that would evolve into hominids split from their ape-like cousins around seven million years ago. A more up-to-date, and equally enjoyable, narrative of this development can be found in Richard Dawkins's *The Ancestor's Tale: A Pilgrimage to the Dawn of Evolution* (New York: Mariner Books, 2004.

10 Desmond Morris, *The Naked Ape* (New York: Dell, 1967), 18.

11 There are some who have suggested, with good evidence, that primates are highly social creatures. Jared Diamond's book *The Third Chimpanzee: The Evolution and Future of the Human Animal* (1991). Diamond goes on to argue that it is because of the extensive socialization of the "higher" brain functions that we can explain the rise of civilization.

12 Richard Dawkins, *The Ancestor's Tale: A Pilgrmage to the Dawn of Evolution* (New York: Houghton Mifflin Harcourt, 2004), 84.

13 This idea is explored in detail in chapter three of David Deutsch's most recent book *The Beginning of Infinity: Explanations That Transform the World* (2011). This is a sentiment shared by most evolutionary biologists who see the development of culture as a pivotal turning point in human development. Jared Diamond has termed this axial period the "Great Leap Forward."

14 Desmond Morris, *The Naked Ape* (New York: Dell, 1967), 34.

15 Steven Pinker has superbly summarized this debate in his book *The Blank Slate: The Modern Denial of Human Nature* (2002), a debate that proves to be more about social policy and politics than it is about biology. As is true of most things the truth of the nature versus nurture debate lies somewhere in the middle between these two extremes.

16 Daniel Wolpert, "The Real Reason for Brains," a lecture given at TED in July 2011.

17 Barry J. Gibb, *A Rough Guide to the Brain* (London: Penguin Books, 2007), 21-25, 36-41.

18 Rush W. Dozier, *Fear Itself: The Origin and Nature of the Powerful Emotion That Shapes Our Life and Our World* (New York: St. Martin's Press, 1998), 80.

19 Ibid., 3-25.

20 Ibid., 11, 76, 119-127.

21 Daniel Gardner, *The Science of Fear: Why We Fear the Things We Shouldn't—and Put Ourselves in Greater Danger* (New York: Dutton, 2008), 16, 3, 46-58, 30-31, 85.

22 Rush W. Dozier, *Fear Itself: The Origin and Nature of the Powerful Emotion That Shapes Our Life and Our World* (New York: St. Martin's Press, 1998), 43, 79, 92, 108-110, 132, 159.

23 Daniel Gardner, *The Science of Fear: Why We Fear the Things We Shouldn't—and Put Ourselves in Greater Danger* (New York: Dutton, 2008), 20, 36.

24 Ibid., 36, 40, 87-101, 102-124.

25 See Thomas S. Kuhn's *The Structures of Scientific Revolutions* (Chicago: University of Chicago Press, 1962). In this book Kuhn suggests that science proceeds slowly because it is often an attempt to prove a prevailing theory rather than to challenge it, and that the only time science experiences a revolution is when an observed anomaly raises questions that cannot be answered by the prevailing theory. Therefore, science is ultimately a gradual, conservative process, which is also counter-revolutionary because of its added dimen-

sion of being a social endeavor.

26 Daniel Gardner, *The Science of Fear: Why We Fear the Things We Shouldn't—and Put Ourselves in Greater Danger* (New York: Dutton, 2008), 244.

27 Rush W. Dozier, *Fear Itself: The Origin and Nature of the Powerful Emotion That Shapes Our Life and Our World* (New York: St. Martin's Press, 1998), 177-194.

28 Michael Shermer, *The Believing Brain: From Ghosts and Gods to Politics and Conspiracies—How We Construct Beliefs and Reinforce Them As Truths* (New York: Henry Holt and Company, 2011).

29 Rush W. Dozier, *Fear Itself: The Origin and Nature of the Powerful Emotion That Shapes Our Life and Our World* (New York: St. Martin's Press, 1998), 129-130.

30 Ibid., 148.

Chapter Four - The Psychology of Fear

1 There may be some artistic license here since most were already dead from hanging or disembowelment prior to being drawn and quartered.

2 Ernest Becker, *The Denial of Death* (New York: The Free Press, 1973), 1-8, 12, 11-24. Freud spoke of this act of annihilation within the collective, which serves the purpose of not only making us immortal but more powerful. See Sigmund Freud, *Civilization and Its Discontents* (1930). Much of the material in Becker's book has also been profiled in a documentary film entitled "Flight From Death: The Quest for Immortality" (2005).

3 Why do we laugh at bathroom and sex jokes? These bodily functions are not really all that funny when you think about it. Could it be because we are afraid to enjoy these things? Could it be that enjoying them forces us to admit how important they are, and how physically vulnerable that makes us?

4 Ernest Becker, *The Denial of Death* (New York: The Free Press, 1973), 25-46.

5 In the film "Flight From Death: The Quest for Immortality" several researchers: Sheldon Solomon, Tom Bozinsky, and Jeff Greenberg, suggest that culture reflects a response to death anxiety. Origin stories give people meaning, and the cultures built on those origin stories become a constant in an uncertain world, which is why people react with such vitriol and violence against those who threaten both the origin story and the culture of which it is a product.

6 Ernest Becker, *The Denial of Death* (New York: The Free Press, 1973), 47-66.

7 This can be found in Book I of Aristotle's *Politics*.

8 Ernest Becker, *The Denial of Death* (New York: The Free Press, 1973), 67-96. In Joseph Campbell's *The Hero With a Thousand Faces* (Princeton, NJ: Princ-

eton University Press, 1949) we learn the story of Prince Five-Weapons who defeats an ogre not with the physical weapons he had trained in but with the knowledge that he could not really be killed. The story is meant to show how knowledge of death is the beginning of enlightenment, 85-89. Any other approach serves merely to cloak our fear, but when the cloak proves inadequate we develop a neurosis, Ernest Becker, *The Denial of Death* (New York: The Free Press, 1973), 92.

9 Ernest Becker, *The Denial of Death* (New York: The Free Press, 1973), 93-124.

10 Nathaniel Hawthorne, "Young Goodman Brown" (1835).

11 The popular Harry Potter series explores this theme as the main character and his friends search out what are called *horcruxes*, in which are stored parts of the main villain's soul. The idea is that if a part of the soul is kept safe it can somehow survive physical death. What more than this is the culture we hold on to for dear life?

12 Ernest Becker, *The Denial of Death* (New York: The Free Press, 1973), 147.

13 Ibid., 127-158. According to Sheldon Solomon capitalism and communism are also "death-denying ideologies." See film entitled "Flight From Death: The Quest for Immortality" (2005).

14 See Karen Armstrong's *Holy War: The Crusades and Their Impact on Today's World* (New York: Anchor Books, 2001).

15 There are more examples of this animus. The anti-Irish Catholic movement of the 1840s even bred a political party called the "Know-Nothings." In the late nineteenth century the Chinese Exclusion Act (1882) put a decade-long ban on Chinese immigration into the United States. In the 1920s there was a move to "Americanize" the new influx of immigrants from southeastern Europe. This was also the point at which the first modern immigration laws began to emerge. Today the cultural focus has turned toward illegal immigrants from Latin-American countries. This is problematic since most of these immigrants are integral to keeping wages low, which favors industry and the consumer over the American worker. So far economics has won out over cultural concerns.

16 See documentary film "Flight From Death: The Quest for Immortality" (2005).

17 Ernest Becker, *The Denial of Death* (New York: The Free Press, 1973), 166.

18 Ibid., 159-175.

19 Michael Shermer's book *The Believing Brain* (2011) argues that we are by nature animals who believe or want to believe. Shermer differs from Jung and Campbell in that he thinks we should try to mitigate the effects of the believing brain with the discipline and practice of science.

20 Ernest Becker, *The Denial of Death* (New York: The Free Press, 1973), 176-207. The term "creatureliness" might also be called "the human condition," a reference to the contradictions of human experience. The desire to be wanted while we need others is a paradoxical state, a situation of flux that might at any one time make us both a master and a servant of others. One of the great

novels to explore this paradoxical kinship between dominance and servitude is W. Somerset Maugham's *Of Human Bondage* (1915).

21 The French and Germans have supposedly coined the term "the little death" to describe the human orgasm, so it is not surprising that sexual escapades would play a part in our pursuit of a death-denying ideology.

22 Ernest Becker, *The Denial of Death* (New York: The Free Press, 1973), 208-252. This should not be mistaken for the view that every mental illness can be cured with therapy. Clearly there are those who require extensive medical treatment and drug therapy for ongoing mental illness. Becker is here referring to those who fall into the great middle, those capable of recovering naturally from neurosis or psychosis, or those who can at least learn to live with these conditions.

23 See Jean Paul Sartre, *Being and Nothingness* (1943), and Albert Camus, *The Stranger* (1942) and *The Plague* (1947).

24 Ernest Becker, *The Denial of Death* (New York: The Free Press, 1973), 253-285, 281.

25 David Deutsch's book *The Beginning of Infinity* (2011) is an example of a philosophical viewpoint that could easily be turned into a death-denying philosophy. We will talk more about this in the chapter on technology, where I profile the ideas of the late Neil Postman.

26 The term "risk society" is associated with the work of Ulrich Beck and Anthony Giddens, who have extensively researched the role of risk in modern-day decision-making. Others have used the term "riskless society" in order to describe their view that society has over-reacted in organizing itself against risk. Sheldon Solomon refers to capitalism and communism as "death-denying ideologies" in the film "Flight From Death: The Quest for Immortality" (2005).

Chapter Five - Burning the Village to Save It

1 H. L. Mencken, *In Defense of Women* (New York: A. A. Knopf, 1922) [Originally published in 1918].

2 The particularly bad circumstances into which the world has fallen is convincingly explained in Carmen M. Reinhart and Kenneth S. Rogoff's *This Time Is Different: Eight Centuries of Financial Folly* (Princeton, NJ: Princeton University Press, 2009).

3 The UK experienced extensive rioting in 2011 because of austerity programs put in place by the government, but things appear to have settled down, and a slow economic recovery may be in process in both Europe and the United States.

4 Not all are engaged in this Chicken Little scenario. For example, some scientists take a sober view of environmental devastation, calling us back to being good stewards of our limited resources on the planet. Jared Diamond's

recent book *Collapse: How Societies Choose to Fail or Succeed* (2005) is a good historical treatment of past environmental horror stories. Diamond does not leave us to stew, though, in apocalyptic darkness, suggesting that we have it in our power to change things, and avoid the worst effects of a system that uses up resources without any thought for the future.

5 See chapter three of David Deutsch's latest book *The Beginning of Infinity: Explanations That Transform the World* (2011).

6 The amount of fear that the control of outer space still engenders among strategic defense planners can be seen in the work of someone like George Friedman whose book *The Next 100 Years: A Forecast for the 21st Century* (New York: Doubleday, 2009) argues that the United States must continue to dominate space, and possibly even establish a base on the moon. Friedman is not a member of the survivalist-fringe. He has spent much of his life in government and is now the head of STRATFOR, a private intelligence agency that consults often with the United States government. Much of the thesis of his book rests on the changing demographics of the planet over the next one hundred years, a time during which he and others argue we will see peak, then decline dramatically.

7 Corey Robin, *Fear: The History of a Political Idea* (New York: Oxford University Press, 2004), 2, 23.

8 Ibid., 48.

9 Ibid., 52-54.

10 Ibid., 75-76.

11 Ibid., 208.

12 Ibid., 98-129.

13 Richard Hofstadter, *The Paranoid Style in American Politics, and Other Essays* (New York. Vintage Books, 1967), viii xiiii.

14 Ibid., 3-40, 14.

15 I am thinking here mostly of the popular novels of Dan Brown. His novel *The Da Vinci Code* (2003) has sold 81 million copies worldwide. His previously lesser known novel *Angels and Demons* (2000) explored the same theme of secret conspiracies involving the Catholic Church and the Illuminati. His most recent book *The Lost Symbol* (2009) digs deeper into the Masonic tradition and how its tentacles extend throughout the world of business and politics.

16 Richard Hofstadter, *The Paranoid Style in American Politics, and Other Essays* (New York: Vintage Books, 1967), 3-40, 38.

17 Ibid., 42-65.

18 Ibid., 141.

19 Corey Robin, *Fear: The History of a Political Idea* (New York: Oxford University Press, 2004), 3, 9.

20 Ibid., 2.

21 Ibid., 6.

22 Ibid., 9, 16.

23 Ibid., 19.

24 Ibid., 228.

25 Ibid., 20-21.

26 Barbara Ehrenreich, *Nickel and Dimed: On (Not) Getting By in America* (New York: Metropolitan Books, 2001), 199-207.

27 Ibid., 210.

28 Corey Robin, *Fear: The History of a Political Idea* (New York: Oxford University Press, 2004), 167-198, 210-211. Barbara Ehrenreich has also followed up her earlier work with another book called *Bright-sided: How the Relentless Promotion of Positive Thinking has Undermined America* (2009). In this book Ehrenreich takes to task businesses who not only look for good employees to perform certain tasks but who also encourage them to always be a cheerful member of the team. For some companies this could be the difference not between raises and promotions but between you and the street.

29 Corey Robin, *Fear: The History of a Political Idea* (New York: Oxford University Press, 2004), 228.

30 Ibid., 239.

31 Ibid., 142-144, 165.

Chapter Six - If It Bleeds, It Leads

1 Most of those watching their televisions today probably do not tie together a recent ad for structured settlements and this famous scene from *Network*. This advertisement for J. G. Wentworth features a series of people sticking their heads out their windows and yelling, "It's my money and I need it now."

2 This idea was put forth wonderfully in Neil Postman's *Amusing Ourselves to Death: Public Discourse in the Age of Show* (1985). One of the central ideas in Postman's book is that television, and now electronics in general, have driven us away from the printed word. We have entered into a Huxley-an world where the medium frames everything. Television encourages a passive mindset where entertainment rather than engagement is sought. Postman argues that the printed word provides an alternative to this passive experience.

3 Thomas Jefferson, letter to Edward Carrington, January 16, 1787. The Papers of Thomas Jefferson, ed. Julian P. Boyd, vol. 11, p. 49 .

4 In 1967 *The New Yorker* came out against the war in Vietnam and saw their advertising revenue plummet. The irony is that it was not the position *The New Yorker* took but its changing demographic when it came to readers. The magazine's subscriptions went through the roof, but the subscriptions were to those with less disposable income. Advertiser's abandoned ship not because

of the content of the magazine but because *The New Yorker's* readers were now simply unable to afford the products that were previously advertised, Ben H. Bagdikian, *The New Media Monopoly* (Boston: Beacon Press, 2004), 218-232.

5 Paul Starr, *The Creation of the Media: The Political Origins of Modern Communications* (New York: Basic Books, 2005), 395.

6 Monopolization was made possible by the Newspaper Preservation Act (1970), which exempted newspapers from the Sherman Antitrust Act (1890). This legislation shows the tendency of large corporations to seek monopolistic protections from government once these entities have established themselves as players in the market. Of course, the free market is good for everyone but the entrenched corporation, Ben H. Bagdikian, *The New Media Monopoly* (Boston: Beacon Press, 2004), 204-217.

7 Ben H. Bagdikian, *The New Media Monopoly* (Boston: Beacon Press, 2004), ix-xix, 1-54.

8 Bagdikian argues that the Internet is radically changing the way information and entertainment is being distributed, but that does not extend to how and for what purpose the content is actually created, Ben H. Bagdikian, *The New Media Monopoly* (Boston: Beacon Press, 2004), 55-73. On January 18, 2012, dozens of companies participated in a protest against SOPA, http://www.washingtonpost.com/politics/sopa-protests-to-shut-down-websites/2012/01/17/gIQA4WYl6P_story.html, accessed on February 28, 2012. As a result of this protest the SOPA legislation was scuttled, but it is likely to come back in somewhat diminished form since there is general agreement that intellectual property needs to be protected, especially from international electronic pirates.

9 Edward S. Herman and Noam Chomsky, *Manufacturing Consent: The Political Economy of Mass Media* (New York: Pantheon Books, 2002), 1-35, 298.

10 Ben H. Bagdikian, *The New Media Monopoly* (Boston: Beacon Press, 2004), 74-113. In the PBS documentary *Buying the War* (2007) Bill Moyers explores the press coverage in the run-up to the 2003 invasion of Iraq. Knight-Ridder News Service and a handful of others questioned the motivations for this war while most of the major newspapers, and other media, swallowed the Bush administration's official argument hook, line, and sinker.

11 Ben H. Bagdikian, *The New Media Monopoly* (Boston: Beacon Press, 2004), 114-130, 177-203, 233-256. Bagdikian argues that five things can be done to correct this imbalance of power: 1) breakup conglomerates, 2) repeal 1992 Telecommunications Act, 3) reinstate the "fairness doctrine," 4) allow the public to have a voice in how media licenses are distributed, 5) establish a digital commons, and 6) encourage challenges to the dominant media companies, ibid, 150-51. It is unlikely that any of these things will ever be done, especially with near universal support for anti-piracy measures, which will benefit existing media conglomerates.

12 Ben H. Bagdikian, *The New Media Monopoly* (Boston: Beacon Press, 2004), 153-176.

13 Eric Alterman, *What Liberal Media? The Truth About Bias and the News* (New York: Basic Books, 2003), 2, 11, 13. More evidence that the mainstream media is not necessarily liberal is their almost unanimous dislike of Al Gore

in the 2000 election cycle. Alterman says that George W. Bush proved to be a master at hob-knobbing with the press while Gore seemed smug and dismissive of the press. This may also explain why with the exception of CBS's Dan Rather the media avoided discussion of Bush's questionable military service and his dealings with Harken Oil, Ibid, 148-174.

14 Eric Alterman, *What Liberal Media? The Truth About Bias and the News* (New York: Basic Books, 2003), 17-18, 23, 25, 122; Daniel Gardner, *The Science of Fear: Why We Fear the Things We Shouldn't—and Put Ourselves in Greater Danger* (New York: Dutton, 2008), 167.

15 Eric Alterman, *What Liberal Media? The Truth About Bias and the News* (New York: Basic Books, 2003), 30, 28-44.

16 Ibid., 81-103.

17 See Stephen J. Gould's *The Mismeasure of Man* (New York: W. W. Norton and Company, 1981). This book was revised in 1996 to address directly the points made in Herrnstein and Murray's book.

18 Eric Alterman, *What Liberal Media? The Truth About Bias and the News* (New York: Basic Books, 2003), 45-80.

19 http://www.washingtonpost.com/blogs/political-bookworm/post/weaker-sales-for-ann-coulters-latest-demonic/2011/06/15/AG1d7MXH_blog.html, accessed on February 28, 2012.

20 Eric Alterman, *Sound and Fury: The Making of the Punditocracy* (Ithaca, NY: Cornell University Press, 2000).

21 Here I am speaking about the Tea Party Movement which was given premature birth on the floor of the Chicago Mercantile Exchange when Rick Santelli delivered a rant against mortgagees who had gotten in over their head. Then, the Fox News Channel incubated this preemie political movement until it became a force in the 2010 election cycle.

22 AT&T is now running an ad that subtly plays on our fear of getting caught out of the loop. The old adage about knowledge being power has been transformed into useless information is power if everyone thinks it important.

Chapter Seven - Stand Aside...I'm an Expert!

1 Selling the house for $1 million would yield $200,000 in capital gains. Twenty thousand of those capital gains would be paid to cover the loan for the down payment and you would be left with $180,000 which you made using the leverage of your $2,000 in savings. That is a return of 9000% (180,000/2,000*100).

2 The asterisk is part of the title which continues *Scientists, Finance Wizards, Doctors, Relationship Gurus, Celebrity CEOs, ...Consultants, Health Officials and More.*

3 David H. Freeman, *Wrong: Why Experts* Keep Failing Us—and How to*

Know When Not to Trust Them *Scientists, Finance Wizards, Doctors, Relationship Gurus, Celebrity CEOs, …Consultants, Health Officials and More (New York: Little, Brown and Company, 2010), 5-7.

4 Ibid., 9.

5 Los Angeles Times reporter William Lobdell talks about this in his book *Losing My Religion: How I Lost My Faith Reporting on Religion in America and Found Unexpected Peace* (New York: Harper, 2009). The book is a broader treatment of Lobdell's loss of faith in Christianity resulting from his inability to reconcile his faith with his reporting on the Catholic scandals involving priests who had sexually abused children for decades, and with the Church's knowledge. However, it is interesting to read about how Lobdell tried to later hold onto his faith by attributing his success at the LA Times to God. In the end Lobdell began to understand that it was just a coincidence that he succeeded at the Times after becoming a Christian. It was he, Lobdell, who had made the pivotal decisions that led to advancement in his career, not God.

6 The same happened recently when CERN suggested they had observed particles traveling faster than the speed of light. It is now thought that some faulty wiring might be the problem. There has been no resolution to the issue as of this time.

7 See Daniel Gardner's *Future Babble: Why Expert Predictions Are Next to Worthless, and You Can Do Better* (Toronto: McClelland & Stewart, 2011).

8 David H. Freeman, *Wrong: Why Experts* Keep Failing Us—and How to Know When Not to Trust Them *Scientists, Finance Wizards, Doctors, Relationship Gurus, Celebrity CEOs, …Consultants, Health Officials and More* (New York: Little, Brown and Company, 2010), 78.

9 Chapter three of Gladwell's book *Blink* is entitled "The Warren Harding Error: Why We Fall for Tall, Dark, and Handsome Men." In it Gladwell explains how our unconscious minds cannot help form opinions about others because of the way they look.

10 All of these ideas are presented in Daniel Kahneman's recent book *Thinking, Fast and Slow* (New York: Farrar, Straus and Giroux, 2011). Much of Kahneman's research over the last forty years has been used extensively by other authors mentioned in this book, authors like Daniel Gardner, Malcolm Gladwell, and Rush Dozier.

11 This is actually a technique used more often by business leaders who try to attribute the success of a particular company solely to their leadership. However, it has been statistically proven that many factors contribute to the success of a company, the least of which is who stands as the face of the company. Macro- and micro-economic factors are more sure statistical determinants of success, especially the mere act of being "first to market," David H. Freeman, *Wrong: Why Experts* Keep Failing Us—and How to Know When Not to Trust Them *Scientists, Finance Wizards, Doctors, Relationship Gurus, Celebrity CEOs, …Consultants, Health Officials and More* (New York: Little, Brown and Company, 2010), 12-145.

12 David H. Freeman, *Wrong: Why Experts* Keep Failing Us—and How to Know When Not to Trust Them *Scientists, Finance Wizards, Doctors, Relationship Gurus, Celebrity CEOs, …Consultants, Health Officials and More* (New

York: Little, Brown and Company, 2010), 203-230.

13 Ibid., 101, 146-167. See also Nassim Nicholas Taleb's discussion of the "wisdom of crowds" in his book *The Black Swan: The Impact of the Highly Improbable* (2007), and Neil Postman's comments in *Amusing Ourselves to Death* (1985) about how experts must first become celebrities before they are taken seriously by the public. [Get specific references.]

14 http://www2.fbi.gov/ucr/cius2009/offenses/expanded_information/homicide.html, accessed June 5, 2011.

15 This is a fear that Philip Alcabes has addressed in his book *Dread: How Fear and Fantasy Have Fueled Epidemics From the Black Plague Death to Avian Flu* (New York: Public Affairs, 2009). Alcabes argues that this fear is rooted more in fiction than science, and that epidemics get a lot of press because that is where most of the funding for research goes, so there is an incentive to keep epidemiological research in the public mind so that the financing of research will continue. Alcabes argues that Tuberculosis, sleeping sickness, malaria, diarrhea, and AIDS are for more devastating diseases but because they occur mostly outside the developed world they get short-shrift. Again, Alcabes presents us with the argument that the fear of epidemics is one way politicians gain power in order to achieve their "political agendas and moral crusades," 218, 219, 230.

16 James Wesley Rawles, *The End of the World As We Know It: Tactics, Techniques, and Technologies for Uncertain Times* (New York: Plume, 2009), 5.

17 National Geographic and the Discovery Channel have begun to get into the doomsday business with their shows "Doomsday Preppers" and "Doomsday Bunkers." After a few episodes you realize that most of the people profiled are working some economic angle. They are either providing survival kits or building the bunkers.

18 Daniel Gardner, *The Science of Fear: Why We Fear the Things We Shouldn't—and Put Ourselves in Greater Danger* (New York: Dutton, 2008), 244.

19 Andrew Keen, *The Cult of the Amateur: How Today's Internet Is Killing Our Culture* (New York: Doubleday), 62.

20 Jeremy Rifkin has written a whole book on this topic, *The End of Work: The Decline of the Global Labor Force and the Dawn of the Post-Market Era* (New York: Putnam Publishing Group, 1995). In it he argues that technology is slowly and inexorably eliminating jobs, creating a class of people who are no longer needed in the production process. This, he suggests, is a problem since governments must respond to the needs of these people even if they are unable to find employment.

21 Andrew Keen, *The Cult of the Amateur: How Today's Internet Is Killing Our Culture* (New York: Doubleday), 16, 83.

22 Chris Mooney, *The Republican War on Science* (New York: Basic Books, 2005). The problem, according to Mooney, is not that people debate scientific ideas—we have been doing that for centuries; the problem is that the methodologies of science are being put into question, making any objective knowledge itself seem impossible. The political left has also contributed to this spirit of distrusting any objective facts with its post-modernist and deconstruction-

ist interpretation of all human knowledge. They argue that everything, even science, is tainted by subjectivity, and so nothing can really be known. Keith Windschuttle has addressed this problem in his book *The Killing of History: How Literary Critics and Social Theorists Are Murdering Our Past* (New York: Encounter Books, 2000).

23 Neil Postman, *Building a Bridge to the 18th Century: How the Past Can Improve Our Future* (New York: Knopf, 1999), 61, 68.

24 We rank at nearly the bottom in science and math when compared to other countries, http://bottomline.msnbc.msn.com/_news/2012/02/10/10366521-us-workers-behind-in-science-and-math?lite. Some debate whether this comparison is relevant, but when you drill down the argument of those who think the U.S. has no problem are really arguing that American kids are getting "just enough" math to function in job market, see http://www.princeton.edu/futureofchildren/publications/docs/19_01_03.pdf and http://www.hks.harvard.edu/pepg/PDF/Papers/PEPG10-19_HanushekPetersonWoessmann.pdf.

25 Neil Postman, *Building a Bridge to the 18th Century: How the Past Can Improve Our Future* (New York: Knopf, 1999), 79.

Chapter Eight - The Dystopian Vision

1 I first encountered this phrase while watching a documentary entitled "Flight From Death: The Quest for Immortality" (2005). According to Sheldon Solomon capitalism and communism are both "death-denying ideologies" because they attempt to allay our fear of death through excessive attention to the economic aspect of life.

2 This is a reference to Frederick Jackson Turner's thesis that the American frontier had a distinctive impact on American society and culture. We discussed this thesis in the previous chapter.

3 A recent segment on PBS's *Newshour* (July 11, 2012) featured Ray Kurzweil who thinks we are on the verge of immortality as information technology reaches the point where we will be able to store all our memories, and possibly our personalities, in a machine.

4 This is a major theme also found in Daniel Boorstin's *The Discoverers* (1983).

5 Neil Postman, *Technopoly: The Surrender of Culture to Technology* (New York: Vintage Books, 1993), 71.

6 Carl Sagan addressed this same issue in his book *Demon-Haunted World: Science as a Candle in the Dark* (New York: Random House, 1995).

7 Neil Postman, *Technopoly: The Surrender of Culture to Technology* (New York: Vintage Books, 1993), 147.

8 Ibid., 185.

9 Ibid., 179.

10 Ibid., 187.

11 In two other books by Neil Postman we are encouraged to abandon the principle of technology for technology's sake. In his book *Amusing Ourselves to Death: Public Discourse in the Age of Show Business* (1985) Postman argues that television tends to cut up political and social dialogue into so many small and isolated segments that there is no way to create the complex, coherent narrative needed for a democratic dialogue. In a later book *Building a Bridge to the 18th Century: How the Past Can Improve Our Future* (1999) Postman talks about the importance of placing science and technology within the context of the Enlightenment tradition.

Chapter Nine - In the Beginning: The Origin of Cosmos

1 Joseph Campbell, *The Hero With a Thousand Faces* (Princeton, NJ: Princeton University Press), 43-44.

2 The theoretical physicist and author Michio Kaku has published two books about the future promise of science: *Visions: How Science Will Revolutionize the 21st Century* (1998) and *Physics of the Future* (2011). A simple summary of these books is that they both argue that what science has not yet figured out it soon will and that most future technology is merely a question of working out the details of what we already know.

3 This is not always true, as we will point out in a later chapter. Many Christians in America are convinced that God wants them to be rich and that they should work toward the Christianization of the nation. These are not views that would normally be associated with standard premillennial evangelicalism.

4 This is a topic on which I intend to write myself. A book-length treatment of faith and science from the Renaissance to the twentieth century should be available within the next two years. In this book I make the argument that leaders within the Christian movement made a mistake when they tried to integrate theology and science, beginning with the work of Thomas Aquinas in the thirteenth century. By the middle of the nineteenth century there was a full-blown intellectual war between science and religion, centering around Darwinism, but not limited to the biological sciences. One of the key issues in this struggle is the notion that science provides us with a certainty that religion can no longer offer. I argue that this is a misinterpretation of the goals of science and that religion abandoned a fundamental class of existential and ethical arguments by abandoning the stance of faith alone.

5 This Lamarckian view that morphological characteristics like muscle size and intellectual power could be passed down from one generation directly to the next was eventually superseded by the Darwinian and neo-Darwinian view. These latter views argue that inherited characteristics result from a mixing of genetic material. This means that morphological characteristics may or may not be passed down from one generation to the next.

6 This story is chronicled in Virgil's *Aeneid* (c. 29-19 BCE).

7 Marie Tanner, *The Last Descendant of Aeneas: The Hapsburgs and the Mythic Image of the Emperor* (New Haven: Yale University Press, 1993).

8 There are many books that one can consult on this topic. I would recommend anything by Karen Armstrong. See the bibliography. Bart Ehrman has also written extensively on this topic, but he tends to favor the New Testament and the apocalyptic traditions of Christianity.

9 Barbara C. Sproul writes that we should distinguish primal chaos from the chaos gods and monsters of a later age, *Primal Myths: Creation Myths Around the World* (New York: Harper Collins, 1991), 18. For example, a primal chaos god who is not necessarily concerned about order, he just is. Later deities will be associated with the destruction of order itself, which could also be seen as a desire to return to primal chaos. It is not clear from mythology that the oldest of the primal chaos gods care one way or another about either the existence of order or whether it is destroyed. There seems to be an assumption in most cultures that chaos will eventually swallow up order at some distant point in the future. The exception is the linear apocalyptic view adopted by Zoroastrians and Christians.

10 There are literally hundreds of creation myths that exist around the world. Barbara C. Sproul has published a nearly encyclopedic collection of these myths in her book *Primal Myths: Creation Myths Around the World* (New York: Harper Collins, 1991).

Chapter Ten - The Birth of the Hero

1 I have purposely avoided extending my topic to include the Asian notion of Yang and Yin or the Mandate of Heaven. This is obviously a universal theme, but my concern is the direct line of history between ancient Middle Eastern myth and Christian utopianism. This is also why this book does not give much space to the present interest in Mayan prophecies, since the interest in this subject is primarily a result of already existing notions of apocalyptic fate resulting from western civilization being influenced by Christian apocalyptic thought and its secular by-products.

2 Mircea Eliade, *The Myth of the Eternal Return* (New York: Pantheon Books, 1965), 122.

3 Ibid., 5. The name Babylon derives from the word *Bāb-ilāni*, which means "gate of the gods," Ibid., 14.

4 Norman Cohn, *Cosmos, Chaos, and the World to Come: The Ancient Roots of Apocalyptic Faith* (New Haven, CT: Yale University Press, 1993), 6.

5 Ibid., 9-10.

6 Ibid., 21-27.

7 Ibid., 33-37.

8 Ibid., 38-40.

9 Ibid., 42-49, 52-53, 55-56.

10 Ibid., 60, 61, 67, 63.

11 Ibid., 65, 67-68, 73.

12 Joseph Campbell, *The Hero With a Thousand Faces* (Princeton, NJ: Princeton University Press, 1949), 4.

13 Ibid., 30-40.

14 Barbara C. Sproul, *Primal Myths: Creation Myths Around the World* (New York: Harper Collins, 1991), 135-142; Norman Cohn, *Cosmos, Chaos, and the World to Come: The Ancient Roots of Apocalyptic Faith* (New Haven, CT: Yale University Press, 1993), 82-83.

15 Norman Cohn, *Cosmos, Chaos, and the World to Come: The Ancient Roots of Apocalyptic Faith* (New Haven, CT: Yale University Press, 1993), 77, 79, 95.

16 Ibid., 97-99.

17 Ibid., 100-101.

18 Ibid., 82-83, 92.

19 Ibid., 90.

20 Ibid., 85, 88.

21 Ibid., 95.

22 Ibid., 114.

23 Ibid., 121-126.

24 Ibid., 135, 138, 139-140.

25 *Henotheism* is the believe in more than one god, but the belief that one's own god is the strongest of all the gods.

26 Norman Cohn, *Cosmos, Chaos, and the World to Come: The Ancient Roots of Apocalyptic Faith* (New Haven, CT: Yale University Press, 1993), 147, 151.

27 Ibid., 141-162, 155, 159. For more on this topic see Karen Armstrong, *The Case for God* (New York: Knopf, 2009) and Bart Ehrman, *The Lost Gospel of Judas Iscariot: A New Look at Betrayer and Betrayed* (New York: Oxford University Press, 2008).

28 Norman Cohn, *Cosmos, Chaos, and the World to Come: The Ancient Roots of Apocalyptic Faith* (New Haven, CT: Yale University Press, 1993), 163-175.

29 There is debate over whether the sect at Qumran were Essenes or another independent group. Whether they were the same group or not they all ascribed to an apocalyptic vision which probably had its roots in Zoroastrianism.

30 Norman Cohn, *Cosmos, Chaos, and the World to Come: The Ancient Roots of Apocalyptic Faith* (New Haven, CT: Yale University Press, 1993), 176-194.

31 Ibid., 195, 194-211. Of course, we may never know what Jesus actually preached or believed, we can only know what people at different times

thought his message was or was not. We can see this in books like Bart Ehrman's *Lost Christianities: The Battles for Scripture and the Faiths We Never Knew* (New York: Oxford University Press, 2005).

32 Norman Cohn, *Cosmos, Chaos, and the World to Come: The Ancient Roots of Apocalyptic Faith* (New Haven, CT: Yale University Press, 1993), 212-219.

Chapter Eleven - Behold I Come Quickly

1 Paul makes clear in his first letter to the Corinthians (15:13-14) that the resurrection of Christ is central to his version of Christianity, and this is even today the dominant view of Christians.

2 The Church would fill the political void left by the decline of the Roman Empire. The difference between the eastern and western parts of the empire would be that the east would continue to fuse church and state while in the west there would develop an uneasy alliance between the Church and the nascent states of Europe, especially the Frankish kingdoms of what are now France and Germany. See Sidney Painter's *The Rise of the Feudal Monarchies* (1951).

3 *Zurvanism* was a version of Zoroastrianism, which was adopted by the Persian Empire sometime before or during the Sassanid era (226-651 CE). Zurvanism emphasized a gradual making over of the world, not an immediate and otherworldly intercession of God.

4 The story of Mohammed is ably dealt with by Karen Armstrong in her book *Muhammad: A Biography of the Prophet* (1992). References to the Roman and Islamic "lake" can be found in the works of Henri Pirenne, whose book *Economic and Social History of Medieval Europe* (1936) is still a must read for those interested in medieval European history.

5 This is not to say that other anti-icon movements did not occur later. There are always groups of individuals wanting to return to the primitive Christian experience, which includes neither icons nor saints. This was one of the distinct characteristics of many Protestant movements after 1500 CE.

6 There are three wonderful books dealing with these topics. The first is Jacques Le Goff's *Medieval Civilization, 400-1500* (1988). The second is Barbara Tuchman's *A Distant Mirror: The Calamitous Fourteenth Century* (1978). The third is Marc Bloch's two-volume work *Feudal Society* [1961].

7 Both the term Europe and Christendom became part of the lexicon in the late medieval and early modern period. See John Hale's *The Civilization of Europe in the Renaissance* (1993).

8 See Jeff Irvin, "Christian Reconquest of Spain" in *The Encyclopedia of World History* (2008), and Bailey W. Diffie, *Prelude to Empire: Portugal Overseas before Henry the Navigator* (Lincoln, NE: University of Nebraska Press, 1960).

9 *Eschatology* is a theological term meaning "the study of last things."

10 See the work of Michael Barkun, *Disaster and the Millennium* (1974) and *Crucible of the Millennium: The Burned-Over District of New York in the 1840s* (1986). There is a point where economic life inextricably intersects the social sphere, a point at which production and consumption cease to be merely about satisfying a need and enter the realm of ego satisfaction. The frequently forgotten or maligned work of Thorstein Veblen on "conspicuous consumption" helps us to better understand the idea of *relative deprivation*. We all to some extent measure our worth by our wealth, which is always relative to someone else's.

11 Norman Cohn, *The Pursuit of the Millennium* (New York: Oxford University Press, 1957), 15.

12 Ibid., 16.

13 Ibid., 19.

14 A satirical take on this history can be found in the film *Life of Brian*, another Monty Python contribution to the zeitgeist. During one section of the movie someone keeps asking what the Romans have ever done for the Jews, and people keep listing things like roads, sanitation, education, wine, etc. Eventually the questioning stops when the someone says, "Yea, but what have the Romans done for us lately?"

15 Norman Cohn, *The Pursuit of the Millennium* (New York: Oxford University Press, 1957), 20-24.

16 See Bart Ehrman's *Lost Christianities: The Battles for Scripture and the Faiths We Never Knew* (New York: Oxford University Press, 2005). In this book Ehrman discusses a Jewish sect called the Ebionites. They followed Jesus Christ but did not believe him to be God or fully divine. They also believed that Christian believers should still practice all the traditions of Judaism.

17 This is a reference to the idea that the kingdom of God would come only after a great war where there would be much death and destruction. This is based on the many predictions attributed to Jesus Christ in the gospels and on the scenario sketched out in The Book of Revelation.

18 Norman Cohn, *The Pursuit of the Millennium* (New York: Oxford University Press, 1957), 25-36.

19 Ibid., 37-52.

20 This was an attempt by the Church in the late tenth century to stop the incessant warfare that raged between the feudal princes of Europe. The movement lasted up until the thirteenth century, and may have been obviated by the growing centralized power of monarchs in Western Europe.

21 Norman Cohn, *The Pursuit of the Millennium* (New York: Oxford University Press, 1957), 53-70.

22 Ibid., 75-80.

23 Ibid., 83, 89-107.

24 Joseph Campbell relates a similar story from Hindu myth in which the king Muchukunda is allowed by the gods to sleep forever in a cave. Waking him is fatal, as the enemies of Krishna find out when he tricks them into waking the

king, *The Hero With a Thousand Faces* (Princeton: Princeton University Press, 1949), 193-196.

25 Norman Cohn, *The Pursuit of the Millennium* (New York: Oxford University Press, 1957), 108-126.

26 Ibid., 127-147.

27 Ibid., 148-186.

28 Ibid., 187-197.

29 David Koresh led a group of Christians who were a sect of the *Branch Davidians*, an offshoot of the Seventh Day Adventist Church. In April of 1993 Koresh and all his followers were killed after engaging federal authorities who were attempting to serve warrants on the Davidian compound. The allegations were that children were being sexually abused or placed in harm's way.

30 Norman Cohn, *The Pursuit of the Millennium* (New York: Oxford University Press, 1957), 198-280.

31 This was a phrase used by the late William F. Buckley Jr. It meant the attempt to realize in this world the promise of the next, which, being a good Catholic, Mr. Buckley rejected.

32 Norman Cohn, *The Pursuit of the Millennium* (New York: Oxford University Press, 1957), 286.

Chapter Twelve - The Utopianism of Science

1 Thomas S. Kuhn explored this idea extensively in his book *The Structures of Scientific Revolutions* (1962). His theory was that scientific revolutions only occurred when there were anomalies which the present scientific paradigm could not explain. Prior to that attempts are made to shoehorn all data into the dominant paradigm. This means that scientific revolutions tend to be rare, and that the scientific community tends to be rather conservative in its pursuits, more often trying to prove the existing paradigm rather than challenging it.

2 The less celebrated case of Giordano Bruno (1548-1600) did not end as well as it did for Galileo. Bruno was burnt at the stake for heresy while Galileo lived the rest of his life under house arrest.

3 John Gray, *Black Mass: Apocalyptic Religion and the Death of Utopia* (New York: Farrar, Straus, and Giroux, 2007), 28.

4 Rene Dubos, *The Dreams of Reason: Science and Utopias* (New York: Columbia University Press, 1961), 9.

5 Nathan O. Hatch, *The Sacred Cause of Liberty: Republican Thought and the millennium in Revolutionary New England* (New Haven: Yale University Press, 1977), 43-49.

6 William Wordsworth, "The Tables Turned" (1794).

7 William Blake, *Songs of Experience* (1794).

8 Job 40:2.

Chapter Thirteen - The Apple of His Eye

1 This is a term used by religious leaders to describe the idea that Israel would be politically restored to the physical geography of Palestine.

2 Hopkins, Samuel. *A Treatise on the Millennium Showing from Scripture Prophecy, That It Is Yet to Come; When It Will Come; In What It Will Consist; and the Events Which are First to Take Place, Introductory to It* (Boston: Isaiah Thomas and Ebenezer T. Andrews, 1793), 55, 60-65, 69-73, 51, 84.

3 Ruth H. Bloch, *Visionary Republic: Millennial Themes in American Thought, 1756-1800* (Cambridge, England: Cambridge University Press, 1985), xiii, 53, xiii-4; and Nathan O. Hatch, *The Sacred Cause of Liberty: Republican Thought and the millennium in Revolutionary New England* (New Haven: Yale University Press, 1977), 17, 43.

4 Michael Barkun, *Disaster and the Millennium* (New Haven: Yale University Press), 45.

5 One of the best synthetic treatments of this era is Charles Sellers's *The Market Revolution: Jacksonian America, 1815-1846* (New York: Oxford University Press, 1994).

6 This can be seen in the work of Samuel Davies Baldwin who wrote in the 1850s about the role the United States would play in Christian prophecy. Baldwin thought the kingdom would be brought about gradually, that Israel would not be reconstituted either before or after the return of Jesus Christ, and that the United States would play a major role as the "new Israel" in the establishment of God's kingdom here on earth. See his book *Armageddon; or the Overthrow of Romanism and Monarchy; the Existence of the United States Foretold in the Bible, Its Future Greatness; Invasion by Allied Europe; Annihilation of Monarchy; Expansion into the Millennial Republic, and Its Dominion Over the Whole World* (Nashville: Southern Methodist Publishing House, 1854). Baldwin does admit that Israel might be restored to "carnal" glory but it would only be as a Christianized version of its former self, 65.

7 William Gannaway Brownlow, *Ought American Slavery to be Perpetuated? A Debate* (Philadelphia: J.B. Lippincott and Co., 1858), 43; Baldwin, *Armageddon*, 51; *Richmond Christian Advocate* reprinted in *Annals of Southern Methodism for 1856*, Charles F. Deems, Ed. (Nashville: Stevenson and Owen, 1857), 307.

8 Peter Toon, "Conclusion," in *Puritans, the Millennium and the Future of Israel; Puritan Eschatology 1600 to 1660*, ed. Peter Toon (Cambridge, England: James Clark and Co., Ltd., 1970), 128.

9 The word "radical" derives from a Latin word that means "roots" or "origin." So, one can see how "radical" agendas always tend to hark back to the "primi-

tive."

10 R.G. Clouse, "The Rebirth of Millenarianism," in *Puritans, the Millennium and the Future of Israel; Puritan Eschatology 1600 to 1660*, ed. Peter Toon (Cambridge, England: James Clark and Co., Ltd., 1970), 66.

11 Edward Johnson, *The Wonder-working Providence of Sion's Saviour in New England*, part of the *Original Narratives of Early American History Series*, ed. J. Franklin Jameson (New York: Charles Scribner's Sons, 1910), 23-25.

12 This is a church mentioned in the third chapter of *Revelation*. It is a church that had grown "lukewarm" in its faithfulness to Christ and which was, therefore, in danger of judgment. (Revelation 3:14-22)

13 This is yet another prophetic reference. (I Thessalonians 5:2, 3)

14 Sacvan Bercovitch, *The American Jeremiad* (Madison: University of Wisconsin Press, 1978), 7, 58-59.

15 Ibid., 9.

16 Ibid., 17, 176.

17 Ibid., 91-92, 93.

18 David R. Williams, *Wilderness Lost: The Religious Origins of the American Mind* (Cranberry, NJ: Associated University Press, 1987).

19 Ibid., 145. See also Ralph Gabriel's *The Course of American Democratic Thought* (New York: Ronald Press Co., 1940).

20 Alan Heimert, *Religion and the American Mind: From the Great Awakening to the Revolution* (Cambridge, Mass.: Harvard University Press, 1968), 59, 60-94, 60.

21 Ruth H. Bloch, *Visionary Republic: Millennial Themes in American Thought, 1756-1800* (Cambridge, England: Cambridge University Press, 1985), 13.

22 Nathan O. Hatch, *The Sacred Cause of Liberty: Republican Thought and the millennium in Revolutionary New England* (New Haven: Yale University Press, 1977), 43-49.

23 George H. Williams, *Wilderness and Paradise in Christian Thought: The Biblical Experience of the Desert in the History of Christianity & The Paradise Theme in the Theological Idea of the University* (New York: Harper and Brothers, 1962), 65-131.

24 Ruth H. Bloch, *Visionary Republic: Millennial Themes in American Thought, 1756-1800* (Cambridge, England: Cambridge University Press, 1985), 54 .

25 Mark A. Noll and others, eds. *Eerdman's Handbook to Christianity in America* (Grand Rapids, Michigan: William B. Eerdmans Publishing Company, 1983), 167.

26 Ruth H. Bloch, *Visionary Republic: Millennial Themes in American Thought, 1756-1800* (Cambridge, England: Cambridge University Press, 1985), 114.

27 Alan Heimert, *Religion and the American Mind: From the Great Awakening to the Revolution* (Cambridge, Mass.: Harvard University Press, 1968), 94-95, 547.

28 Ruth H. Bloch, *Visionary Republic: Millennial Themes in American Thought, 1756-1800* (Cambridge, England: Cambridge University Press, 1985), xiii, 53, xiii-4.

29 Nathan O. Hatch, *The Sacred Cause of Liberty: Republican Thought and the millennium in Revolutionary New England* (New Haven: Yale University Press, 1977), 17, 43. This is also an interesting example of how history repeats itself since there is a large number of Christians who believe that pluralism and multiculturalism is a frontal assault on Christian faith. Writers like David Limbaugh equate the "war on Christmas" or the teaching of evolution with a broader assault on Christian faith. See *Persecution: How Liberals are Waging a War Against Christians* (Washington, DC: Regnery, 2003).

30 Glenn T. Miller, "Images of the Future in Eighteenth-Century American Theology," *Amerikastudien/American Studies*, n.s. 1 (1975): 100.

31 Ernest Lee Tuveson, *Redeemer Nation: The Idea of America's Millennial Role* (Chicago: University of Chicago Press, 1968), 51.

32 Frederick Jackson Turner, "The Significance of the Frontier in American History" presented at the American Historical Association, 1893.

33 Gar Alperovitz, *Atomic Diplomacy: Hiroshima and Potsdam* (New York: Simon and Schuster, 1965).

Chapter Fourteen - The American Theocratic Empire

1 Http://www.washingtonpost.com/politics/senate-panel-examines-contractor-spending/2012/03/29/gIQAdNlsjS_story.html and http://www.washingtontimes.com/news/2012/may/17/defense-contractors-eye-cuts-to-jobs-plants/, accessed on June 14, 2012.

2 For an excellent history of how all this happened see Anthony Sampson's *The Seven Sisters: The Great Oil Companies and the World They Shaped* (New York: Viking, 1975).

3 Kevin Phillips, *American Theocracy: The Peril and Politics of Radical Religion, Oil, and Borrowed Money in the 21ˢᵗ Century* (New York: Viking, 2006), 338.

4 This is called by historians the "price revolution," and it was exacerbated in the sixteenth century by the importation of gold and silver from the New World. It heavily impacted Spain and Portugal but also influenced economics throughout Europe, Earl J. Hamilton, *American Treasure and the Price Revolution in Spain, 1501-1650* (Cambridge: Harvard University Press, 1934).

5 Peak oil theory does necessarily propose that oil will no longer be produced, only that it will be less abundant and more expensive to extract from the ground. For more information on this see the website for the Association for the Study of Peak Oil and Gas, http://www.peakoil.net/.

6 We still have this problem today, which is why many Americans do not understand that gasoline and oil prices are set at a world level. That is why gasoline is shipped out of the United States to other national markets, even during times of high demand, because suppliers can make more money for each barrel of oil or gasoline they sell somewhere else. By the 1970s the Japanese and German economies began to compete with the United States for markets and resources. U.S. legacy costs in the automotive industry have also dragged these industries down because they have been unable to change fast enough. This has only gotten worse as China, India, and other Asian nations have joined the world market. From 1970 through 1980 oil went from $3.00 a barrel to $31.00 a barrel. This prompted a nationwide effort to conserve energy, which ended in the 1980s as oil prices began declining and Americans fell in love with gas-guzzling SUVs, Kevin Phillips, *American Theocracy: The Peril and Politics of Radical Religion, Oil, and Borrowed Money in the 21ˢᵗ Century* (New York: Viking, 2006), 27, 40, 31-67, 25-30.

7 This scenario is generally held to by most premillennial evangelical Christians and is said to be in accordance with the events mapped out in the *Apocalypse of John*, commonly called in the New Testament the *Book of Revelation*. These ideas have also been fleshed out in fiction. Carol Balizet's *The Last Seven Years* was written in 1978 and is still in print. Salem Kirban's *666* was written in 1974 and is also still in print. Most recently Tim LaHaye and Jerry B. Jenkins have sold millions of books from their multi-volume series entitled *Left Behind*. All of them present a fictionalized account of the what evangelical Christians call "the great tribulation" and the rise of the antichrist.

8 During the First Gulf War John F. Walvoord published *Armageddon, Oil, and the Middle East Crisis: What the Bible Says About the Future of the Middle East and the End of Western Civilization* (1990). The title says it all.

9 Kevin Phillips, *American Theocracy: The Peril and Politics of Radical Religion, Oil, and Borrowed Money in the 21ˢᵗ Century* (New York: Viking, 2006), 68-96.

10 Ibid., 100, 119, 128.

11 John Gray, *Black Mass: Apocalyptic Religion and the Death of Utopia* (New York: Farrar, Straus, and Giroux, 2007), 1, 2, 28, 21.

12 Kevin Phillips, *American Theocracy: The Peril and Politics of Radical Religion, Oil, and Borrowed Money in the 21ˢᵗ Century* (New York: Viking, 2006), 171-217. Phillips believes that the GOP has become a de facto religious party in their opposition to so-called "secular liberalism" and that the Southern Baptist Convention is as close as the U.S. has gotten since the Revolution to having a single dominant religious denomination. The SBC recently suggested changing its name to the Great Commission Baptists, and they have elected their first ever black leader of the convention. An interesting historical point is that the Southern Baptist Convention was created when the Baptists split in the mid-1840s over the issue of slavery. It will be interesting to see whether this move eliminates the political edge Republicans have when it comes to the "southern strategy," the use of race issues to divide the electorate. According to some studies there is a statistical correlation between religious commitment and racism in America, Sam Harris, *The Moral Landscape: How Science Can Determine Human Values* (New York: Free Press, 2010), 146.

13 John Gray, *Black Mass: Apocalyptic Religion and the Death of Utopia* (New York: Farrar, Straus, and Giroux, 2007), 55-69.

14 Ibid., 75, 84, 85-86, 93. If you are a believer in man as a rational economic actor then PBS's *Nova* episode "Mind Over Money" (2009) may rattle your belief structure. This episode surveys the work being done by scientists about how people make decisions, a field largely inspired by the work of Daniel Kahneman and others.

15 John Gray, *Black Mass: Apocalyptic Religion and the Death of Utopia* (New York: Farrar, Straus, and Giroux, 2007), 123, 111, 121, 134-145.

16 Ibid., 146-161, 171, 161-174, 174-183. Francis Fukuyama famously came out against the neo-conservative desire to export democracy through violence, http://www.newyorker.com/archive/2006/03/27/060327crbo_books. What made this amazing was that Francis Fukuyama's earlier work, *The End of History and the Last Man* (1992), can be seen as a seminal work in neo-conservative thinking. In this book Fukuyama argued that we were approaching an end-point in history, a point where liberal capitalism would dominate the planet. This book had shades of utopianism, and was part of a long secular tradition. Much of Fukuyama's thought was based on Hegel and his idea that history was constantly progressing. Karl Marx was also a proponent of this view when he wrote *Das Kapital* (1860). In the 1930s Pierre Teilhard de Chardin wrote *The Phenomenon of Man*, which was not published until 1955 because it had been placed on the Catholic Church's Index. Teilhard was a Catholic priest and an evolutionist. He proposed that mankind was progressing through a divinely guided process of natural selection toward what he called the "omega point." Once mankind had reached it would mean that mankind was in perfect harmony with both himself and God.

17 John Gray, *Black Mass: Apocalyptic Religion and the Death of Utopia* (New York: Farrar, Straus, and Giroux, 2007), 184-192, 192-204, 204-210, 207. On the question of the unknowable God, of which there is a long tradition in history, see Karen Armstrong's *The Case for God* (New York: Knopf, 2009).

18 Andrew Bacevich, *The Limits of Power: The End of American Exceptionalism* (2008), 1-13, 13.

19 Ibid., 15-66.

20 Ibid., 124-169.

21 Kevin Phillips, *American Theocracy: The Peril and Politics of Radical Religion, Oil, and Borrowed Money in the 21st Century* (New York: Viking, 2006), 218-62, 99-131.

22 This is a general summary of Chris Hedges's *American Fascists: The Christian Right and the War on America* (New York: Free Press, 2007). On its face Hedges's analysis might seem overwrought, but it is only an analysis of less than ten percent of the American population, and although everything he says may not apply to all evangelical Christians it applies directly to many. Most evangelical Christians are not outright fascists but they could definitely be called "fellow travelers." Hedges uses Umberto Eco's definition of "ur-fascism" to describe what he means by American Christian fascists. This is a combination of the following: a cult of tradition, a rejection of modernism, action for action's sake, suppression of dissent, xenophobia, appeal to a distressed social

class, hyper-nationalism, vilification of the rich foreigner, life depicted as always a battle for survival, contempt for the weak, praising the "heroic virtues," power and sexuality are intertwined, the common man is praised but society is run by an elite group of pseudo-commoners, and it has a language all its own meant to dumb down discourse or eliminate it altogether, http://www.themodernword.com/eco/eco_blackshirt.html, accessed on July 4, 2012.

23 Richard Hofstadter, *Social Darwinism in American Thought* (Philadelphia: University of Pennsylvania Press, 1944).

24 Jim Wallis, *God's Politics: Why the Right Gets It Wrong and the Left Doesn't Get It* (San Francisco: Harper, 2005).

25 Kevin Phillips, *American Theocracy: The Peril and Politics of Radical Religion, Oil, and Borrowed Money in the 21st Century* (New York: Viking, 2006), 276, 281, 338, 298-318. See also Kevin

26 Ibid., 329.

Chapter Fifteen - Tiger, Tiger, Burning Bright

1 The argument of many Christians is that the "secular liberal agenda" has grown increasingly worse since the 1925 Scopes Trial. For example, the Supreme Court's decisions in 1962 and 1963 to prohibit state-sponsored prayer and Bible readings in public schools. These did not prohibit students from or staff from these things; they could simply not be part of the curriculum. A decade later the landmark decision on women's reproductive right, decided in the case of Roe v. Wade (1973), only increased the animus of the evangelical community toward a society that they saw as increasingly ungodly. Evangelicals and their pseudo-intellectual mouthpieces in the Republican Party argued that the social problems plaguing American society were not the growing economic disparity between the rich and poor or the decreasing economic opportunity among the American working class; it was the relativism and immorality promoted by secular liberalism that was at the root of all American social problems. They contended then and still do that returning to the past and to God is the only sure way Americans can hope to renew their society.

2 The evidence for this can be had in two cases. The first is the attempt by a school district in Dover, Pennsylvania, to get "intelligent design" taught alongside evolution. A U.S. federal court ruled in December 2005 that "intelligent design" was not science and therefore could not be given equal time in science classes in the Dover Area School District. The second example is the case of the Texas school board, which in 2010 approved changes to its history curriculum in order to balance what it thought a pro-liberal agenda in standard history textbooks, http://www.nytimes.com/2010/03/13/education/13texas.html.

3 For an accessible treatment of this topic read Richard Dawkins's *The Greatest Show On Earth: The Evidence For Evolution* (New York: Free Press, 2009).

4 *Euhemerism* is the term used to designate those individuals in mythology

who have exhibited superhuman qualities and who may have originally been based on ordinary historical human beings of great achievement.

5 In the 1650s Bishop James Ussher (1581-1656) established a chronology of human history by working backward through the text of the Bible. Using this method he determined that the date of the earth's creation occurred on Sunday, October 23, 4004 BC.

6 Stephen Jay Gould also argued for this position, using what he called the principle of *non-overlapping magisteria*. This is the idea that science and religion have non-intersecting bailiwicks. Religion cannot comment on the validity of scientific data and science cannot knowledgably comment on morality or existential questions, on which religion is expert, *Rocks of Ages* (New York: Ballantine Books, 1999).

7 Armstrong refers to this as the *apophatic* tradition, the idea that God cannot be known, only experienced—usually in silence and with very little intellectual activity, *The Case for God* (New York: Anchor Books, 2009), Kindle edition.

8 Richard Dawkins, "Man vs. God," *Wall Street Journal*, September 12, 2009, accessed on June 26, 2012.

9 Michael Shermer, *The Believing Brain: From Ghosts and Gods to Politics and Conspiracies—How We Construct Beliefs and Reinforce Them As Truths* (New York: Henry Holt and Company, 2011), 2-3; a poll conducted in December 2010 found that 4 out of 10 Americans believe in "strict creationism," which means they reject the notion of an unguided process of natural biological selection, http://www.gallup.com/poll/145286/four-americans-believe-strict-creationism.aspx, accessed on June 23, 2012.

10 The western world has a long tradition of criticizing religion without abandoning the idea that God exists. Medieval mystics were constantly criticizing the Church for its worldliness and the lack of attention to the Church's central mission: evangelism and ministering to the poor. Modern believers do not necessarily attend religious services on a regular basis but they are convinced that God can be found there when they need him.

11 Hans Küng makes this argument in his book *Does God Exist? An Answer For Today* (New York: Doubleday, 1980). In brief he argues that because all human philosophy eventually results in nihilism we must believe that God exists. If we do not then life becomes meaningless. I will let you figure out what logical mistake has been made here.

12 William James, *The Varieties of Religious Experience: A Study In Human Nature* (New York: The Modern Library, 1902), 7, 8, 16, 27, 47-48, 74.

13 Ibid., 86-87, 109.

14 Ibid., 159, 181.

15 This was the subject of research at the turn of the century. E. D. Starbuck, a former student of James's, wrote a book called *The Psychology of Religion* (1899). In it he showed that all teenagers exhibit a pronounced brooding period during which they feel disconnected and alienated. This leaves them vulnerable to easy conversion. George A. Coe, another James contemporary, found a correlation between those who could be easily hypnotized and those who were susceptible to religious conversion, William James, *The Varieties*

of Religious Experience: A Study In Human Nature (New York: The Modern Library, 1902), 195, 235.

16 William James, *The Varieties of Religious Experience: A Study In Human Nature* (New York: The Modern Library, 1902), 312, 359, 366.

17 Ibid., 422, 497, 501.

18 Michael Shermer, *The Believing Brain: From Ghosts and Gods to Politics and Conspiracies—How We Construct Beliefs and Reinforce Them As Truths* (New York: Henry Holt and Company, 2011), 145, 7, 59-60, 62.

19 The fusiform gyrus, which sits in the lower interior of the brain, is involved in facial recognition, and it is always on, Michael Shermer, *The Believing Brain: From Ghosts and Gods to Politics and Conspiracies—How We Construct Beliefs and Reinforce Them As Truths* (New York: Henry Holt and Company, 2011), 70. Is it any wonder that people see Jesus in their grilled cheese or the Virgin Mary in a stained bed sheet? See pages 261-276 of Shermer's book for a long list of biases that reinforce our existing views. Michael Shermer's book *Why People Believer Weird Things: Pseudoscience, Superstition, and Other Confusions of Our Time* (1997) also explores many of the fundamental thinking mistakes we make, and argues that science is the only way to free us from this faulty type of thinking.

20 Michael Shermer, *The Believing Brain: From Ghosts and Gods to Politics and Conspiracies—How We Construct Beliefs and Reinforce Them As Truths* (New York: Henry Holt and Company, 2011), 5, 6-7, 35-36, 43. People who tend to believe their lives are controlled by an outside force (*external locus*) also tend to believe in ESP, spiritualism, reincarnation, and mystical experiences, ibid., 77.

21 This idea is put forth by Jennifer Whitman at UT-Austin and Adam Galinsky at Northwestern University, Shermer, 80.

22 Michael Shermer, *The Believing Brain: From Ghosts and Gods to Politics and Conspiracies—How We Construct Beliefs and Reinforce Them As Truths* (New York: Henry Holt and Company, 2011), 168, 174, 172, 119, 135, 258, 322.

23 Sam Harris, *The Moral Landscape: How Science Can Determine Human Values* (New York: Free Press, 2010), 1-25, 45.

24 Ibid., 82.

25 Ibid., 27-52, 63.

26 Ibid., 99.

27 Ibid., 93, 121, 97.

28 Jonathan Haidt has written a whole book on this, *The Righteous Mind: Why Good People are Divided By Religion and Politics* (New York: Pantheon, 2012).

29 Sam Harris, *The Moral Landscape: How Science Can Determine Human Values* (New York: Free Press, 2010), 123, 126-27, 158.

30 Jonathan Haidt, *The Righteous Mind: The Righteous Mind: Why Good People are Divided By Religion and Politics* (New York: Pantheon, 2012), Nook Book.

31 Sam Harris has written about this in his eBook *Free Will* (New York: Free

Press, 2012). Steven Pinker has also devoted much ink to this topic in his book *The Blank Slate: The Modern Denial of Human Nature* (New York: Penguin, 2002).

32 Stephen Prothero has made a compelling case for American illiteracy when it comes to religion, even when it comes to the religions Americans claim to practice, *Religious Literacy: What Every American Needs to Know—and Doesn't* (New York: Harper One, 2008).

33 Daniel Dennett, *Breaking the Spell: Religion As a Natural Phenomenon* (New York: Viking, 2006). For those of you who do not have the time to read through Daniel Dennett's book, here is a short summary of his hypothesis. First, Dennett argues that religion is a powerful natural force in society and politics and, therefore, deserves to be subject to the scrutiny of science, regardless of the reticence of many to challenge the sacred, and largely unquestionable, assertions of religion. Second, because religion is a natural phenomenon we must treat it like any other natural phenomenon, and the best theoretical framework with which to study the development of religion is the theory of evolution by natural selection. Dennett then goes on to explain how religion might have developed from our rudimentary observation that anything that is complicated and moves must have intelligence behind it. This he maintains is how folk religions began; they were a response to the inability to explain the world around us without employing some idea of "agency." Folk religions, though, are only simple, informal ways of understanding the unknowable. That is why religion, as we understand the term today, had to develop. It was made possible by other developments like language and other forms of symbolism. All along, from primitive folk religions to complex religious beliefs and practices, there was a constant adding and subtracting, resulting in ever more complex and useful ideas for individuals and societies. It is at this point that religion began to develop what we might consider some of its more dangerous aspects. Religion began to adopt rituals, creeds, and doctrines that could not be questioned. Those who protected these aspects of the religion— Dennett calls them "stewards"—would go to any lengths to keep the secrets of their religions, including deception and techniques making it impossible to disconfirm what they were saying. Next, Dennett argues that religions prey on our natural inclination to join groups, what some call the "herd instinct." However, Dennett says these allegiances are complicated by language, culture, and sometimes the competition between alternative religions. A fundamental problem that develops in the study of religion as a natural phenomenon is the rise of "belief in belief." Dennett claims this is a modern phenomenon where belief in God becomes an argument so complex that even scholars of theology cannot unravel the "mysteries." This makes it nearly impossible for the average person to address the question, which, in turn, makes it superfluous. This is a strategy to protect religion from being questioned, especially among those who claim that belief in God and religion are the equivalent of one another. Lastly, Dennett asks his most controversial question, is there any need for religion in the modern world? The answer appears to be "No" since religion cannot give us a proper understanding of God, and is not the only means of providing morality and existential meaning. Furthermore, those who continue to argue that religion does supply these things ignore the cost factor of belief over non-belief. Dennett ends by suggesting that much more research needs to be done in this area; however, he leaves us thinking that the case for religion, from a scientific standpoint anyway, is not as strong as some would

have us believe. At best it is a system that will have to experience extensive mutations if it is to survive in a world dominated by science.

This idea that religion must adapt if it is to survive is also made by Bishop John Shelby Spong of the Episcopal Church. His book *A New Christianity for a New World: Why Traditional Faith Is Dying and How a New Faith Is Being Born* (2001) is a controversial manifesto on how Christian theology must adapt to the modern view of the world if it is to survive. Spong is definitely outside mainstream Christianity with his views on Christology and soteriology, and there is little reason to believe that these doctrinal changes could occur without major structural changes to the Christian Church. I doubt these changes will occur, and that atheism is more likely to prevail in a world where economic prosperity is largely shared and where all major diseases are eliminated.

34 The process of separation can happen suddenly and without the conscious desire of the hero. He may be compelled by fate or the opening of some door through which he cannot resist traveling. Once on the other side of the door, often represented as the "world navel," the hero usually goes through a series of trials meant to strip him of his identity. This is necessary for him to become the "new creature" he is fated to become. The hero is frequently helped by a guide (*mystagogue*) and some type of talisman that gives him power or assistant along the road. The return is often a conflict of interest for the hero since now that he has achieved enlightenment or a boon he sees no reason to return, but in the end the hero's journey is about coming back to his society and sharing his discovery. The real purpose of the hero is to move society forward, to break with the old ways and light the way to a new path, Joseph Campbell, *The Hero With a Thousand Faces* (New Jersey: Princeton University Press, 1949), 81, 91, 97, 101, 337, 384.

35 Joseph Campbell, *The Hero With a Thousand Faces* (New Jersey: Princeton University Press, 1949), 19.

36 Ibid., 104.

37 Ibid., 23.

38 Ibid., 249.

39 Ibid., 270.

40 Ibid., 164-165.

41 Ibid., 45.

42 Ibid., 180.

43 Ibid., 388.

44 Ibid., 79, 162, 238.

Chapter Sixteen - Our Brave New World

1 http://www.lettersofnote.com/2012/03/1984-v-brave-new-world.html, accessed on July 16, 2012.

2 *Soma* appears to be a hallucinogenic drug that heightens one's senses while reducing inhibitions. A modern comparison might be MDMA, or *Ecstasy*.

3 Christopher Lasch, *The Culture of Narcissism: American Life in An Age of Diminishing Expectations* (New York: W. W. Norton, 1979), xvi.

4 Ibid., 248. This is an observation that the late Christopher Hitchens made in his autobiographical account *Hitch-22: A Memoir* (2010). Hitchens speaks of a moment when he is attending a rally at one of England's leading educational institutions and everyone is standing up saying, "Speaking as a …, I think this should be done." For Hitchens this was an axial moment because he realized that the "movement" which he had joined, and led in some respects, had simply become a way of complaining about one's lot in life, not about really changing society. [get reference]

5 Thomas Frank has given this idea substance in his book *One Market Under God: Extreme Capitalism, Market Populism, and the End of Economic Democracy* (New York: Anchor Books, 2000).

6 Thomas Frank has addressed this in his book *What's the Matter With Kansas? How Conservatives Won the Heart of America* (New York: Henry, Holt and Co., 2004).

7 See Stephen Pinker's *The Blank Slate: The Modern Denial of Human Nature* (New York: Viking, 2002).

8 Thomas Frank, *What's the Matter With Kansas? How Conservatives Won the Heart of America* (New York: Holt, 2004), 7, 157-178, 28-66, 1-10.

9 Ibid., 179-190.

10 Ibid., 67-77.

11 Ibid., 237-251; Michael Sandel has recently published a book titled *What Money Can't Buy: The Moral Limits of Markets* (New York: Farrar, Straus and Giroux, 2012) which deals extensively with the intrusion of the market into every aspect of life. Can everything be bought? The answer is "No," not if we want to maintain aspects of our lives not measured in dollars and cents.

12 Left and right, some have decided that there is no solution that government can provide; it is simply too corrupt. Chris Hedges and P. J. O'Rourke stand at opposite ends of the political spectrum but both suggest a turning away from politics. "Why bother," they ask. Reading through Hedges's *The World As It Is: Dispatches on the Myth of Human Progress* (2010) gives one visions of warm baths and razor blades. However, even Hedges cannot help but still be a little hopeful that we will one day institute a morally-infused democratic socialism,

renounce American empire, and work for Palestinian justice. Sure, why not? P. J. O'Rourke, always in a much better humor, simply says "stop encouraging the bastards!" His book *Don't Vote: It Just Encourages the Bastards* (2010) argues that the disease is not too much business being done but too much government. O'Rourke believes the common wisdom of the modern economic libertarian, if we just got government out of the way the market would solve all our problems.

13 Daniel Bell, "The Cultural Contradictions of Capitalism" in *Morality and the Market*, Eugene Heath, ed. (New York: McGraw-Hill, 2001), 533-542, 541.

14 Aristotle mentions this in Book I of his *Politics* (Part XI) and Adam Smith mentions it in his discussion on the division of labor, Book V, Chapter I of *An Inquiry into the Nature and Causes of the Wealth of Nations* (1776).

15 This is one of the central themes of Thomas Frank's book *One Market Under God: Extreme Capitalism, Market Populism, and the End of Economic Democracy* (New York: Anchor Books, 2000).

16 The best book-length treatment of the effects of this movement is E. P. Thompson's *Customs in Common: Studies in Traditional Popular Culture* (New York: New Press, 1992).

17 For a fascinating history of the discovery of Australia and its development as a prison colony read Robert Hughes's *The Fatal Shore: The Epic of Australia's Founding* (New York: Alfred A. Knopf, 1986).

Epilogue

1 This idea is the source of Hegelian and Marxian thought. It was given recent new life in Francis Fukuyama's *The End of History and the Last Man* (1992). It can also be seen to a lesser degree in the work of others who cheerlead for the death-denying ideology of the modern liberal capitalist state. Niall Ferguson's *Civilization: The West and All the Rest* (2011) is one of those cheerleaders.

2 Most recently Representative Louis Gohmert (R), a member of the U.S. House of Representatives, suggested that the shooting in Aurora, CO, that occurred on July 20, 2012, was a result of the U.S. abandoning the Judeo-Christian ethic. It is this kind of simplistic moralism that gets us nowhere, which is why those with better insight should attempt to marginalize these folks as much as possible when it comes to any public debate on morality.

Index